From the Library of

Gordon Sandford

A FUTURE FOR ENGLISH MUSIC

In series with this volume:

ELGAR, O. M. *A Study of a Musician*
LETTERS AND OTHER WRITINGS OF EDWARD ELGAR
LETTERS TO NIMROD *From Edward Elgar*

Professor Sir Edward Elgar, portrait by Talbot Hughes

A FUTURE FOR ENGLISH MUSIC

and other Lectures

BY

EDWARD ELGAR

Peyton Professor of Music in the
University of Birmingham

EDITED BY

PERCY M. YOUNG

FOREWORD BY

ANTHONY LEWIS

Peyton and Barber Professor of Music in the
University of Birmingham

London : Dennis Dobson

FIRST PUBLISHED IN GREAT BRITAIN IN 1968
BY DOBSON BOOKS LTD, 80 KENSINGTON CHURCH STREET, LONDON W8

MADE AND PRINTED IN GREAT BRITAIN BY
THE GARDEN CITY PRESS LIMITED
LETCHWORTH, HERTFORDSHIRE

SBN 234 77046 5

CONTENTS

ILLUSTRATIONS

Music examples relevant to the text are inserted according to Elgar's
indications throughout

ACKNOWLEDGEMENTS

I am greatly indebted to Mrs. C. Elgar Blake and the Trustees of the Will for permission to publish the lectures, preparatory notes and drafts for the same, as well as other original material of the late Sir Edward Elgar, and to the Library of the University of Birmingham for access to relevant documents and to the letters of Elgar in the possession of the Library. I otherwise wish to acknowledge the assistance of the City Librarians of Birmingham, Leeds, and Manchester, the Librarian of the Gesellschaft der Musikfreunde, Vienna, the staff of the Music Room of The British Museum, Professor Dr. Dorothea Siegmund-Schultze, Mr. Frank Singleton, of *The Guardian*, Mr. F. W. Rushton, and Mr. Alan Webb, Curator of the Elgar Birthplace, Broadheath, Worcestershire.

Illustrations appear by courtesy of the Trustees of the Elgar Will, the Barber Institute of Fine Arts and the Library of Birmingham University, the City Libraries of Birmingham and Manchester, and the Gesellschaft der Musikfreunde, Vienna.

P. M. Y.

FOREWORD

by

ANTHONY LEWIS

Peyton and Barber Professor of Music in the
University of Birmingham

The considered thoughts on music of a composer of the stature of Elgar would be of great interest in almost any form, even the most fragmentary. But in these Birmingham lectures we have Elgar's ideas on a number of central topics set out in a systematic and continuous fashion, such as we possess from few other composers of his eminence. What is more, thanks to Dr. Percy Young's admirable editorial scheme, we can observe the process of Elgar's ideas taking shape and being formulated and developed. We are enabled, as it were, to see the lectures in depth and to note which of his tenets he intended to have forefront emphasis and what amongst the rest was essentially supporting and background matter. In this sense we can, perhaps, appreciate them more clearly than some of Elgar's contemporaries who, to judge from some of the press comments, mistook marginal aside for main thesis.

Too often the giving of these lectures has been passed over by biographers as an irrelevance in Elgar's life, an undesirable distraction from his creative work. Dr. Young's carefully compiled narrative of events leading up to Elgar's acceptance of the Peyton Chair makes it clear, I would think, that Elgar himself did not regard the lectures in this light. He saw in them an opportunity to marshall views that had been evolving at random in his mind for some time and to present them in concrete and connected terms. I think there is evidence that he needed this kind of release at this stage of his career, and that although it cost him an effort, he made that effort willingly and thought it not only worthwhile but necessary. Certainly the benefit and stimulus musical life derived from his lectures was very real.

For if there is one myth that is finally dispelled by the publication of these lectures and the correspondence connected with them, it is the myth that Elgar was totally uninterested in the Birmingham Professorship, that he never had any intention of taking its responsibilities seriously and that he in fact achieved nothing for the University except a certain notoriety derived from the more controversial passages in his lectures. When he accepted the Chair Elgar was already a composer of established international reputation, while Birmingham University had only recently come into being. What the University needed to establish its new Chair was an outstanding personality capable of conferring status by his acceptance of the post, the setting by him of an appropriate artistic and intellectual standard, and the laying of a sound and imaginative basis on which future activities could develop. All these things Elgar provided, not just perfunctorily, but with a sense of purpose and even of mission. His lectures were carefully prepared and were challenging and thought-provoking; they also contained much sound guidance regarding academic policy. Almost his first act was to set up a Music Library, for which he chose many of the books himself and saw that available Collected Editions of the great masters (including Purcell) were secured. He immediately established good relations with the Birmingham School of Music and set in hand the formation of a University orchestra and choral society. The University Musical Society sprang into being and benefactors came forward with donations for equipment. Altogether the situation would seem to have been highly favourable for further advance and at this point, having completed his most useful contribution, Elgar quite understandably and logically withdrew. Why Richard Peyton should have been so disappointed it is difficult to imagine; perhaps he was too near events to grasp their implications for the future. In any event, I think I can say with confidence that all those who have had the rather daunting privilege of following Elgar in the Birmingham Chair have been profoundly grateful to him for his initiative.

PREFACE

By the nature of his occupation the editor of the works of a great composer, or writer, is obliged to consider that the material which he is called upon to handle has some special, if not unique, significance. The present editor is no exception to the general rule.

It has long been apparent that an edition of the lectures which Elgar delivered at the University of Birmingham in 1905–6 was called for. In the first place they represent Elgar's only consistent attempt to formulate his aesthetic and musico-social principles, and must therefore compel the attention warranted by his lasting eminence among the creative geniuses of his age and country. In the second, it was intended that they should be published.[1] Thirdly, and most important, they add considerably to our knowledge of the operation of Elgar's creative processes, and therefore inevitably enlarge our understanding of his music. Finally, since it has been a temptation to previous biographers and critics to quote passages from the lectures and since this practice will doubtless continue it is as well to show not only what Elgar wanted to say, or what he might have said, or what others thought he said, but what he did say. And not only what he did say, but how he came to say what he did, and what happened after he had done so. Behind the lectures lies also a vivid picture of musical life in an English provincial city at the turn of the century, and also of musical life in England in general.

The exact story is a tangled one. It is also a fascinating one, illuminating many corners of musical history, if not of history itself. For it shows an English artist in relation to English society at a particular point in time, and in so doing upsets more than one apple-cart. What was a tract for the times remains, perhaps, a tract for the times.

In this connection the outstanding feature of the lectures is not the lectures themselves, but the furore they created when delivered. To be truthful it was not their delivery—before an adulatory Birmingham audience—but their publication that caused the trouble. Faithfully on the day after the event the lectures (with one exception) were reported in the Birmingham and a number

---

[1] The typescripts prepared by Lady Elgar and May Grafton were supplemented by tentative Indexes, while Ernest Newman stated that the lectures were "about to be issued in book form", adding that "they must, of course, be taken into account in any volume dealing with the life-work of Elgar". *Elgar*, London, 1906, p. 177.

of national papers. Their frequent contentiousness, more often than not the result of unpremeditated interjections, was kept warm by later re-issue of the reports in *The Musical Standard*, and by selected citations published elsewhere. When those outside Elgar's immediate circle read what appeared some were affronted, others appalled. The Professor had slapped down the conventions of discretion that were supposed to prevail in other than political oratory (in that field it was the age of Keir Hardie); he had spoken more like a man than a gentleman; unpardonably he had said many things that were true.

Some exercise of the imagination is called for to get the situation in perspective. At the present time hardly a day passes without some professor or other saying something about something. Even Professors of Music make public utterances. The enquiring mind of the general public, however, is rewarded only with a quarter-column—if that—in the local evening newspaper. The one exception, of course, is the subject of sex: the animadversions of a professor on this theme may make the nationals. Elgar kept conscientiously and closely to his own subject; he received more publicity than all the University Professors of Music collectively have achieved since. And very unwelcome it was. Among musicians at large the only present challenge to Elgar's then controversial status comes not from the centre of the profession but from the eminently notorious, or notoriously eminent, fringe. And here, again, the general cause of discord is unrelated to music.

It may be said that in the first decade of this century people had time in which to read. That, in a sense, is true. But it does not affect the fact that they were under no compulsion to read about music. The newspaper editors (whom Elgar rather unfairly and most injudiciously lambasts on p. 165) knew what they were about, however, and following principle calculated their columns according to what their readers might have been supposed to have wanted. Hence—Elgar, at length, on music.

This raises the question as to whether the English were then so unmusical as they have often been said to have been. After which we must ask ourselves whether we have progressed as far as we think we have done. The answer to the first question is certainly a negative one, if, as it seems, there were those who were prepared to achieve martyrdom in defence of the cause of "absolute" music, or the contrary cause of "programme" music. No doubt the great problems—and they *are* great problems—are now more suavely dealt with, by eminences well trained in musicology, philosophy and psychology, behind a Third Programme fence or in secluded groves reserved for critical disputation. But this is not the point. What is, is that the public at large at the present time could hardly care less, but that in Elgar's day the same kind of public cared a great deal. Socially speaking, music mattered.

It mattered too to Elgar, for, as he quickly points out, he was a composer, *et praeterea nihil aliquod*, and he claimed no prerogative in other fields. Least of all was he a professor, or a teacher, or a critic, or a public orator. However, he did his best to qualify conjointly in each of these functions. And in eight lectures he did as much to influence musical thinking in England as most are able to do in a lifetime of exposition.

The image of Elgar as the Edwardian and the Imperialist has of late years been somewhat veiled; partly because that image is false, partly because of an apparent necessity always to accommodate the actions and ideas of great men to changes of mood and critical opinion. Whereas once the positive facets of Elgar's music were applauded it is now the dubieties and uncertainties that arrest sympathy and awaken sensibility. If the lectures show a belligerence that matches up with the temperament of "Pomp and Circumstance" the manner in which they were prepared demonstrates to what extent this was a mask behind which were hidden many hurts and resentments, and a haunting sense of incapacity. When we look at the rough and scattered notes which were the first, spontaneous, and undisciplined, approaches to a formal definition of his views we see one Elgar; when we read the final version—or the newspaper account punctuated with audience reaction—we see another. In the connection between the two, written into the progressive revisions and the ultimate co-ordination of first thoughts, lies a significant part of his biography.

In the broad sense of the phrase Elgar was, and sometimes appeared to glory in being, a self-made man. In this he was, as I believe the tenor of these lectures emphasises, a typical Victorian; not least of all in his desire to cover up such inadequacies as he supposed himself to possess. Having concluded formal education by the age of fifteen it is not surprising that Elgar's handling of words was often irregular. That it was also at times inspired is also true; but when faced with a sheet of paper on which to set down ideas through the verbal medium for a formal purpose Elgar was aware only of insecurity. Aware that the professors with whom he would mix had enjoyed educational privileges denied to him he was apprehensive—so apprehensive that the whole pro-fessorial episode reduced him to a state of almost complete nervous debility.

In a number of letters written to Jaeger in 1903[1] Elgar reacted violently, though with humour, to Jaeger's use of the word "crude". A degree of obsession with the word persisted, as is seen in the reference to Elgar's Introduc-tion to a book by his friend Hubert Leicester on p. 155. In the rough notes for the lectures what would be considered crudities of opinion or, even more clearly, of style, abound. In the preliminaries to the lecture on *Critics* there is a selection of relatively violent examples. Elgar particularly hit out at the "educated"—those from whom "no amount of education no amount of the polish of a university, can eradicate the stain from the low type of mind we call commonplace", and at those "needy inebriates of the weekly reviews" who set themselves up as arbiters of critical opinion.[2]

---

[1] See *Letters to Nimrod*, p. 194 et seq.

[2] The nature of Elgar's thoughts is frequently reflected in many passages marked for reference (and sometimes annotated) in the books in his library. So, in this connection, attention is drawn to A. Smythe-Palmer, D.D., *The Ideal of a Gentleman* (an anthology), London, n.d., p. 132: "He is neither vulgar nor genteel, nor any compound of these two

Having in this way eased himself of his inner tensions and resultant prejudices Elgar then proceeded to refine his ideas and his language. It was a slow and tortuous business. He went through all the stages of literary improvement—as might have been advised in a course of night-school classes—until both vocabulary and syntax, though overdressed, appeared to him as fit for survival in the world of letters. Fortunately, however, Elgar recognised that a lecture was also a talk and he tended to forsake the set script from time to time, preferring to come closer to his audience by way of the extemporised phrase. It should be said that those who crowded into Elgar's lectures were wholeheartedly on his side; because of this he ploughed through his prescribed course.

Elgar's struggle to educate himself is indicated not only by his exercises in manipulating prose style, but also by his affection for the recondite allusion, or the impressive quotation. He was, of course, an omnivorous reader, but in the way in which he advertised the extent of his reading he was more than a little self-conscious. On the other hand the relatively narrow field from which references to musical works are drawn indicates the small resources on which his talents had been nurtured. Most of the works (excepting those of Strauss) to which reference is made were within the repertoire of the Worcestershire Philharmonic Society, of which he was the conductor, or were known to him through other amateur activities of his early years in the West Midlands. The notable instance of a work that he had encountered in youth and which exercised a continual fascination for him was Mozart's G minor symphony (K. 550), the model for his own first exercise in symphonic form and the subject of one of the lectures. In this lecture, the most fragmentary of all and the only one lacking journalistic amplification, and in the annotation on his score, Elgar reveals for the most part not the considered conclusions of his maturity but the tutored analytical probings of his apprenticeship. Yet, limited as he was in youth, Elgar reached out to the wider world. On p. 100 a hitherto unknown detail of biography comes to light, in regard to his championship of Brahms,[1] in Malvern, in the 1880s.

In the composition of the lectures the reasons for Elgar's radicalism, which is the kernel of their content and the cause of their immediate notoriety, become apparent. Elgar had a "chip on the shoulder", but he saw no reason to suppose that others should be obliged to wear the same chip because of the culpable inertia or indifference of those in authority. He was scathing in respect of bad composers, whose misfortune it was to be regarded as good. He was angry at the irresponsibility of the leaders of society in respect of the arts. He was energetic in his challenge on behalf of the under-privileged, with whom he was able to identify himself.

---

kinds of vulgarity. He has the manners of no class, but something of quite a different order. His manners are a *part of his soul*, like the style of a writer of genius. His manners belong to *the individual*. He makes you think neither of clown nor gentleman, but of *Man*." John Foster [1770-1843, correctly noted by Elgar as a "Baptist minister".]

[1] cf. *Elgar O.M.*, p. 57.

In declaring himself he ran hard up against reaction. An editorial in the *Birmingham Post* reminded him of the sanctity of the essential principle of English freedom, somewhat curiously and naively interpreted: ". . . Sir Edward forgot that ours is a free country," thundered the leader-writer in deference to the most influential among his readers, "free to neglect as well as to accomplish. We may, and do, neglect art, especially music, and leave it to those who treat it commercially. Truly artistic enterprises mostly spell ruin. The chief Continental nations are before us in education, and the art of music is cared for and supported, as are the sister arts. But the peoples of these countries are not free to do as they like, and such 'free' lectures as those of the Birmingham Professor would probably not be acceptable to the heads of Continental Universities."[1]

Elgar prided himself on his provinciality. Again, the repetition of a phrase in the lecture notes implies an obsession. In a letter about the Morecambe Musical Festival, quoted by *The Musical Times*[2] and alluded to in one of the lectures,[3] he said: "Some day the Press will awaken to the fact, already known abroad and to some few of us in England, that the living centre of music in Great Britain is not London, but somewhere farther North." "Somewhere farther north", the caption chosen by *The Musical Times*, rings through Elgar's career symbolising his abhorrence of the smugness of official musical life.

That Elgar was patriotic is a truism. Those statements reproduced in this book relating to the theme give an idea of the true shape of his patriotism. He was concerned about the quality of English life; about the amelioration, at least by way of the arts, of the condition of the "working-classes"; about the hypocrisies under which native music laboured. "English music is white, and evades everything",[4] he said in one striking, memorable, and permanently relevant phrase. The whole argument that arose about his ambiguities on the "absolute" was a revelation of this, to him, unacceptable "whiteness".

In following Elgar's concept of the function of national music one is struck by the similarity of his attitude to that subsequently expressed by Vaughan Williams. Elgar managed to avoid a special appeal to folk-music (for the reason that his origins did not allow him to review the activities of the "folk" quite so objectively or theoretically) but the advice to young composers to "draw their inspiration more from their own country, from their own literature, and . . . from their own climate",[5] to consider the "larger audience",[6] and to aim at what is "sincere, honest, healthy" is completely in tune with the views expounded by Vaughan Williams, the apostle of "sincerity, simplicity and serenity".[7] At the same time Elgar, his reputation rapidly developing at this time abroad, felt himself also to be a European, with reciprocal rights in the Common Market of music.

---

[1] December 14, 1905.
[2] July 1, 1903, p. 461.
[3] See p. 154.   [4] p. 49.   [5] pp. 51, 203.
[6] p. 37.   [7] *National Music*, London, 1934, p. 121.

Elgar knew how he had become a composer. In his lectures—which, it should be emphasised, were not designed for a professional audience—he described, both directly and indirectly, how this had come to pass. By doing so he gave more valuable counsel than he would have done had he restricted his aims to a merely technical end. Not unnaturally he comes down heavily in favour of the meaningfulness of music. One may venture to suggest that had he answered his critics in the winter of 1905 by observing that music, in his view, was meaningful in an absolute sense he would have neatly got himself off the hook.

Tovey, who was especially interested by Elgar's views on Brahms, understood what Elgar was driving at. In his note on the Violin Concerto, for example, he wrote with some relevance to and, perhaps, a backward glance towards the argument: "Of all external subjects for music the illustration of human character is the most purely musical; if indeed it can be an external subject at all. Music either has character, or it is meaningless, and the character either has human interest or none."[1]

The matter of significance was, precisely, a matter of social significance and as Elgar contemplated it as such his thoughts began to move towards a particular philosophy of our own times. If his background and development led him in the general direction of "commitment" and thus imbued some of his general statements with a prophetic quality they also enabled him to see some of the possible consequences of the antithesis—the cult of "whiteness". "But if we give up absolute music where are we logically to end? Are we to be led back by symbolism to ideograms & is music to become a mere series of labels or chemical formulae of the emotions[?]"[2] The music of Elgar stands high in public esteem because it is not ideographic; in which sense it is absolute music.

One reason for publishing the literary remains of a composer is, as has been suggested, that one hopes that fresh light will be thrown on his music. In this instance I believe that we gain much from what follows, for from the form and content of the lectures we can the better appreciate Elgar's intentions and methods as a creative musician. Within limits we can discover more about his responses to the music of other composers. Most of all, however, we benefit in that we can examine the act of creation at close quarters. There is the repository of scattered ideas, not always choately formed, the refinement of these in a succession of stages, their final unification, and their interpretation in performance. There is also to be noted a superfluity of idea. What was considered for one lecture is often, therefore, ultimately to be found incorporated in another, or merely lost by the wayside. The way in which the lectures were composed is the same as in respect of the music. Here also rough notes exist—in the fragmentary motives of the Sketch Books. These were scribbled in as they occurred to Elgar in the hope that at some time they should find a home; but at the time of notation there was little or no certainty regarding their final

[1] *Essays in Musical Analysis*, London, 1934, III, p. 152.
[2] pp. 192, 208.

destination. In many cases the rough notes were—"crude". The processes of refinement (in contrast to the lectures rather more in the mind than on paper) and unification were undertaken as was the case with literary concepts; and in the end there was a complete work.

In substance the lectures show the breadth of Elgar's interests—from chemistry to theology. Recondite allusions, as to classical literature, to seventeenth-century drama, or to the eschatological speculations of Jean Hardouin and Giovanni Pietro Pinamonti, illustrate a natural zest for accumulating knowledge, but also Elgar's hidden intention to out-professor the professors. But in one way or another such allusions can without too much difficulty be referred to the character of his music. In this connection examination of his vocabulary is also relevant: "triumphant", "noble", and the Pindaresque "splendour-loving", for example, are sensuously evocative of transmutable concepts.

In a famous phrase Elgar described the Cello Concerto and by implication the rest of his music as "a man's attitude to life". The lectures delivered at Birmingham University annotate the attitude.

The lectures not only give additional material in respect of Elgar but also provide further evidence on which the role of Lady Elgar may be assessed. From some of the errors which crept into her transcriptions of her husband's rough notes it becomes clear that he was from time to time talking of things that were some way beyond her comprehension. But this only serves to make the fact of her faith in his genius the more moving. The lectures imposed a strain on Elgar, but no less a strain on his wife. In addition to nursing him away from his depressions, and standing firm against the grievances she entertained on his behalf, she valiantly got down to her task of amanuensis. She not only did not always understand what she was copying. She could not always correctly read what Edward had written—an inability that is to be understood. But what she wrote on his behalf she took to be of supreme authority. When the lectures were delivered she sat by, a copy of the typescript in her hand. The touching, perhaps slightly pathetic, testimony to the anxiety with which she followed the proceedings is shown in her pencilled additions to the text of the inaugural lecture—*laughter*, *applause*, etc. More than anything she wanted him to be a success.

SOURCES AND EDITORIAL PROCEDURE

The material on which this edition is based consists of:

(*a*) Rough notes.
(*b*) Manuscript drafts and "fair copies" in Elgar's own hand, or by Lady Elgar, or their niece, May Grafton.
(*c*) Preparatory drafts in typescript.
(*d*) Final typescript.
(*e*) Newspaper and periodical reports of the lectures, together with corres-

pondence from or to Elgar, or between other interested parties, or published in the press.

The lecture material is preserved in seven volumes kept among the archives at the Elgar Birthplace, Broadheath, near Worcester. Each volume holds the relevant documents for a single lecture. Frequent corrections and emendations by Elgar occur in (b) and (c) above. If not otherwise clear these are marked (E), while any (other than in respect of correction of palpable copyists' errors) by Lady Elgar are designated by (C.A.E.).

The final typescripts have been taken as the basis of the authentic version which it is here intended to show. In respect of the lectures on the symphonies of Brahms and Mozart, however, the fragmentary character of the final typescripts make it necessary to rely to a considerable extent on the published reports of these lectures. What is to be considered as the authentic version is printed on the right-hand page, while textual variants are shown on the facing page. Supplementary information is given below the main text in the form of footnotes.

The substance of the rough notes is placed before the appropriate lecture. Manuscript drafts and copies are defined thus—Ms. 1, Ms. 2, etc.; typescripts as Ts. 1, Ts. 2, etc. These definitions are shown marginally.

In the final typescripts there are many errors of typing. These are not reproduced. In the alternative versions of passages shown in the textual commentary all insertions, whether marginal or interlinear, are italicised. Where Elgar himself used underlinings such words or passages are in small capitals. Cancelled sections, preceded by δ, are printed within square brackets.

Specimen passages of textual variant thus read:

(1) . . . it is [δ not] *no longer* PRACTICAL in many ways . . .
(2) We must [δ give] *meet* them [something better] *in a nobler way* than *by* [songs] publish[ed]*ing* [at] *songs & [2d] pianoforte music at twopence a sheet.* . . .

So far as is possible such sections are set facing the passages of the main text to which they refer. Key words in the main text (shown on right-hand pages) are italicised to facilitate textual comparison. These italics are solely a guide to the eye. Capital type is therefore introduced where, in his final version, Elgar occasionally used underlining.

Square brackets are reserved for editorial use throughout. Where Elgar occasionally introduced them they are here replaced by round brackets.

P. M. Y.

CHAPTER I

THE CULT OF THE PUBLIC LECTURE

THE Birmingham lectures of Elgar may be viewed from different angles. They represent, of course, an attitude towards music. But they also represent an attitude to society, of society to music, and to the place of music in society. Inevitably they have a relationship to education. In themselves they are in fact an Elgarian conclusion to an age of educational emancipation and reform and they therefore show Elgar—sometimes ill at ease—as a Victorian. These lectures were delivered under the sponsorship of a University but they are in no sense what would now be understood as University lectures. They were addressed, as Elgar assumed music should be addressed, to a "larger audience".

The mainsprings of educational reform in England during the nineteenth century were philanthropic idealism, self-help, and popular agitation, and a great deal depended on adult education. This was cultivated on two planes. On the one hand there was class-teaching, primarily aimed at the elimination of illiteracy; on the other the public lecture based on the principle that culture was a generally desirable social acquisition. In both cases a moral issue was implicit, for the frequently expressed intention was to improve society. Unfortunately in so far as music was concerned the intention was often frustrated through a lack of funds. Elgar, the beneficiary of Victorian education and non-education, did not attempt to disguise a moral purpose, as is shown particularly by his loaded adjectives and his inspirational quotations from other writers. Nor did he fail to draw attention to the responsibility that should be borne by those who controlled the nation's wealth.

Apart from their musical content these lectures will be seen to synthesise the two main traditions of Victorian adult education. So too did the foundation which sponsored the lectures.

Adult schools were inaugurated at the end of the first stage of the Industrial Revolution, early examples being those founded in Nottingham, in 1798, by William Singleton and Samuel Fox,[1] and in Leeds, in 1816, by Dr. Thomas Pole. An Adult School was established in Birmingham by Joseph Sturge in 1842. These institutions were stimulated largely by the zeal of Quakers and Methodists, while further encouragement was given by the Bible Society, founded in 1804. During the first half of the nineteenth century so-called Mechanics' Institutes came into being, generally as a result of a collective desire for self-improvement and for material advancement. This being the case it is

[1] See James Lomax, *A History of Quakers in Nottingham, 1648–1948*, Nottingham, 1948.

not surprising that there was resistance to the idea of extended opportunities for intellectual improvement: ". . . there existed amongst the upper and middle classes a strongly pronounced feeling of hostility to Mechanics' Institutions, as having inherent in their nature something of the revolutionary spirit".[1] Awareness of such hostility, still strong at the time of his lectures, lay behind Elgar's attitude to the particular problems of musical education. The development of adult education in Birmingham during the first half of the nineteenth century was thus described by one of the pioneers:

> Prior to 1850 Birmingham had made several attempts to establish a literary and scientific institution, where, by means of lectures, reading rooms, museums, &c., the people of Birmingham might have an opportunity of acquiring some scientific and literary knowledge. The old Philosophical Institution in Cannon Street had, in the early days of last century, done good work, and had amongst its members such names as Boulton, Watt, Darwin, Wedgwood, and others equally well known. Then came the old Mechanics Institution [f. c. 1825] in Newhall Street, where our late talented townsman, Mr. George Shaw, first acquired his scientific knowledge. This was followed by the old Polytechnic, whose home was in that fine Jacobean building in Steelhouse Lane opposite the Upper Priory. All these flickered for a time, and finally went out, and in 1850 we were fairly stranded, and Birmingham was entirely without any society of the kind. At this time, when all thoughtful men were deploring this state of things, some half-dozen gentlemen called a meeting to consider the possibility of founding an institute such as the present one, and foremost among them were Mr. Arthur Ryland, Captain Tindal (manager of the Birmingham Branch of the Bank of England), Mr. John Dawes (of Bromford Ironworks, Oldbury), Sir John Jaffray, Messrs. John Hebbert, George Dixon, Follet Osler, Peter Hollins, William Mathews, and myself, and later on Mr. Mathews's two brothers, George and Charles Edward, the loss of whom we so much deplore, and several others. But the life and soul of the whole movement was Mr. Arthur Ryland, who, by his devotion, energy, and tact, succeeded in holding together a capital working committee, and finally, by very hard work, we raised sufficient funds to encourage us to commence the building of the present Midland Institute. By way of starting with due eclat Mr. Ryland sought and obtained the services of the late Prince Consort who most graciously came down to Birmingham on the 22nd day of November, 1855, and laid the first stone. Since then the institute has done a grand and useful work, and has helped to bring up a class of intelligent artisans second to none in the kingdom.
>
> I may remind you before concluding that soon after the institute was opened Mr. Ryland induced Charles Dickens to read his 'Christmas Carol' for us in the Town Hall, and the proceeds made a very handsome addition to the fund.[2]

[1] *History of the Nottingham Mechanics' Institution 1837–1887*, London, 1887.

[2] From a letter from Sir Henry Wiggin, member of first committee of the Midland Institute, to Whitworth Wallis, honorary secretary, on the occasion of the Jubilee of the laying of the Foundation Stone of the Institute, November 22, 1905.

The foundation of the Birmingham and Midland Institute was a direct consequence of the powerful influence of the public lecture. For it was Charles Dickens who planted the idea in the course of a lecture in Birmingham in 1852. In 1869 Dickens served as President of the Institute.

In this case the fashionable aspect of the lecture by a notability paid dividends. Elgar's lectures, as will be seen, also attracted fashionable attention and their often self-conscious literary style (from which, however, Elgar departed from time to time) is a reminder that the Victorian lecturer was to some extent expected to be a combination of preacher and entertainer.

At the beginning of the century people of refinement—as well as those generously endowed with moral scruples—avoided the theatre, of which, it was considered, the values had declined, lectures by Sir James Mackintosh, the philosopher, at Lincoln's Inn,[1] by John Flaxman, sculptor and artist, at the Royal Academy,[2] and by the scientist, Sir Humphrey Davy, at the Royal Institution,[3] proved highly successful; but less so than those of the Rev. Sydney Smith whose opinions, delivered with his customary wit and polish, on *Moral Philosophy* caused chaos in Albemarle and Grafton Streets in 1804–5 as hundreds of patrons attempted to dismount from their carriages at the same time. On the scientific side the popular lecturers in addition to Davy were John Dalton and Michael Faraday. Literature was served by Coleridge[4] whose lectures varied so greatly in quality and intelligibility that audiences quickly dropped away, and by Hazlitt.[5]

In 1818 Hazlitt gave a course on the English poets at the Surrey Institution (f. 1807) in Blackfriars Road. Here there was a different audience from that to be found at the Royal Institution. The fashionable were unwilling to cross the river and Hazlitt had to be content with the lower middle-class, largely Dissenting, congregation (many belonged to the near-by chapel made famous by Rowland Hill), that came, as Thomas Talfourd said, with "a hankering after the improvement of the mind".

The most effective agent in the dissemination of popular culture during the Victorian era was undoubtedly Charles Dickens, whose provincial tours were sensationally successful. When he spoke at a conversazione given by the Birmingham Polytechnic in February 1843 the Town Hall was filled. "In his speech he welcomed the Polytechnic idea as being neither sectarian nor class and as something in which honest men of all degrees and every creed may associate. It was an idea that might even prevent men working at machines from degenerating into machines . . ." In Liverpool two nights previously he

---

[1] *The Law of Nature and Nations*, 1799.

[2] *Lectures on Sculpture*, published London, 1829.

[3] 1801, courses on *On the New Branch of Philosophy*, *Pneumatic Chemistry* (after the last lecture free anaesthetisation by nitrous oxide was offered to members of the audience), and *Chemistry*.

[4] *Shakespeare and Milton, in Illustration of the Principles of Poetry*, 1811, at the rooms of the Philosophical Society, Fleet Street.

[5] *The History of Human Philosophy*, 1811, at the Russell Institute, Great Coram Street.

had said of the Mechanics' Institute in that city: "I look forward from this place as from a tower, to the time when high and low, rich and poor, shall mutually assist, improve and educate each other."[1] The influence of Dickens was strong in the democratisation of adult education, but his powerful maxims on the subject were but summaries of the faith and practice of many less prominent workers in this field.

Among Victorian musicians there were many who, having had to work out their own salvation in a basically uncongenial environment, possessed the missionary instinct. Almost every choral society fulfilled an educational function; even more so the singing-classes that sprang up to provide prospective choral society members with sufficient techniques and sufficient musical literacy to be able to essay the popular oratorios without embarrassment. In the broader sphere of musical education the outstanding names were those of Samuel Wesley (1766–1837), William Crotch (1775–1867), William Sterndale Bennett (1816–75), and John Hullah (1812–84)—the principal precursors of Elgar in his role of lecturer.

Wesley's lectures, given between 1810 and 1820, were delivered at the Bristol Institution (he was born in Bristol), at the Royal Institution, the Surrey Institution, and at the "Green Man" in Blackheath. Judging from his copious notes[2] Wesley had a rare facility for presenting scholarly material with ease and humour. He also ranged widely, as is shown by the syllabus of his spring lectures of 1826 at the Royal Institution.

1. On Music, considered in the two-fold Sense of a Science, and an Art.
2. On Musical Taste.
3. On Musical Prejudice.
4. On the Distinction between Sublime, Beautiful, and Ornamental Styles.
5. On the General Management of Musical Performances in England.
6. On the Advancement and Improvement of Musical Knowledge and Taste.

Crotch, more pedagogic than Wesley, dug deep into the scientific and stylistic properties of music and in so doing helped to lay musicological foundations. Nevertheless he was in great demand and from the beginning of the century delivered many series at the Royal Institution in addition to those given in his Professorial capacity at Oxford.

Crotch's Royal Institution lectures of 1824 covered much ground, and were copiously illustrated by examples played on the pianoforte:

1. Remarks on the National Music of Various Countries . . . Remains of the Music of the Greeks. Jewish chants. The National Music of Ireland.
2. The National Music of Scotland—Highland and Lowland. The National Music of Wales.
3. National Music supposed to be English; that of France, Italy, Switzer-

[1] *Charles Dickens*, Una Pope-Hennessy, London, 1945, pp. 202–4.
[2] B.M. Add. Mss. 35014–6.

land, Germany, Spain and Portugal, Hungary, Poland, Scandinavia and Norway, Denmark, Russia, Sclavonia, Turkey, Arabia, Persia, the East Indies, China, Java, Otaheite, Canada and Norfolk Sound.
4. Superiority of Vocal over Instrumental Music. Remarks on Mozart's Comic Opera of *Cosi fan Tutte* concluded. Character of Mozart.

A daunting catalogue; and one wonders how the audience survived the third lecture. Overall, however, Crotch's lectures published in 1831 as *The Substance of several courses of lectures on Music read at Oxford and in the Metropolis* [Royal Institution], bearing marks of eighteenth-century philosophising (often in a moral way) on music and aesthetics in England, point towards the philosophical attitudes attempted by Elgar. In his opening address Crotch defined his audience and his pontifical relationship with it: ". . . but as his classes never consisted, at the University or the Metropolis, wholly, or even principally, of philosophers or composers, but rather of lovers of music, performers, and perhaps a few young composers, the lecturer has generally made his principal object an endeavour to improve the taste."[1] Like Wesley on the one hand and Elgar on the other he referred back to Sir Joshua Reynolds, saying that art and principles of art "should be considered in their correspondence with the principles of other arts, which, like this, address themselves primarily and principally to the imagination".[2] In a well-argued passage[3] Crotch turned away from the mimetic principles enunciated in James Harris's classical *Three Treatises* —on Art, Music, Painting and Poetry, and Happiness—(1744) towards an idealisation of the "absolute", defined as "Sublimity, . . . the highest walk of our art as of every other".[4] Sublimity was to be found in the "true church style" of the seventeenth and eighteenth centuries. Since it was absent from the church music of Crotch's day, then, "our art is . . . on the decline". At this point Elgar was in general more optimistic than Crotch, and unwilling to beatify the madrigalists or even Purcell in such lavish terms as Crotch used.[5] In his conclusions Elgar, however, was more pessimistic. He would hardly have turned a final flourish in these terms: "The result, then, of these statements, is, that the public taste of this nation is in a gradual state of improvement; and, notwithstanding the decline of the art itself . . . has attained a higher stage of advancement than it has known for half a century."[6]

[1] "Introductory", pp. 3–4.
[2] "On the three Styles of Music; the sublime, the Beautiful, and the Ornamental", p. 26.
[3] "On Musical Expression", p. 45.
[4] "The Rise, Progress, and Decline of the Art", pp. 71–3.
[5] "The Names of the Most Distinguished Composers in various styles", p. 86 f., pp. 104–9.
[6] "On the Present State of the Public Taste of this Nation", p. 158.
Crotch published three volumes of *Specimens of Various Styles of Music referred to in A Course of lectures . . . and Adapted to Keyed Instruments* (R. Birchall, n.d.; 2nd ed. Cramer, Addison, and Beale, n.d.). His primary object was "To improve the taste by introducing the performer to every kind of excellence, and thereby prevent his being bigoted to particular sorts of music, or particular masters."

Sterndale Bennett, more realistic than Crotch, was a pioneer in the presentation of lectures in which the quality of the performance of the musical illustrations was an important consideration. In 1859 he visited Sheffield to deliver
two lectures (for an honorarium of forty guineas) at the Literary and Philosophical Society. The first of these lectures leads directly to the first of Elgar's
series. It was thus synopsised by the *Sheffield Independent*, of April 30.

On Wednesday evening Professor Sterndale Bennett delivered his first
lecture on 'The state of music in English private society and the general
prospects of music in the future.' . . . Stirling Howard, Esq., the president,
introduced the lecturer as a fellow-townsman of whose eminence in his
profession Sheffield ought to feel proud. Professor Bennett said the object of
his lecture was to inquire into the state of music in English private society.
When asked whether England was a musical nation, his first idea had been,
'Who can doubt it?' Looking at the great advances made in music in
London, the large number of concerts given compared with what was done
formerly, the immense number of amateur performers in choral societies,
and the popularity of the Italian opera, he was inclined to say that musical
taste was extending. In the provinces, too, there were now regularly held
great musical gatherings called Festivals—as that at Birmingham, Bradford
and Leeds. These facts showed the popularity of concerted music, but he
asked what had been done for music at home? In addition to the smaller
pieces that might be culled from the larger works, there was a very large
class of music called chamber music, properly adapted for the private
drawing room. Some of the great masters had written pieces of this kind,
but their works were not generally found in English private society. The
most popular pieces were selections from the Italian operas and fantasias—
light, frivolous pieces. It was a mistake to suppose that good music was
necessarily heavy, as he hoped to convince them by his examples. But with
all his complaints, he did not despond. There was perhaps only one country
in Europe whose musical chances he would exchange with our own, and
that was Germany. Germany took up and maintained good music when
Italy had allowed it to decline. . . . Take up the music of an English
drawing room, and what a medley collection it was. Some pieces from the
Italian operas, sentimental songs, a few negro melodies, &c. The second
point in which England suffers in comparison with Germany was the
excitement necessarily inseparable from concerts. No concert which began
before eight o'clock was fashionable, and the programme must last till
eleven or twelve. In many households they are dreaded, because they
disturb domestic arrangements, and a great part of the public are prevented
from becoming musical because of the late hours. . . . Professor Bennett
then proceeded to perform upon a fine-toned pianoforte an admirable
selection. He was assisted by Mr. Percival Phillips and Miss Seale. The
manner in which the selection was performed elicited loud applause.

John Hullah, like Elgar, was born in Worcester and, also like Elgar, was
largely self-taught. At the age of seventeen he went to London and, after having
some instruction from William Horsley and Domenico Crivelli, made a name

for himself as a popular singing instructor. A disciple of Guillaume Wilhem, whose methods had proved so effective in French musical education, Hullah, a friend of Sir James Kay-Shuttleworth who was a chief architect of the Foster Education Act of 1870, became in due course the chief adviser to the Board of Education on school music and the training of teachers. At the same time Hullah had developed his interest in the history of music. In 1847 he arranged historical concerts of English vocal music at Exeter Hall, and in 1865 published the series of lectures given by him at the Royal Institution. These lectures[1] (dedicated to W. E. Gladstone) are of exceptional interest, dealing in some detail with the Baroque music of England, Italy, and Germany.

It will be seen that the Royal Institution was the focal point both for general and musical cultural exposition. Had Elgar not been unsure of himself in an academic role he would have joined the main stream before the question of the Birmingham professorship arose. The lectures that he ultimately gave in Birmingham might very well have been delivered a year earlier in London; in which case, presuming that he would have found the task as difficult and worrying, he might have refused the Birmingham offer altogether.

On February 19, 1903, the Assistant Secretary to the Royal Institution wrote to Elgar as follows:

Dear Sir,
    Many thanks for your prompt reply. I feel sure the Managers will regret to hear that you are unable to lecture here after Easter, and they will no doubt desire that it may be possible for you to arrange to give a Course of lectures next year either before or after Easter.
                                                    Yours truly,
                                                    Henry Young

The next series of lectures on music at the Royal Institution were given in 1905 by Sir Alexander Mackenzie, whose subject was "Bohemian Music". It remains to show what kind of a University it was that invited Elgar to deliver his lectures. It was, in fact, an institution that had grown out of the cult of the lecture.

In 1825 a series of lectures on Anatomy were delivered in the city and a year later "The Royal School of Medicine and Surgery in Birmingham", incorporated by William IV, was set up in one room. After twelve years this body was converted into a residential college of the Church of England which, in turn, was incorporated as Queen's College in 1843. In this year the Queen's Hospital was built and three years later its students were prepared for degrees of London University. Queen's College specialising more and more in theology left room for a more specifically medical institution, and in 1851 Sydenham College, conducted by a group of medical practitioners, was founded in association with the General Hospital. In 1880 Mason College, founded by Josiah Mason (1795–1881), a wealthy manufacturer and philanthropist, and

---

[1] *The Third or Transition Period of Musical History.*

endowed with £200,000, was opened on broader university lines but with a necessary and desirable inclination to technology. Six years later, with Joseph Chamberlain as President, Alderman Clayton as Chairman of Council, and Dr. R. S. Heath as Principal, Mason College became a University College. In 1900, by which time the Day Training College for Teachers had been taken over as well as the medical faculties and Chairs in Education and Economics had been endowed by generous benefactions from George Dixon, and additional donations had come from Sir George Kenrick, the College became a University.[1]

As Principal of the University Sir Oliver Lodge, physicist and psychical researcher, was energetic in stimulating a general intellectual renaissance. In some of his utterances he was well ahead of his time. "It may be long," he wrote, "in this slow-moving country before the influence of brain-power in history is recognised as fully as the influence of sea-power has been." And— "Hitherto the ideas of this country in education and scientific research have been conceived on a wholly inadequate scale. . . ."[2] Lodge was indefatigable in the field of the public lecture. So too was Muirhead, the Professor of Philosophy. Of the then professorial staff the one most interested in music was the Professor of German, H. G. Fiedler,[3] son of a German music director, who was appointed Dean of the Faculty of Arts in 1904.

In this year the Chair of Music was endowed by Richard Peyton, the condition being that its first occupant should be Elgar, whose associations with Birmingham were already strong. After a good deal of negotiation it was decided that Elgar's only settled duties would be to deliver a series of lectures. From a communication from Peyton to Fiedler[4] it would seem that the idea of a Chair was in the first place fed by Fiedler to Lodge and by him (invoking the name of Elgar) to Peyton.

[1] See Sir Oliver Lodge, "Early History of the University and its Present Institutions", in *Birmingham Institutions*, ed. J. H. Muirhead, Birmingham, 1911, p. 62 et seq.

[2] "The Requirements of the University of Birmingham" (*Nature*, January 1, 1903), reprinted in Sir Norman Lockyer, *Education and National Progress*, London, 1906, pp. 258–62.

[3] Hermann Georg Fiedler (1863–1945) was a native of Zittau in Saxony and a graduate of Leipzig University. He came to Birmingham in 1890 as Professor of German Language and Literature at Mason's College. In 1907 he left Birmingham, where he was also Chairman of the University Musical Society, for Oxford. Sometime tutor to the then Prince of Wales he published the *Oxford Books of German Poetry and Prose*.

[4] November 7, 1904.

CHAPTER 2

FOUNDATION OF A CHAIR OF MUSIC

RICHARD PEYTON, founder and benefactor of the Chair of Music in Birmingham University, was a typical figure of his age. He deserves commemoration whenever the Roll of Honour of Victorian worthies is called; not least on account of his willingness not only to recognise Elgar's genius but also to do something about it. Peyton's family roots were in Worcestershire, and in days when local patriotism ran high this may have had something to do with it.

Born in Moseley, Birmingham, Peyton, a Unitarian, was educated in Liverpool and Moseley before being sent to study in Heidelberg. In due course he joined the prosperous family firm of manufacturing chemists, Peyton and Son. His business interests—from which he retired relatively early in order to have time for his main enthusiasms—are of no concern here except in so far as they provided a solid foundation for a variety of useful voluntary undertakings. He became a town councillor as a Liberal Unionist, trustee and benefactor to many charitable institutions, and a magistrate. The owner of an estate in Montgomeryshire he was liberal in improving the amenities of his tenants, and he had an enlightened sense of responsibility so far as the countryside was concerned. An amateur artist he sat on the committee of the Art Gallery, to which he gave a number of paintings.

Peyton's devotion to music was passionate, inspired, no doubt, by the fact that as a young man he had been present at the first performance of *Elijah*, conducted by Mendelssohn, in Birmingham Town Hall. (In due course Peyton, whose talents were of a practical order, was responsible for the better lighting and ventilation of the Town Hall.) In 1857 he founded the Birmingham Amateur Harmonic Association and twenty-five years later saw to it that the Library of this body was passed to the Midland Institute. He was for many years an honorary officer of the Birmingham Triennial Musical Festival and was always prepared to travel to the Continent (at his own expense) to negotiate with notable artists. It was due to him that Ferdinand Hiller,[1] Max Bruch,[2] Camille Saint-Saëns,[3] and Niels Gade,[4] appeared in Birmingham. With a

[1] For first performance of *Nala und Damajanti*, Op. 150 (1870 Festival).

[2] For first performance of *Das Lied von der Glocke* Op. 45 (1879 Festival).

[3] For first performance of *La Lyre et la Harpe*, Op. 57 (1879 Festival). Regarding the Birmingham choir Saint-Saëns wrote: "Je voudrais que les personnes qui refusent tout sentiment musical aux anglais puissent entendre les choristes de Birmingham. Justesse, précision de la mesure et du rhythme, finesse des nuances, charme de la sonorité, ce choeur merveilleux réunit tout", "Les Festivals de Birmingham", article of August 1879 reprinted in *Harmonie et Melodie* (1885), pp. 141–54; see also Arthur Dandelot, *La Vie et l'Oeuvre de Saint-Saëns*, Paris, 1930, p. 92.

[4] For first performance of *Psyche*, Op. 60 (1882 Festival).

particular sense of responsibility for choral music Peyton assisted in the running of various of the choral societies of the city, and also selected the singers for the Handel commemorations in the Crystal Palace. The obvious representative of Birmingham, he served on the Council of the National Training School for Music,[1] where he endowed a scholarship.

Conscious that the welfare of music depended on the adequate provision of educational facilities Peyton saw an opportunity when the Council of the new University showed a disposition to encourage a broad view of culture. On December 7, 1904, the following letter was read to the Council by Joseph Chamberlain, Chancellor of the University:

Dear Mr. Chamberlain,—I address myself to you as Chancellor of the University of Birmingham, in order to make a proposal which, should it be approved by the authorities of the university, may I hope be to the advantage of the university and for the advancement of musical art. The proposal I have to make arises from the fact that there is at the present time a special opportunity of offering an appointment to a chair of music in the university to one of the most eminent of English musicians whether of the past or the present time; and the offer which I have the honour and pleasure to make is to contribute a sum of ten thousand pounds for the endowment of such a chair, the only condition being that it should in the first instance be offered to and accepted by Sir Edward Elgar, Mus.Doc., LL.D. Should that gentleman be willing to accept the position, his name would I feel sure at once command universal respect and confidence; and the study of music under his guidance and leadership would in the future ensure a high appreciation elsewhere of the value to be attached to such musical degrees as would be conferred by the Birmingham University. The city of Birmingham has a certain musical reputation, derived in a great degree from its triennial musical festivals which commenced in the year 1768; of which forty-one have now been held; and to which the world of music is indebted for the production of considerable numbers of new and important works by composers of many different nationalities, who have been induced by reason of the reputation of the festivals and the excellence of the performances to compose expressly for Birmingham. The city may also be considered musical by reason of the large number of persons who annually—whether as performers or audience—attend the concerts of the festival, choral and various other large and important musical societies; and there should be ample scope for the advantages to be derived from a university education, were such obtainable, not only to local students of the art but also to those whom the reputation of its musical professor would attract from elsewhere. I have always taken a deep interest in the musical life of the city, and hope (should my proposal be accepted) that the results would enhance the reputation which Birmingham already

[1] Founded in 1875 this institution was re-formed into the Royal College of Music in 1881.

enjoys; and that in the not distant future it would become one of the most important centres of musical art.

Yours sincerely,
RICHARD PEYTON

Moved by the Chancellor, seconded by Alderman Martineau, a resolution was passed accepting the offer and endorsing the nomination of Elgar for the Chair by the donor. (Lodge, however, was not willing to make this a precedent, foreseeing the possibility of wealthy benefactors of uncertain discrimination packing the institution with professors of dubious academic quality.[1]) The meeting also resolved that the Chair should bear the name of the donor. To end a happy meeting Sir John Holder came forward with a further offer of £1,000 "towards a fund for providing the necessary instruction—which will be supplemental to the establishment of the Chair of Music".

Elgar was put in a position of some difficulty. Either he accepted an uncongenial occupation, or the University was denied its Chair. Elgar's dislike of teaching (of which he had had more than enough as a visiting teacher in girls' schools in his younger days) was intense. Only half a year before the Birmingham appointment came up he had refused a generous offer from Manchester,[2] and, as has been seen in the previous chapter, he put off the Royal Institution when there was an opportunity to lecture there. He had, however, a strong connection with Birmingham. In youth he had played in Stockley's orchestra. His first success as a composer—modest though it was—came when his *Intermezzo Moresque* was given its first performance at the Town Hall, under Stockley, on December 13, 1883. *The Dream of Gerontius* (although the performance left much to be desired whereat the composer was miserable) was first given in Birmingham. So, too, in 1903 was *The Apostles*. The score of *Gerontius* was presented to the Oratory in Birmingham, where Father William Neville was an old friend and, as Newman's former private secretary and later as his literary executor, invaluable adviser.[3] Since 1900 Granville Bantock, whom Elgar held in high regard, had been Principal of the School of Music in the Midland Institute. Elgar was a supporter of George Halford,[4] the enterprising successor to Stockley as chief orchestral conductor in Birmingham, and

---

[1] Letter from Lodge to Fiedler, November 9, 1904.

[2] In Peyton's letter of November 7 there is a curious comment: "I understood you to say", he wrote to Fiedler, "that the [Birmingham] appointment in question was of Dr. [*sic*] Elgar's own seeking, that he had declined an offer from Manchester & had been in communication with Leeds". This sequence of activity on Elgar's part is not otherwise confirmed.

[3] Neville died on March 16, 1905, at the age of eighty. Educated at Winchester and Trinity College, Oxford, he worked as a priest of the Church of England at St. Saviour's Mission, Leeds. Under the influence of Newman he became a Roman Catholic in 1847 and was ordained six years later.

[4] George Halford (1859–1933) was born at Chilvers Coton, Warwickshire (George Eliot's "Shepperton"), was taught music by his father (a violinist) and the organist of

his championing of Richard Strauss gave great pleasure to Elgar. Respect for Halford increased when the Elgars heard his performance of *Cockaigne* and the *Pomp and Circumstance Marches* (Nos. 1 and 2). There were, remarked Lady Elgar, "Yells of delight after marches".[1] The next day Halford wrote to Elgar. The substance of the opening paragraph of his letter has relevance to the character of Elgar's lectures:

> I must [wrote Halford] just write you one word of thanks for coming here yesterday. I think it was awfully kind of you to come when you didn't know me and hardly anything about me but now I hope we may always be friends. We are both working for one object, the advancement of our art, and we are also doing what we can for *English* music. Therefore we have *something* in common . . .

On December 20, 1904, Richard Strauss conducted one of the Halford Concert Society's concerts[2] and afterwards the Elgars had a delightful reunion

---

Holy Trinity Church, Coventry. After holding various posts as organist he came under the influence of Dr. Swinnerton Heap by whom he was introduced to the Birmingham public as pianist. Halford conducted the Birmingham Musical Association, the Birmingham Choral and Orchestral Association, and the Midland Institute Madrigal Choir. In 1896 he commenced the Halford Concerts (ten each year). "One of Halford's seasonal achievements was to give the city in successive programmes the symphonies of Beethoven. It was he, too, who first familiarised the Midlands with the compositions of Tchaikowsky and Richard Strauss. But for him the Birmingham of his day would have had no high-class music except that to be found at the annual Sir Charles Hallé concert and at the Triennial Festival." *Birmingham Post*, February 14, 1933.

[1] Diary, January 21, 1902.

[2] "Musically the visit of Dr. Richard Strauss to Birmingham was looked forward to as one of the events of the season. True, we had an opportunity of hearing him as a pianist at one of Mr. Max Mossel's drawing-room concerts last season, and several of his works had been introduced by Mr. Geo. Halford. But, for all that, of the man and his music—that is, his greater works, we knew little. Therefore we were glad of another opportunity of judging him not only as a composer but also as a conductor. A number of vacant seats were noticed, and undoubtedly some few people appear somewhat afraid of attempting to listen to a concert composed wholly of Strauss music. It was a bold undertaking on the part of Mr. Halford to ask his patrons to listen to the music of one man, but the audience present—among whom one noticed many influential people in the musical world—must have been gratifying both to the promotors and to the composer-conductor. The programme was as follows: 'Don Juan,' Op. 20; Violin Concerto in D minor, Op. 8; Tone-poem 'Tod und Verklärung,' Op. 24; 'Ein Heldenleben,' Op. 49. The novelty of the concert was the Violin Concerto, and, as its opus number indicates, this is an early work, but as music it is excellent in every respect. It is formed on classic models, but contains some real melodies, which charm the listener by their beauty. Speaking personally it did not appeal to the writer as a great work; but played as it was by Mr. Max Mossel, it certainly created a most favourable impression. Mr. Mossel gave his part excellently. The 'Lento' was charmingly played, while the 'Rondo' went with a most inspiriting swing. The first movement appeared to contain the most solid scoring. Under Dr. Strauss the orchestra gave just the requisite accompaniment.

"As regards the orchestral selections, Mr. Halford had evidently prepared his ground well, especially as regarded the 'tone-poems,' all of which, however, have been dealt with in detail in previous issues of this journal. The 'Don Juan' 'poem' is a work of great

with him at the Clef Club.[1] By now, Elgar, after many misgivings and many consultations, had committed himself. He was the Peyton Professor elect.

It would appear that a subtle means of persuasion was employed to overcome Elgar's known reluctance to accept academic office. The Prize-giving of the Midland Institute was held in the Town Hall, Birmingham, on October 12, 1904. Sir Oliver Lodge, Principal of the University, delivered the Presidential address, his subject being *Mind and Matter*. The Vote of Thanks was proposed by the Lord Mayor (Sir Hallewell Rogers), who introduced the seconder—

They had with them to second the resolution [he said] a gentleman to whom he should like to give a very hearty welcome to the city, Sir Edward Elgar (Applause). They had listened many times in that hall [the Town Hall] with great pleasure to Sir Edward Elgar's works, and they would be glad to hear him speak, particularly as he had come to Birmingham specially to attend the meeting. Sir Edward had the welfare of the Midland Institute at heart, as he was a visitor to the school of music (Applause).

Sir Edward Elgar, who was received with applause, seconded the resolution, observing that he had the honour to be connected with the Midland Institute in the department of music. He came to that meeting with a great deal of pleasure, because music he thought, might be considered to be, to put it colloquially, looking up (laughter). That was to say, in years gone by music was considered sufficient as an amusement, or in the higher degree a solace, but in these later days they managed to get a little intellect into it, and sometimes they were allowed to teach and to lead. He had heard with pleasure and reverence the references of Sir Oliver Lodge to the art of music, and he quite felt the dignity with which the art was now treated. Apart from the progress music had made he wished to say how finely it was progressing at the Midland Institute, and how Birmingham, as usual, was going forward and was not content only to import, but to create (Hear, hear). He had looked with much pleasure to the work done in Birmingham,

---

power, but, to my way of thinking, does not depict the idealist in his best light. The orchestral colouring is in places most vivid, and several of the themes are beautiful, and one must say the composer imparted a certain individuality to the performance. One of the best performances was undoubtedly that of 'Tod und Verklärung.' There was nothing in this poem which struck a repellent chord, while the realism of some sections, especially that of the dying struggles of the unhappy man, was excellent. This performance created great enthusiasm. 'Ein Heldenleben' has been the subject of special articles in this paper, and therefore does not call for any special comment as to its merit. Its powerful scoring is admittedly great, while in places its beauty is impressive; but it is such a combination of beauty and ugliness that, as a work of art, I am loth to place it. Sometimes, it must be confessed, one appears to be listening to a musical joke. Certainly the performance of the work was magnificent in every respect, every point being accentuated. The majority of the audience remained until the close, and Dr. Strauss met with a reception which must have assured him of the high estimation in which he was held by the audience. Shouts of 'bravo!' at the close of the concert were a startling demonstration on the part of the audience, and undoubtedly the Strauss Concert will long be remembered by many."
The Musical Standard, January 14, 1905, p. 27.

[1] Diary, December 2, 1904.

and he was grateful to the Birmingham people for the sympathetic hearing they always gave him (Applause). He was pleased to see the art enlarging and becoming not merely an amusement, but really doing some good (Applause). If musicians were going rather a little ahead and putting a little intellectuality into their music and were trying to be considered reasonable beings instead of mere puppets to amuse them, the lords of science and literature must not be angry with them. The sun did not hide the morning star although it ushered in the dawn (Applause).[1]

Lady Elgar was pleased, noting in her Diary: "E. made very nice speech." Afterwards there was a "nice talk with Sir O. Lodge". A month later, on November 12, Professor Fiedler came over to Hereford, where the Elgars had taken a house in the previous July, to talk "over Chair". On November 14 Elgar wrote to Fiedler declining the offer of nomination, on the grounds that "the duties would take up too much time". But on November 17 Alfred Hayes, then Secretary of the Midland Institute, and Bantock came to discuss the matter further. Three days later, busy with the last pages of *Pomp and Circumstance No. 3* Elgar was in a state over the professorship and "very anxious how to decide Birmingham".[2] Taking his indecision to London on November 12 he had consulted Alfred Littleton of Novello's who advised him to accept. On November 25 Charles Harding took Elgar to meet Peyton. Elgar liked Peyton and before leaving for Germany for the performance of *The Apostles* at Mainz wrote his provisional acceptance of the Professorship on November 25.

Mr. Harding wrote to Lady Elgar on November 28: " 'Joy & joy for ever'. We have heard the welcome answer! and I hasten to express our happiness with prospect of our city and the Midlands of England, being in touch with one, whose influence on music will be so ennobling and uplifting!

"Of course it will be a little time before the news is made public, but I could not resist writing to you—and please tell Sir Edward how glad I am, and I fancy the fact of being connected with the *new* University (with its fresh aspirations) will appeal to him?"

Mrs. Harding supplemented her congratulations with a copy of an extract from F. W. H. Myers's poem, *On Art as an aim in life*.[3]

On December 2 Alfred Hayes wrote to say, "I hope and believe that the position will prove agreeable to him under the conditions which he has wisely laid down.[4] The benefit which he is thus conferring on the cause of musical culture and progress cannot be over-rated." Hayes also sent as appendix to his

---

[1] *Birmingham Post*, October 13, 1904.

[2] Lady Elgar, ibid., November 20, 1904.

[3] Florence, 1871; see Frederic W. H. Myers, *Collected Poems*, London, 1921, pp. 192–202.

[4] On November 18 Elgar had indicated to Fiedler that after the first year special lecturers should be engaged, "each on a modern subject & generally to direct the influence of Music into Modern & *practical* ways". Cf. list of 1907–8 lectures given on p. 282. On November 22 (while looking forward to a long tenure of office) he indicated to Fiedler: "if I find the increasing duties interfere with my composition I may resign the post, say after three years. . . ." See *Elgar O.M.*, pp. 125–6.

& kind regard

Yours sincerely

Edward Elgar

Plas Gwyn

Hereford

Nov 25 1904

Dear Professor Fiedler,

My scruples, save those I hold as to general unfitness, have been removed, and I write to say that if the professor-ship is offered to me on the lines already decided upon I will accept it & will do my best for the University

letter a copy of his own first book *The Last Crusade* (1887).[1] On the day following Brodsky came to Malvern with his Quartet and when asked what his views were on Elgar's acceptance of the Chair observed—while hiding his disappointment over the refusal of Manchester—that he had *"no* feeling about Bir[m.] except pleased for any thing wh. wd. be good for E."[2]

Sir Oliver Lodge was the next correspondent, his letter of December 7 expressing "the joy with which the announcement of the proceedings at Council today will be welcomed by every member of the Staff, and to signify our cordial concurrence in the invitation which is being conveyed to you by the Vice Chancellor". And on the following day Mrs. Fiedler joined this "chorus of congratulation", saying how glad she was that her husband has been allowed to help in this memorable work—"for I am sure that it will have far-reaching effects in the History of Music!"

Much publicity had surrounded the appointment and Elgar was expected to work wonders. In the *Birmingham Post* of December 21, 1904, a "Special Contributor" published an inspired article (see telegram of December 10, p. 17) on *The Universities and Musical Degrees,* in which he wrote:

> ... And now a Chair of Music having been founded in the University by Mr. Richard Peyton, which by a unique good fortune has been accepted by the most eminent living English composer, the one thing most wanted, a great and inspiring leader and organiser, has been secured. It is, of course, to [*sic*] soon to indicate the lines on which Sir Edward Elgar is likely to work—he will probably foreshadow his plans in his inaugural address—but of this we may be sure, that he will develop music and musical teaching on modern and practical lines.[3] Sir Edward is most anxious to develop the School of Music, of whose co-operation he is assured, so that it may prove the practical training ground for his students. He believes there is no reason why the Birmingham School of Music at the Midland Institute should not some day rival the older institutions in Manchester and London, if only the necessary financial support can be secured. If in the future a Faculty of Music should be established in the Birmingham University, it will no doubt be a working faculty with a number of additional teachers; and the degrees, if such are granted, will be made to mean a great deal more than the present musical degrees at other Universities, representing as much culture, theoretical knowledge, and professional skill as, say, the M.D. in the case of the medical profession.

We have every confidence that the beginning of Sir Edward Elgar's

---

[1] Alfred Hayes (1858–1936), son of the Town Clerk of Wolverhampton and, later, of Birmingham, was educated at grammar schools in both towns and at New College, Oxford. When he retired in 1931 he had been connected with the Midland Institute, as Secretary and Head of the Education Department, for forty-two years. He wrote several books of poetry as well as verse dramas and made translations from Tolstoy and Pushkin. Until 1900, when Granville Bantock was appointed Principal of the School of Music, Hayes was responsible for music in the Midland Institute.

[2] Diary, December 3, 1904.

[3] cf. p. 14, fn. 4.

POST OFFICE TELEGRAPHS.

EYRE & SPOTTISWOODE, LONDON.

Office Stamp.

KING'S NORTON
BIRMINGHAM
10 DE 04

| Charges | £ | s. | d. |
| to pay } | | | |

Handed { in at } Regent St   at 1.52 p.m.,   Received { here at } 2.23 P.m.

TO { Professor Fiedler Elford Grove Kings Norton

Just teak am a rehting offer
let the proposed article appear
but with no definition of
future ideas and developments
                    Edward Elgar
        2360a Queen St Westminster

activity in Birmingham will mark a new epoch in British music, and that he will be the rallying point and inspiring influence for the rising school of English musicians. The musical world in England and abroad will watch with keen interest the developments which are sure to take place in our city under the guidance of Sir Edward Elgar.

The *Musical Opinion*, however, introduced a somewhat cynical note:

> Sir Edward Elgar is one of Fortune's favourites. It is only a few months since he received a knighthood; now a chair of music has been created especially for him. . . . Sir Edward has intimated his acceptance of the appointment and everybody concerned is happy. "I have only what I can earn by my compositions," said our latest musical knight in protesting against the music pirate business; now he will have an income of at least four hundred pounds from another source. It should be added that a thousand pounds has been gifted by another Birmingham magnate for the working expenses of the music chair.[1]

A sceptical note was also introduced by the Rev. Joseph Wood who, at the Annual General Meeting of the Midland Institute asked "Is Birmingham musical?" He hoped that Sir Edward would be able to do something to improve the situation but doubted whether much progress could be made. As an example of a really musical city he instanced Manchester, where, he said, there was a built-in capacity for musical appreciation in that there were 70,000 Germans resident there.[2]

During January and February, 1905, Elgar was chiefly occupied with the *Introduction and Allegro* for strings, of which he conducted the first performance in Queen's Hall on March 8. A note in the *Musical Standard* of January 7,[3] shows another project, but one that never progressed further than sketches. "Also of interest is the fact that the composer is engaged on a work of quite a new order. It is a pantomime-ballet-divertissement on the subject of Rabelais's 'Gargantua et Pantagruel'." There were many other engagements and, out of the goodness of his heart, he was also busy making a libretto for Ivor Atkins—for the *Hymn of Faith*. But Birmingham was never very far out of mind. On January 11, breaking off from a sitting for Talbot Hughes the painter,[4] Elgar wrote to Peyton:

[Hereford]

Dear Mr. Peyton,

Very many thanks for your kind letter: we have been quite heavily saddened by the death of our friend Mr. C. Harding & feel the deepest sympathy for the family. Your plan, so unhappily interrupted, for a

---

[1] January 1905, p. 258.

[2] See *The Musical Standard*, January 21, 1905. The Rev. Joseph Wood's facts were somewhat astray. The census returns for the German population of Manchester in 1901 were—756 men, 563 women, and in 1911—865 men, 453 women.

[3] p. 3.

[4] The portrait appears as Frontispiece to this book.

meeting at your house with the governors was a very kind thought & I am sorry it cannot be carried out.

Many thanks for your general invitation; this will make my visit to Birmingham, when that does come off, pleasant. I am shortly going to communicate with Sir Oliver Lodge [as to?] plans & if this necessitates my staying the night in Birmingham I will gladly avail myself of your very kind offer.

Believe me
Very sincerely yours
Edward Elgar

On January 17 he wrote to Fiedler:

[Hereford]

My dear Professor Fiedler;

Our deepest sympathy has been with you in the sudden sorrow which has befallen you.[1]

Had it not been for this most sad event I should have written earlier asking if we could meet to discuss one or two matters which I want to proceed with in connection with the University.

I cannot be with you today at the meeting of the Faculty as I am not well —(chill) & I do not make any special effort to come (this would be attended with some risk) as I think you will not really want me (from what I gather from the agenda). Tell me if it would be possible & quite agreeable to you to come over here, either to lunch[2] or stay the night: we should be delighted to see you: if this is not practicable I would hope to come over to Birmingham soon.

Kind regards
Yours sincerely
Edward Elgar:

P.S. Am I appointed to the post yet? That is, am I officially recognised & may I assume the honour *and* responsibility in answering questions etc. connected with the University.

I have had no official notice that I can find beyond the V. chancellor's invitation which I accepted.

Lodge wrote on January 27 to say that Elgar's appointment and stipend had been effective as from January 1. Elgar next wrote to Fiedler from The Warden's

---

[1] Charles Harding (1839-1904), who died on the last day of the year, was Fiedler's father-in-law. A solicitor (retired in 1898), Harding was a keen supporter of musical activities. He had founded ten scholarships at the National Training School for Music, was a Steward of the Birmingham Music Festival until 1903, a Vice-President of the Festival Choral Society, and "with a view to encouraging sight singing in the Board Schools had presented to the School Board a challenge shield to be competed for by the various schools under that body". (*Gazette and Express*, January 2, 1905.) Harding was also a Life Governor of the University and had provided scholarships for the School of Modern Languages. A close friend of Peyton, and intimate with all the interested parties, he had done a good deal of diplomatic work in respect of the Professorship behind the scenes.

[2] The Fiedlers came to lunch on January 28 (Diary entry).

Lodgings, New College, Oxford—where he had been on the occasion of his receiving an honorary Doctorate—on February 7:

> Dear Professor Fiedler:
> I am so sorry I could not get away in time yesterday.
> I think I can manage the date we tentatively fixed for the inaugural address—I see this is on your list for tomorrow but it had best be *not* publicly announced until after I return home (Thursday next) & have communicated with you.
>
> In haste
> Yours sincy
> Edward Elgar

A week later, writing on Birmingham University notepaper from his home in Hereford, Elgar confirmed date and title:

> Dear Professor Fiedler
> Yes: Thursday March 16th at 6.30.
> Subject
> "A Future for English Music"
> In greatest haste
> Yours very sincerely
> Edward Elgar

This was followed by a further communication on February 23, the score of the *Introduction and Allegro* having been completed ten days previously and proofs of *Pomp and Circumstance No. 3* having been checked.

> [Hereford]
> My dear Professor:
> I am now 'through' the arduous work which has held me tight & for a few days I can look round. I should like to 'look round' the University & shd want a cicerone. Would you have any free time next week Tuesday, Wednesday or Thursday?
> Failing either of these days I could manage Monday—on Friday I go to London
> Yours sincerely
> Edward Elgar
> I have sent a line to Sir Oliver Lodge saying I hope to be able to come next week.

On the same day Elgar seriously began to initiate his plan for putting down the foundations for music in the University. He wrote to H. V. Higgins, Chairman of the Covent Garden Opera Syndicate, whom he knew through the Elgar Festival held at Covent Garden that year.

> My dear Higgins:
> In connection with the chair of music I am hoping to raise a fund to be expended in aiding the performance of works of young composers and generally assisting deserving compositions to an adequate performance. I

do not propose to ask for a lump sum to *invest* as that method might lead to another Chantrey Bequest, – – a thing very much to be avoided. I ask for subscriptions, – – a certain sum annually for not less than three years. If at the end of that time, or any other time agreed upon, the subsriber [*sic*] feels that the fund is not justifying its existence he can withdraw his support.

This is more 'alive' than a permanent fund and will give the administrators a feeling of continued active responsibility.

For the moment I only want a definite promise: later a committee will be appointed, but I shall be responsible for the actual distribution and I need not tell you that the influence would be quite modern. I am very anxious to have the name of the Syndicate as supporters; the thing will in no sense be local, but endeavour will be made to find out and help 'genius' anywhere.

With kindest regards,

Yours very sincerely,[1]

As will appear Elgar was also busy thinking on the establishment of a music library in the University. On March 1 he went to Birmingham "to prospect all day".[2] Still suffering, on and off, from the chill already detailed—but more truthfully from a mild depression not helped by the ever nearer ordeal of public speech—he survived the first performance of the *Introduction and Allegro*—helped by Lady Elgar's "bag of restoratives",[3] and settled down to put his notes in order. On the day before the Inaugural Lecture he was "busy with shorthand writer, having address typed".[4]

[1] Only a carbon copy of this (typewritten) letter exists.
[2] Diary entry, March 1.
[3] Ibid., March 8.
[4] Ibid., March 15.

CHAPTER 3

THE INAUGURAL LECTURE
(March 16, 1905)

THE Elgars, accompanied by Frank Schuster and Alfred Kalisch, music critic of *The World*, travelled from London to Birmingham where they were met by Peyton. After tea the party proceeded to the Midland Institute, where the lecture was to be given. "E. looked most beautiful in his gown and hood. then to lecture—organ played his tunes. crowded hall. E. lectured most splendidly, held his audience breathless . . ."[1]

The Manchester Guardian confirmed Lady Elgar's impression and added to what she wrote: "The large hall of the Midland Institute was crowded, and the staff of the University was on the platform. During the interval of waiting selections from Sir Edward Elgar's works were played on the organ, and were loudly applauded, especially 'Land of Hope and Glory', which was peculiarly appropriate (though we did not know it at the moment) to the confident and hopeful tone of Sir Edward's address. The new professor, who wore the robes of a Doctor of Music of Cambridge, was loudly cheered as he entered with Sir O. Lodge, the Principal of the University, whose prefatory remarks were commendably brief and to the point. . . . [The lecture] was admirably delivered and marked throughout by verbal felicity no less than by originality of thought and breadth of view."[2]

> *Rough Notes*
>
> General mem[a]

page no.[3]

    I   I Inaugural address
           II English composers
         III English executants
         IV English critics

    I v.   I stand here in a position new to me,—made for me: a position of responsibility & of honour; [δ I am fe] while feeling [δ my] how inadequate I am for this post of Peyton

---

[1] Diary entry, March 16, 1905.
[2] March 17, 1905.
[3] Editor's numbering.

Professor of Music in the University of Birmingham I [δ may] will say at once that I intend to shirk neither the responsibility nor the honour, & will try my best to [δ be worthy of both] meet the first &, it may be, add to the second.

The munificence & good will towards our art of Music shewn by the founder of the Chair, Mr Rich Peyton, have been commented upon [δ in many] by many pens in many lands & it is not necessary for me to refer more than briefly to this matter. My own [δ thanks] word of thanks will not be on my own behalf [δ although my] but in the name of the younger school of English musicians. [See p. 29.]

2   Sir Joshua Reynolds, (deploring want of due academic training) asks why those who are "more than boys at sixteen become less than men at 30"—we [δ may] have to ask ourselves why those who were (according to their friendly critics) more than men at 30 *have* invariably dwindle into nonentities between 50 & 60. [See p. 59.]

The Renascence

We are the inheritors of an art which, under the fostering care bestowed upon it during the 20 years between 1880 & 1900, has gained no affection in this country & has obtained no respect abroad

3   Our composers have too frequently written their works as if for an audience of musicians only: the English works (it will be understood that I refer to great attempts at composition only) have been correct & cold

A large audience shall be addressed. let me [δ dref] define the audience. I do not mean the popular public; but our playwrights do not write only for other playwrights & our novelists only for other novelists, or our painters execute their greater works merely for the benefit of other painters.

[δ But] All the composers recognised by [δ all] great musicians of [δ all] every school have written their works with a view to their larger [δ art] audiences [See p. 37.]

4   *dignity & respect*
Hubert Parry the head of the art in England
respect & I will say affection

———

Made on too many occasions the figurehead & apologist for the formal school. [δ we] I claim claim him in spirit as a young man. the young & buoyant spirit is happily with us & no cloud of formalism can dim the healthy influence he [δ still] exerts upon us. [See pp. 48, 49.]

4 v.   [This page is reversed]

Mema

a great conductor Wood

add

audiences [See p. 163.]

The first critic was Lucifer & he criticised—with little effect except to himself it seems,—the Creation [See pp. 155, 157.]

————

Important near end before students refer to Birmingham professors

————

near end—after proposed lectures

Leslie Stephen

We must start from experience. We must begin by asking impartially what pleased men, & then again *why* it pleased them. We must not decide dogmatically that it *ought* to have pleased on his pleased on the simple ground that it is or is not congenial to ourselves". [See p. 57.]

5   I have said that some men stand still
—the difficulty is not with these: but with a certain sect of the fashionable people who boldly declare "we are modern"—anxious to be in the first flight of popularity they sing Ca ira ca ira—to the wrong tune a revolutionary song sung to the old hundredth does not excite anything but pity for the performance. [See p. 41.]

[Amongst ?]

6   The word *Music* in these remarks refers only to what is concisely called 'big' music—oratorio, opera, symphonies & concerto & sonatas. When occasion arises I shall refer to lesser music by name. [See p. 31.]

————

Theatre Music—Shakespeare's incidental music always *Arne*
(bad period) [See p. 43.]

———

Strauss' Düsseldorf speech
    Arne behind Handel etc etc.
    —to Bennett less than Mendelssohn [See p. 43.]

———

mem: imitation.
    it is just as bad, as weak & means no more, to imitate
Richd. Strauss as it was to imitate Brahms. [See p. 50.]

———

modern evolution: where the Mendelssohnians *whined* at
the approach of the new men, the imitators of Brahms
groan. [See p. 49.]

7   Mem: No need for young men to insist; Theophile Gautier
red waistcoat not needed; the *public*? is ready to listen to
anything worthy.
    No eccentricity of costume necessary to draw attention:
that is in this day not a sign of strength but of utter feebleness
& want of ability.
    Imitators of French more deplorable than anything! [See
pp. 41, 51.]

———

Hume's essay. "We have placed our lever in heaven & by
it we can move the world. [See p. 61.]

8   Audiences: gaucherie of English men
not accustomed to lecture in large meetings
    feeling of restraint & *Grobheit* hence horror of any
serious subject in the concert room.
    There have been times in the arts when men have stood
still; men have said this is perfection & I will imitate it.
    Eclectics
        ? Caracci
    3   ⎧ Ludovico
          ⎨ Annibale
          ⎩ Agostino [See p. 39.]

9   *Begin.*
    Opening—refer to foundation of Chair

Mr. Richd. Peyton
a tribute not to me but to the healthy young
english school [See p. 29.]

personal note
not exactly to be my [illegible word]
& I have accepted it   These remarks refer only to big music.

————

Small music England is preeminent
[See p. 34.]

————

Humorous: The English [δ require] *commission* a song writer
or a pianist to compose cantatas or symphonies for their
festivals & it is quite in keeping with the upside down case
of things—that a man without a voice & with no notion of
speaking shd. be addressing this assembly. Here however I
trust the preconceived english idea will break down & we
may get all our [illegible word]

10   I I have referred to young [England ?]
what does it mean
I do not know
I know it means something original & something alive.
—It wishes for life—it desires no annihilation of existing
perfect things. [See p. 39.]
It is opposed to mere imitation.
Kapellmeister music. [See p. 39.]

————

at certain stages in every art men have stood still.
Imitation—Caracci [*sic*] eclectic
[marginal   useless (See p. 39.]
note in
pencil]   ————

Something is moving—what is it again I have no answer,
[δ is it the] quote from [Hume ?] [See p. 61.]
But is it the soul.
go to Plato [See p. 41.]

11   probably when the editor is tired of writing obituary notices
of the great works of his living friends musicians [δ will
receive] the definition will be altered. [See pp. 157, 160, 164f.]
I

12   John Bull
mem: the robust school called English remember Shakespeare, we are in his own country, the ideal Englishman as
drawn by S.—not to confuse the personality of the Man—
the writer with the personality he has drawn for us has more
than drawn, has made living Mercutio, the gallant gentleman,
Fauconbridge the bold [darling?] etc etc. [See p. 51.]

Why should we accept as ideal English music a type that
exists in no other art? [See p. 51.]

13   [Quotations from Hoffmann as on p. 61.]

TEXTUAL COMMENTARY

Ts. 1   Second paragraph appears before first

[δ I fear . . . otherwise]
[δ At the same time] *It*
[δ the] *a* future
   in England. [At head of page] *In addition to the extra-ordinary faculty we have of discovering the greatness of a vocalist after he has lost his voice* [running on to main text] *t*he English custom of giving [δ the] *a* commission

[δ ordinary] *resemblance to ordinary* English custom
will break [δ down] *off*
some movement [δ in other directions]

[δ feeling] acknowledging
Richd Peyton

by *attempting to* draw [δ ing]

I hold it to be . . . .
                    :
                    :
                    :
                    :
            : . . . .*name of Shakespeare*

A FUTURE FOR ENGLISH MUSIC

I fear that in this opening address there may be rather a strong personal note. As I do not intend to be actually formal, this personal note I do not consider to be absolutely unfortunate. As I am speaking from my own experience—experience dearly bought—*I fear that it cannot be otherwise. At the same time* it is my desire to treat the subject which I have chosen—*a future* for English music—in the broadest possible manner. Curious things occur in our art *in England.* The English custom of giving the commission to a song writer or a pianist to compose cantatas or symphonies or oratorios for Musical Festivals has long been in vogue, and it is quite in keeping with the upside-down-ness of things that a man without a voice and with no notion of public speaking, should be addressing this assembly. Here, however, I trust the *resemblance to ordinary English custom will break off,* and that at any rate the matter of this address may give rise to *some movement,* even if it is very lamely set forth.

I stand here in a position new to me, made for me: a position of responsibility and it may be of honour. While *acknowledging* how inadequate I am for this post of the "*Richard Peyton* Professor of Music" in the University of Birmingham, I will say at once that I intend to shirk none of the responsibility, and will try my best to add to the honour of the position by *drawing round me* some of the best minds connected with our art. The munificence and goodwill towards our art of music evinced by the founder of the Chair, Mr. Richard Peyton, have been commented upon by many pens in many lands, and it is not necessary for me to refer more than briefly to this matter. My own word of thanks will not be on my own behalf; but in the name of all that is healthy and sincere in the younger school of English musicians, I thank the founder. *I hold it to be* a happy chance, or, as we are serious to-day, I will say a happy Providence which places this new movement in English music in that district of England which was parent of all that is bright, beautiful and good in the works of him whom we know and love under the *name of Shakespeare.*

In choosing an indefinite title for this address I was following my

Ts. 1   [δ idea] *conviction*

concerto and [δ in some cases Sonatas] *so forth*

critics. [Marginal note:] *These three factors are necessary to form
a complete art* [at foot of page] *& among the critics I actually
include the intelligent audience. Cf. Birmingham Post:* ". . . Sir
Edward made it quite clear that his lecture was purely introductory, and that it would be followed by three others, in
which he proposes to develop his views and intentions more
minutely, dealing in turn with the three factors essential to
form a complete Musical Art—Composers, Executants, and
Critics, using that last term in the broad sense of an educated
and intelligent audience".
[δ work] *picture*   over—*but to fulfil its mission*

    the public *which*

[New paragraph marked]

as [δ before] *with the author*
The publisher has to be called in to *print and* present [δ this]
the work, *in a tangible form* but the vast [δ difference] *gulf which
separates musical from literary authorship* is [δ that] *the fact* the
work remains practically unheard and not understood without the help of [δ the] executants.
To these & to [δ T] *the* third living factor in our art, the
critics,
        [δ who frequently do more harm than good,]
Ts. 1   material [δ for] *upon*

own *conviction*—that the result of the address would also be indefinite. What THE future of English music may be, no man can say, but during the course of this address and three others which I will name presently, I will endeavour to foreshadow A future for English music—a future based on my own experience and on my hope.

Music in these remarks, refers only to what is called "big" music—oratorio, opera, symphony, concerto, *and so forth*. When occasion arises I shall refer to lesser music specifically.

A living art of music consists not only of composers, as some of the race seem to imagine, but also executants, and—I will dare to add—*critics*. Composers are in a different position from painters or literary authors.

The painter finishes his *picture* and his labour is then *over:—but to fulfil its mission* the picture must be hung and exhibited, and thus it meets its public and there is nothing to stand between the *public which* the artist addresses and himself.

With the literary author the case is rather different. His personal work ends when his manuscript is finished, but he has to call in the help of the printer to present his work in such form that it may reach the public. In the case of some lady novelists, I believe, the friendly services of the publishers go so far as to correct the spelling and amend the syntax—but that is beside the present point. But with the composer of music, a different state of things exists. His own personal work, *as with the author*, ends when his manuscript is finished. *The publisher has to be called in to print and present the work*, but the vast gulf which separates musical from literary authorship is that the work remains practically unheard and not understood without the help of *executants*. By executants I mean singers, players, and above all, conductors. *To these and to the third living factor in our art, the critics,* I shall refer in another address. But I should like to insist on the belief that the living art of music should consist of these three factors—the composer, the executants and the critics; the composer providing the *material upon* which

[δ advice] opinion   luminous *advice*
[δ and]   *by*
[δ In the light of some recent developments I should like to
make clear that the action referred to is not a libel action.]
[δ *I said "action",—we had better understand at once that the
action*]

Ts. 2   [δ In the light of some recent developments I] *It* should
[δ like to make] *be* clear*ly understood* that the "*action*" referred
to is not a libel action.

Ts. 1   I do not [δ mean] by any means *wish to indicate*

              and a *piece of*

[δ constrained] *inspired*

[δ As I have said] *T*oday

In looking [δ back to find] *for*

ordinary *commercial* lecture [δ of commerce]
. . . preceding 1880. **C**
Some of us who *in that year 1880* were [δ then] young

the other two classes subsist; the executants rising to the level of the composer in doing their best to give a worthy performance of such things as are provided for them; while the critics—with not necessarily *friendly opinion* but large-minded and *luminous*—should help to a better understanding of the composer *and* the audience that he addresses; that is to say that these three factors should have a definite 'action' one upon another for the advance of music. *It should be clearly understood that the 'action' referred to is not a libel action.*[1]

Now I have used the word audience—and I should like it clearly understood what I mean by the word. *I do not, by any means,* wish to indicate the general POPULAR public. A work of art is none the less a work of art if it is never seen; and a *piece* of sculpture of Michael Angelo or a Symphony of Beethoven would be just as great if buried in a cellar as if in its proper place educating, helping and improving mankind generally by being placed before an audience. But no artist who is *inspired* to create could possibly feel that his labour is justified unless his production is brought before that audience or public for which, in his own mind, he designed it.

To-day, I can only make a few general remarks on English music, reserving for three separate addresses, English Composers, English Executants, and English Critics.

In looking for a practical starting point for anything that may be usefully considered in relation to present day music, I think it unnecessary to go back farther than 1880. I do not say definitely that that is the best starting point, but it is sufficient for the purpose. The history of music from the time of Purcell onwards is well known, and it would be merely a tiresome repetition of the *ordinary commercial lecture* to go over the two centuries *preceding 1880. Some of us who in that year* were young and taking an active part in music—a really active part such as playing in orchestras—felt that something at last was going to be done

---

[1] In the case "Cotton v the Newspaper Syndicate Ltd" heard before Mr. Justice Grantham and a special jury on February 28, 1905, Mrs. Adelaide Mary Cotton (professionally known as Miss Ada Reeve) won her action for libel against the *Weekly Despatch* on account of an article headed " £250 a week—Confessions describing road to success in musical comedy, by the Queen of Comic Opera, Miss Ada Reeve" which, purporting to have been signed by Miss Reeve, had appeared on February 28, 1904 (see *Birmingham Mail,* February 28, 1905).

Ts. 1   An *interest* hitherto unknown [δ interest]

[Marginal note:] [δ Blest pair of Sirens] [* From foot of page:] *Happily for us some still live and give their quota of joy and satisfaction,—such a one is Parry's "Blest pair of Sirens".* Those that live are still before *us* [δ you]:

Ts. 2   not necessary. [At foot of page:] *& happily for us some still give their quota of joy & satisfaction* Those that live are still before [δ you] *us* the greater portion are dead and forgotten, and only exist as warnings to the student of the twentieth century.

Ts. 1   . . . twentieth century. **D**

to find *say in 1900* that we had [δ succeeded to] *inherited*

[At foot of page * :] *like the very bad boy;* I DON'T CARE
[On a page existing only in this draft:]
                    [δ *& one preeminent English Conductor Henry J Wood*] As I have said, my remarks refer only to "big" music; but it is necessary to say that in smaller music England has always held its own and in such things as comic opera and [δ the ballet it is still] *ballad has been & may easily be again* preeminent.
    Our orchestral players are still the best in the world & our choral singers, who have within the last few years justified the increase of musical education by adding to that robust energy which was their chief characteristic a greater range of expression giving us tenderness & romance with [δ happily], no loss of that virile

in the way of composition by the English school. A large number of compositions during the twenty years following, were brought before us, and the whole atmosphere of English music was changed, owing to the spread of musical education, which was out of proportion to the natural growth of the population; or, to put it plainly, that musical taste had increased. *An interest* hitherto unknown was taken in the work of our native composers. Some of us who were accustomed to play the works of Beethoven, Weber and—to come down to the most modern man of that date, Wagner,—while we were anxious to believe all that a friendly Press told us about the glories of the new English school, could not help feeling that the music given us to play, was, not to put too fine a point upon it, rather 'dry'. I am not going to criticise these works in detail: it is not necessary. *Happily* for us some still live and give their quota of joy and satisfaction: the greater portion are dead and forgotten and only exist as warnings to the student of the *twentieth century.* It is saddening to those who hoped so much from these early days, to find that after all that had been written, and all the endeavour to excite enthusiasm for English music—"big" music—*to find that we had inherited* an art which has no hold on the affections of our own people, and is held in no respect abroad.

The last word calls to mind that there are two ways of looking at foreign opinion. I have the advantage to have heard my works frequently played and to have mixed very much with foreign musicians, and can speak with some authority and with some feeling as to the opinion held of English music generally amongst our nearest neighbours. I am not one of those who are continually wondering what the intelligent foreigner *thinks of him.* To me "Britain is a world by itself; and we will pay nothing for wearing our own noses".

force which has been our pride: and we can say with pride that we have produced one great conductor H J. Wood—a world renowned artist.

[δ general]

general causes [Ts. 2 Marginal note.] [δ *twice*]

Ts. 1   [Marginal note:] *Out*

... audience, [δ which I myself like to imagine I am approaching.]
As I have said It must be [Ts. 2] [δ *As I have said*]

Ts. 2   [δ we are pleased]

Ts. 1   ... divisions *into* which I propose to divide the next three addresses [δ into]—

However, we continually see, in criticisms written by Englishmen, that a desire to please the foreign musician is, if not uppermost, continually present.

Without pretending to any exhaustive consideration as to the *general* failure of the works produced during the period named, it is necessary to consider what have been *the causes* of their want of vitality. Our English composers too frequently write their works as if for an audience of musicians only: therefore these works have been correct and necessarily cold. Looking at great creative artists, we find that a totally different attitude has been adopted. The dramatist does not write his work for an audience of other dramatists, and a painter does not paint or produce his pictures for a public consisting of mere technical painters. The novelist certainly does not write merely for other novelists; but the musician always seems to have the fear of other musicians before his eyes. It is quite possible for any student to find errors in the way of fifths and so forth in the works of the great masters; but these men have always written for a *larger audience*. It must be understood distinctly that by these "larger audiences" I do not mean the popular public. Far from that—taking it as a necessary evil that audiences must exist or that music itself must cease to exist, let us consider what sort of audiences we want to please. We like to see scientific men, artists of all kinds, and literary men, actors—in fact everyone who is concerned with art in any shape or form. If our compositions interest and touch some responsive chord in these people, *we are pleased*, and have the gratification of knowing that art has met art, and that in itself is an artistic reward. Is it possible to conceive that Bach or Beethoven or Brahms so wrote for a narrow circle? No, they addressed a larger party, a responsive, human and artistic mass, and amongst these we find our greatest supporters. I am bound to say that the English works have not fulfilled their mission, except in a very few instances.

As the three main *divisions into which I propose to divide* the next three addresses—that is, composers, executants, and critics,—are bound to overlap. I do not propose to go definitely into any musical composition as this moment; any detailed criticism or analysis of work I will leave to the next lecture.

I have spoken of the young English school—what does it mean? I

Ts. 1   [Marginal note] *Out.* We had too much mere imitation of other men's work, and *I understand* it is against this mere imitation [δ and not against the mere thing] that the young men cry out so violently.

         [δ have] *need*   [Ts. 2] *need* only   to   look

Ts. 1   They probably have . . .
& 2

Ts. 1   . . . as great *as* [Marginal note] *? as*

         Carrac[δ h]*ci* [Marginal note] *Caracci*   [δ a technique] *an eclectic* school
           [δ technical] *eclectic*
         which [δ according to their view], *apparently* contained *work equal to*

         [Marginal note] *Out*

confess I do not know; and yet it is for that school that I stand here, and for which in a certain measure I plead. I know that in the best sense it means something original and something alive. It wishes for life, but it desires no annihilation of existing perfect things. It is opposed to mere imitation, and mere "Capellmeister" music. *We had too much imitation* of other men's work and I understand it is against this mere imitation that the young men cry out so violently. Music is such a young art that it is impossible to say definitely where we are; whether we are at the end of practical development or whether we are only at the beginning: this is not worth while to discuss. *But we need* only to look upon the history of other arts and we see that at certain stages men have stood still, and have said: "This is perfection". *They have probably* not said "I will imitate this", but they have done so. The young English school then is against mere imitation. I think I have used the word old-fashioned: that requires at this stage a little explanation. Things that are old are not necessarily old-fashioned. Bach is old but will never be old-fashioned. I need not go through a list of other composers whose music still lives, but I may take a modern instance, Meyerbeer, who is not old but certainly is old-fashioned. The reason for this, without multiplying instances, is that the man who is not old-fashioned represents the greatest advance in his art in his own time: and it is one of the saddening things to consider that the parasite has always existed by the side of the original and has frequently been accepted as being *as great as*, if not greater than, the giant upon whose genius he has lived.

Besides the men who stood still we also see groups of people who have endeavoured to gather together into one focus the canons of art and found a school. I need only refer to the *Caracci*[1] and the disastrous result of their attempt to found *an eclectic school*. We have seen *eclectic composers* in our own day, who have poured out works—symphonies, concertos, oratorios—*which apparently contained work equal to* the best of their contemporaries or their predecessors. These works failed and must always fail. The art that stands still is dead; the art that moves, or I would say progresses, is alive. That brings us to the consideration of what is progress and what is mere *movement*.

[1] Agostino (1557–1602), Annibale (1560–1609), and Lodovico Carracci (1555–1619), whose works, marked by richness of design and colour, were the focus of progressive tendencies in Bolognese painting from about 1582 when they opened an "Academy" in Bologna. In dismissing them as "eclectic" Elgar was repeating a general Romantic opinion. For a full discussion of this term in this connection see D. Mahon, *Studies in Seicento Art and Theory*, London, 1947.

Ts. 1   [Marginal note] *Out*

[δ lead] *leave*

he *and his work* will be accepted . [δ and his work]
There is [δ N] *n*o need

At the present no one who lives in the world of music in England can help feeling that SOMETHING is moving—something which is giving place to the mere imitation. This movement I believe at last comes from within. It may be that the soul, of which Plato speaks, is living in the world of English music.

To revert once more to the word 'Old-Fashioned'. It is not difficult to deal with the men of whom I have spoken who sit by the wayside and say "This is the end of art and the way ends here". They say this when they mean that they see no farther and that their wings have drooped and their souls (if they have them) are tired. It is easy to *leave* THEM by the wayside. More difficult to deal with and more clogging to any real progress in art are those formalists who say: "We are modern and we are in the race": when, as a matter of fact, they are quite out of any running for any artistic prize:—the men who go about assuming that they are most modern and singing revolutionary songs to the wrong tune. It is all very well to sing "Ca ira, ça ira—but the effect is quite lost if it is chanted to the Old Hundredth, and excites nothing but pity for the performer.

On the other hand I find amongst the younger men a quite out-of-date desire for notoriety, as distinct from legitimate fame. Something, as I said, is moving, and we will assume it is the soul of music, and the English are now ready to accept anything and welcome it, which is sincere, honest, healthy and well written. It is no longer necessary for the young man of the present day to pose; he only need be himself, and if his personality is worth anything he *and his work will be accepted. There is no need* for the young man to insist, as Théophile Gautier[1] insisted, by wearing a flaming waistcoat. That historic garment had its use in France, and fulfilled its mission, and its place need not be taken in England by any eccentricity of costume or exuberant length of hair. Such things in this day are not a sign of strength—as it

[1] Théophile Gautier (1811–72), French Romantic critic, poet, and novelist. Like Jean Hardouin (see p. 47) he was educated at the College of Louis-le-Grand, Paris. Regarding the waistcoat—

"La première d'*Hernani* (25 février 1830) est une date fameuse de la vie de Théophile Gautier: c'est ce jour-là qu'il revêtit, pour la première fois et la dernière fois, le terrible gilet rouge qui fit si grand scandale parmi les bons bourgeois, et dont il a dit mélancoliquement: 'Je ne l'ai mis qu'un jour, et je l'a porté toute ma vie!' " Émile Bergerat: *Théophile Gautier: Entretiens, souvenirs et correspondance*, Paris 1879, pp. 43–4.

"He made himself a waistcoat—a doublet—of crimson, 'which he had taken pleasure in composing himself'. This red waistcoat, which was in point of fact bright pink, inaugurated to the sound of the horn in *Hernani*, was talked of in those days. They talked much of it, they talked long, they talk still . . ." Maxime du Camp, trs. J. E. Gordon (Preface by Andrew Lang), *Théophile Gautier*, London, 1893, pp. 27–8.

made at Düsseldorf [end of page; two sheets inserted]
C [Cf. p. 32]

There are enough and to spare of essayists and lecturers giving us useless accounts of men and things whose importance died with them. Mr. Gladstone once said this age "will be looked upon as 'AN AGE OF RESEARCH' *"—I wish he had said useless research.*

Yes: research is a good thing in its way: but most of our musical enthusiasts reciting the deeds of the 16th & 17th centuries are as usefully employed as blind men might be, groping in a churchyard at night trying to read epitaphs in a forgotten tongue. [Cf. pp. 62, 241]
D [Cf. p. 34]

[δ *Few of them ever had a separate existence: there was no true birth; the umbilical cord was never severed & the wretched infant led a miserable life attached to its parent* [illegible erasure] *and they died together.*

This has been the inevitable end of [illegible erasure] *manufactured music: we were told our men were giants,* [δ *equal to Brahms &*] *we find that our best are only* [δ *equal to the*] *Julius O. Grimms* [δ *& the*] *and Reineckes* [δ *of Germany*]]][1]

Ts. 1

were *generally* misunderstood
[At head of page, marked ⋆]
              The words to some had a bitter taste, but if the actual words were RUE *the inferences drawn were hemlock.*   [Marginal note] *Out letters of advice* (*laughter* [C.A.E.])

---

[1] Julius Otto Grimm (1827–1903), minor German composer, chorus-director and teacher, best known as a friend of Brahms. Carl Heinrich Carsten Reinecke (1824–1910), virtuoso pianist, conductor of the Leipzig Gewandhaus Orchestra, writer and composer.

was as far back as Samson's day—but an utter feebleness, and generally want of ability.

I should like specially to look back for one moment and see where our English composers have been—the relation they bore to the great men of their own day. Dr. Richard Strauss[1] in a vivid speech made at *Düsseldorf* three or four years back, threw a brilliant illumination on

this somewhat darkened picture. We all knew, although we dared not say so in so many words, what he then told us: that Arne was somewhat less than Handel; that Sterndale Bennett was somewhat less than Mendelssohn, and that some Englishmen of later day were not quite so great as Brahms. These words were *generally* misunderstood—purposely misunderstood—in some quarters, but the absolute truth, the foundation remains. *The words to some had a* bitter taste, but if the actual words were rue, the inferences drawn were hemlock.

Since the announcement that I was appointed to the position I now hold, I have received from all parts of the world, letters of *advice* (which the writers are pleased to consider good advice) as to the way that the musical department of this University should be conducted. That advice contains strange things. Many of them are anxious that I should say something rude about existing teaching institutions. I may

[1] May 20, 1902: see *Elgar O.M.*, pp. 104–5, also *Neue Zeitschrift für Musik*, June 18, 1902, pp. 369–70: ". . . Alles in allem ist Elgar, wie der Engländer sagt, 'a man of genius', von dem noch manches zu erhoffen ist".

from my intention; (*applause* [C.A.E.])

Ts. 1   [Marginal note] *enlarge*

and transform [δ composers] *persons* of very ordinary intellect[δ s] into *composers* of genius[δ es.] (*laughter* [C.A.E.])

[δ country] *pastoral*

Interior of Birmingham Town Hall, early nineteenth century

Professor H. G. Fiedler

Richard Peyton

The Campanile, Birmingham University, photograph of *c.* 1905

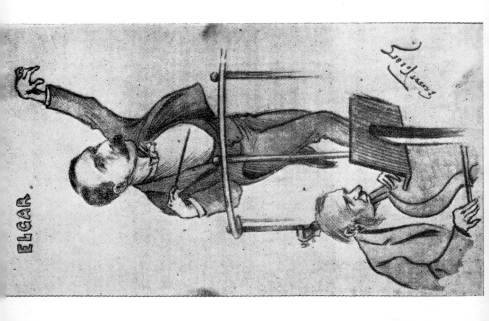

say at once that nothing is further from *my intention*; no one has a greater respect for the real teaching institutions of this country than I have, and it would be impertinent for me to say that they are as well, and in many cases better equipped, than Continental institutions. But judging from the tone of some of these epistles it would seem that the writers have some grievance against the teaching which has hitherto been adopted. As we know, new developments are taking place in the teaching of many subjects, notoriously in the teaching of languages, and it is quite possible to see that some new developments may be suggested in teaching the theory of music. Once more I fear I must disappoint you by saying that I do not mean to go into that to-day. The teaching in this University will be developed later, and will be commenced and enlarged according to the needs of the moment. At present nothing could be better than the teaching at the Music School of the Midland Institute under the direction of Mr. Granville Bantock and the splendid staff of professors, and the University and the Music School of the Institute will work in perfect harmony and goodwill. The word harmony used in another sense brings to mind that one new idea may take root in Birmingham and develop. To put it concisely that harmony in almost the earliest stages should be taught horizontally and not perpendicularly: that is to say, a system is being formulated now by which the student should at once learn the value of one chord in relation to what follows it or precedes it, instead of learning simply from a catalogue and knowing its constituent notes. This is a very crude way of putting into two or three words a system which may revolutionise the teaching of harmony.

But I referred to the people who have been good enough to write to me at this moment. They evidently expect some form of teaching in Birmingham which would more nearly meet their own case, *and transform persons* of very ordinary intellect into composers of genius. That scarcely is within the powers even of the University of Birmingham, and standing on Warwickshire land and with a delicate reference to the grumblings of those people who do not succeed through I fear, their own fault, I would venture to remind them of the old *pastoral* proverb; "Sick sheep make a sorry shepherd".[1]

Well, the movement has begun, and, as I have said before, I am not

---

[1] cf. postscript to undated letter to August Jaeger:

Private

I say: you as chief of yr. dept.,
suffered (slightly) for the sins of your underlings—which calls to my inferior mind the O.E.
proverb "Sick sheep make a SHYTTEN *shepherd"!*

5—AFFEM

[δ Jesuit] *person*

Ts. 1   could possibly be. (*applause* [C.A.E.])

sure if it is the soul or if it is only after all the body. Movements from the head—musical movements—we have had; at any rate they seem to be ceasing, and we hope that something more powerful is taking its place. I am diffident about speculating as to the cause of the movement at the present moment; that has been done in the press—I fear somewhat in the manner of Jean Hardouin.[1] The result of the speculative enquiries of this "most learned fool" as he has been somewhat impolitely called, was the following original idea: "The rotation of the earth was an acknowledged fact after some struggle for existence; he maintained that the rotation of the earth was due to the efforts of the damned to escape from their central fire. Climbing up the walls of hell, they caused the earth to revolve, as a squirrel its cage or a dog a spit".[2] Possibly this erudite *person* was mistaken, as is too often the lot of speculators on first causes and other small matters.

One word more as to the conduct of this Chair. I would warn the exuberant young spirits not to expect any sympathy from me in anything that savours of disrespect to any of the older institutions, to which in the past we owe so much and in the future we look for further help and enlightenment. If they think they cannot learn anything in relation to their art which is useful to them, I should like to say that at any rate they may learn an amount of dignity and goodwill which probably would be more useful to them in their artistic life and their private life than any juvenile gaucherie *could possibly be.*

To return to the English music and the reason of its non-success, and by non-success I do not mean more popular success, but I mean its inability to impress musicians or to captivate amateurs or to hold an abiding place in their affections. I find that it is commonplace as a whole. Critics frequently say of a man that it is to his credit that he is never vulgar. Good. But it is possible for him—in an artistic sense only, be it understood, to be much worse; he can be commonplace. Vulgarity in the course of time may be refined. Vulgarity often goes with inventiveness, and it can take the initiative—in a rude and mis-

---

[1] Jean Hardouin, Librarian of the College of Louis-le-Grand (see p. 41), was an industrious scholar but of a too speculative turn of mind. He was described as "le plus paradoxal des savants anciens et modernes" (*Nouvelle Biographie Générale*, Paris, 1858). In his *Prolegomena ad censuram veterum scriptorum* (published 1765) he propounded the original theory that the majority of classical works were in fact produced by thirteenth-century monks, while in *Doutes proposée sur l'âge du Dante* (1727) he suggested that the *Divina commedia* was the work of a fifteenth-century disciple of John Wyclif.

[2] See James Mew, *Traditional Aspects of Hell (Ancient and Modern)*, London, 1903, p. 308, where the phrase "most learned fool" is ascribed to Peignot (see p. 156). Mew's book, of which Lady Elgar is said to have disapproved, was frequently referred to by Elgar.

. . . evades everything [δ except the commonplace].

Ts. 1   Marginal note   *Walford Davies* EVERYMAN
                                  Bantock THE TIME SPIRIT
                                  Holbrooke QUEEN MAB[1]

Sir Hubert Parry (*applause* [C.A.E.]), the head of our art in this
country, who produced a serious work at the Gloucester
festival: made on too many occasions the figure head and
apologist of the formal school, I claim happily in spirit as a
young man with him no cloud of formality can dim the
healthy *sympathy* and broad influence he exerts and we hope
may long continue to exert upon us. *I am not averse as you
well know to light & amusing music: it has its place, but such
commonplace works shd. never have been allowed in a musical
festival.*

Ts. 2   [δ made on too many occasions . . . as a young man] ? [in
                margin]

[1] *Everyman* and *Queen Mab* (based on Mercutio's speech in *Romeo and Juliet*, I, iv, 53)
were performed at the Leeds Festival on October 7, 1904, on which evening Holbrooke
dined with the Elgars. "E.", noted Lady Elgar, "was *so* good to him." Holbrooke's *Ulalome*
(*Poem, no. 4*, Op. 35, based on E. A. Poe) was given its first performance at a Queen's Hall
Orchestra concert on November 26, 1904. Bantock's *The Time Spirit* (chorus and
orchestra) was performed at the Three Choirs Festival that year.

guided way no doubt—but after all it does something, and can be and has been refined. But the commonplace mind can never be anything but commonplace, and no amount of education, no polish of a University, can eradicate the stain from the low type of mind which is the English commonplace. This applies to other arts besides music. One branch of art never understood and never developed in England is the decoration of the public building. An Englishman will take you into a large room, beautifully proportioned, and will point out to you that it is white—all over white—and somebody will say what exquisite taste. You know in your own mind, in your own soul, that it is not taste at all,—that it is the want of taste—that it is mere evasion. English music is white, and *evades everything*.

But there seems to be hopes that the younger school of England is at last coming to its own—I repeat, to its own, because in the true spirit of chivalry, the younger school, as represented by the best men, does not desire a place which is somebody else's—at least so I read the true character of the young Englishmen. The honours for the last year at the Musical Festivals, which still, unhappily, furnish practically the only opportunities of producing new large works —the honours have fallen, save with one exception to the *younger men*. They have provided us with serious music and they have given us something earnest and something sincere. The one exception is a name which shall be always spoken in this University with the deepest respect, and I will add, the deepest affection- I mean Sir *Hubert Parry*, the head of our art in this country, who produced a serious work at the Gloucester Festival:[1] with him no cloud of formality can dim the healthy sympathy and broad influence he exerts and we hope may long continue to exert upon us.

I have spoken somewhat severely of imitation. But the juvenile composer of the present day in many cases is in no way superior to his predecessors. Where the Mendelssohn imitator whined, the follower

[1] The two outstanding "modern" works at the Gloucester Festival were Elgar's *The Apostles* and Parry's *The love that casteth out fear*. In respect of the former "[This] is not, in short, an English treatment of religious feeling; indeed, it is far removed from national character.

"It is here that the work of Sir Hubert Parry is so different. His treatment of the big subject of the smallness of man and the largeness of Divine Love is full of a manly reverence and force. In his music man acknowledges the greatness of God without abasing himself. There is no sentimental 'whine' in the music. In wholeness of conception, too, the short oratorio is organic. There is none of the wavering between realism and abstract thought that makes the treatment of 'The Apostles' so unequal—an inequality that is the cause of many of Richard Strauss's symphonic poems." E. A. Baughan, "The Gloucester Festival: the new works", *The Monthly Musical Record*, October 1, 1904, pp. 185-6.

Ts. 1   in the *decadents of the* modern French [δ impressionist]
               school
Ts. 2   [δ *lurid realism ?*]
                              in the *decadents of the* modern [French
               impressionist school] *France.*

Ts. 1
                    [Marginal note] *Turner*[1]

Ts. 2   I plead then . . . an English art *Good* [in margin]
Ts. 1   [δ Take an instance.] 20, 25 years ago, *some of* the Rhapsodies
               of Liszt [δ were] *became* very popular . [δ some of them.] I
               think every Englishman *since has* called some work a

[1] Joseph Mallord William Turner (1775–1851), English painter.

of Brahms groaned, and now we seem to be threatened with shrieks transferred from the most livid pages of Richard Strauss. But the last imitators seem carefully to avoid all that is melodious, and I will add sublime, in Strauss,[1] and settle with considerable affection on what it is easiest to reproduce. More pitiful than anything that I have mentioned up to the present moment, are the anaemic followers of the modern French school. Their numbers are happily few, and their influence nil; but the younger generation is never more irritating than when it apes a sickly sentimentality such as we find in the decadents of the modern French School.

What, then, is and can be an English School of Music? It is easy to go back to the days of Purcell and revel in the glories of those days and earlier, when England led the world in the matter of composers; but such thoughts have no practical value on the music of the present day, which in this University is ALL we have to consider. We have been severely lectured many times for the want of robustness, and we have been told that certain boisterous, heavy strenuous choral works have represented the height of English music and represent the English spirit. This is absolutely untrue. John Bull makes an excellent figure for a political cartoon; but I am bound to say none of us ever met John Bull in private life—particularly the John Bull who is supposed to like this particular class of music. I would remind those who still hold this spurious idea of an Englishman, that another man, whose influence at any rate came from a district very near to us here, has drawn for us, not in one character but in many, what I hold to be the ideal Englishman. We are in his own country, and I am not confounding the personality of the man Shakespeare, the writer, with the personalities he has drawn for us—has more than drawn—has made living: Mercutio, the gallant gentleman, Falconbridge, the brave and daring spirit: I need not continue my list. Why should we accept as an ideal for English music a type that exists in no other art? I plead then that the younger men should draw their inspiration more from their own country, from their own literature—and, in spite of what many would say—from their own climate. Only by drawing from any real English inspiration shall we ever arrive at having an English art. Twenty, twenty-five years ago, some of the Rhapsodies of Liszt became very popular. I think every Englishman since has called some work a Rhapsody. Could anything be more inconceivably inept. To

---

[1] See Monthly Musical Record, May 1, 1905, pp. 84–6, for Herbert Antcliffe's "Elgar and Strauss, a Comparison and a Contrast".

Rhapsody.   . . . cannot do.   (*laughter* [C.A.E.])

[Marginal note] *Henry Irving.*[1] *his theatre taken from him &
turned into a music hall*
Did they exist [δ T] *t*hese things would have

Ts. 2   But still [δ something, as I said before,] something moves

[δ Do not . . . cannot say.]

Ts. 1   (*applause* [C.A.E.])

. . . at once furnished, [δ and I may say that it will be a
pleasure on my part to put a sum from the stipend attached
to this Chair at the disposal of the Library Committee.[2]

Fund for the encouragement of young composers.]
[See p. 81.]

[δ should] *must*

[1] See p. 219.
[2] See comment on Library proposal in *Birmingham Post*, p. 62.

rhapsodise is one thing Englishmen *cannot do*. Why take a title simply because it is popular with an Hungarian composer whose very nature it is to rhapsodise. This, you will say, is a trivial incident. So it is, but nevertheless it points a moral showing how the Englishman always prefers to imitate. It is a misfortune for us that we have no living dominant author, no living tremendous painter, and at present *no actors* or actresses of overpowering personality. *Did they exist* they would have—as in the case of Goethe, to give only an instance—a vivifying effect on the art of music.

But still something, as I said before, something moves, and the day is coming, if the younger generation are true to themselves, are strong, if they cease from imitation and draw their inspiration from their own land. Now what part is the University of Birmingham going to play in this advance? *Do not be* disappointed—*I cannot say*. We may depend upon the public spirit and the munificence of the University authorities and their friends to find whatever may be necessary from a pecuniary point of view; but it is impossible to forecast any results unless the material is found to work upon. Many questions have been asked as to the conferring of degrees at this University. I may say at once that it is not my intention at present to recommend that degrees should be given in this University. That may come later, and certainly if things progress will come. To obtain a degree a residence in the University will be absolutely necessary—that I may say *definitely*. But a serious question arises—what advantage is Birmingham itself going to offer to intending students? To begin with we must have a library in the University, a library of musical literature and of music which shall compare favourably with the other branches of literature which are well represented in this city. For that special efforts will have to be made, but I do not anticipate any difficulty on that score, it simply requires to be mentioned, I am sure, for the library to be at once *furnished*.

Then the advantage of the life in a town like Leipzig, which for many years retained its renown as a musical educational centre, was more on account of the music possible to be heard there than of the actual superiority of the teaching staff. In Leipzig the students had the opportunity of hearing the best artists of the day and the best orchestral concerts and rehearsals, and also the advantage of having an excellent Opera to attend at a small fee—concessions were made to them in both cases. Now something *must* be done in Birmingham to make the orchestral concerts a permanent institution. I am well aware that there are excellent orchestral concerts here, but I do not understand that they

To the famous Choral Society . . . Mr. Stockley [added above and below main text]

conscientiously

more frequently

are on a permanent basis. *To the famous Choral Society here*—or Choral Societies—I need not refer, they are too well-known. I look back however with pride and gratitude to my connection with the Festival Choral Society and that I was able to learn something of choral effect in the old days under our revered chief, *Mr. Stockley*.[1] Before we can *conscientiously* invite students to reside in Birmingham for the three most receptive years of their life, we must be sure that we have something for them to hear beyond the ordinary school concerts and school orchestra—excellent though both may be. The question of Opera of course is too indefinite and too impossible to think of at the present moment, but as Opera cannot be heard *more frequently* in any other town we need not fear comparison in that respect. It may be that we shall be able to take the lead and do something in the way of encouraging either English opera or Opera in English.

One other point—and this is an idea which I am very anxious to carry out, but I find it difficult. I have spoken of the want of inspiration in English music. Many respectable and effective works have been written during the twenty years 1880–1900. To me they represent more or less—I will not particularise—such a phase of art as in another way was represented by Lord Leighton.[2] There you had a winning personality, a highly educated man, a complete artist, technically complete, but the result was cold and left the world unmoved. The musical works produced in the period named leave me in exactly the same way: I am amazed at the dexterity displayed in the finish of the works, but there is absolutely nothing new. The student of orchestration, the student of choral writing, will find nothing new and nothing but what may be better learned from French or German composers.

One thing most pleasing to a composer is to count amongst his hearers and supporters the most cultured literary men, artists, sculptors,

---

[1] William Cole Stockley (1829–1919), born in Sidcup, Kent, came to Birmingham in 1850 as assistant to a music- and piano-dealer named Sabin. In due course he became senior partner of the firm which, from 1880, was known as Stockley & Co. An organist, Stockley was appointed conductor of the Festival Choral Society in 1855. He persuaded his committee to engage local orchestral players rather than those from distant towns. Such was his success in the orchestral field that he was in due course able to invite Dvořák, Cowen, Prout, Hamish McCunn, Parry, and others to conduct their own works at his concerts. Stockley was chosen as chorus-master of the Birmingham Festival in 1858. He resigned both appointments in 1895 but in 1900 took over rehearsals of *The Dream of Gerontius* after the death of Swinnerton Heap (see obituary in *Birmingham Post*, September 8, 1919).

[2] Frederick Leighton (1830–96), painter and sculptor, who was knighted in 1878 (as President of the Royal Academy), made a baronet in 1886, and a baron on January 24, 1896. He died on the following day.

Ts. 1   [δ actually] *necessarily*

E *I quote . . . congenial to ourselves"* [on separate sheet following, marked **E**]

(*laughter* [C.A.E.])

Ts. 1   *laughter & applause* [C.A.E.]

[δ somewhat] indefinite

scientists, and in fact all cultivated people not *necessarily* musicians. I am hoping to induce a great critic, a great painter, and an author and so forth, to come to Birmingham and tell us why they like one piece of music and not another. I make this statement quite baldly and coldly because it is exactly what we do not know. *I quote* from Leslie Stephen: —"We must start from experience. We must begin by asking impartially what pleased men, and then *why* it pleased them. We must not decide dogmatically that it ought to have pleased or displeased on the simple ground that it is or is not congenial to *ourselves*".[1]

It is quite easy for one of the students in this music school, as I said before, to point out a consecutive fifth and such-like errors, but we do not want technical instruction. We want to know whether the clever men in other arts find refreshment, maybe amusement, maybe improvement, certainly solace, at any rate interest, in certain compositions and not in others. Why, if a symphony by a certain composer is put down they flock to hear it, and why if a work by an Englishman is put down they studiously stay *away*. By this means, if my scheme is carried through—and I trust it will be—I hope to get six first rate artistic opinions as to the real inspiration, using the word in its highest sense, and find out what the educated, artistic and cultured people miss in music which they hear once and then avoid. From this I know we may learn more as to the natural basis of an art than any amount of text books, any amount of performances, and certainly more than any amount of professorial lectures, even from the Richard Peyton Professor of *Music*.

Now I draw these remarks to a close, conscious that they—as I said at the beginning—are indefinite. That is necessary, because the position of things here is at present *indefinite*. I have endeavoured to sketch for you in the lightest possible way what my feelings are regarding the possible future for English music. There are many possible futures. But the one I want to see coming into being is something that shall grow out of our own soil, something broad, noble, chivalrous, healthy and above all, an out-of-door sort of spirit. To arrive at this it will be necessary to throw over all imitation. It will be necessary to begin and look at things in a different spirit. Sir Joshua Reynolds in his first address to the Royal Academy—but he is deploring the want of

[1] Slightly misquoted. The passage should read ". . . impartially what pleased men, and then inquire why it pleased them . . ."; Leslie Stephen, *English Literature and Society in the Eighteenth Century*, London, 1904, p. 5. This volume, published on the day of Stephen's death (February 24, 1904) contained the Ford Lectures of 1903, which H. A. L. Fisher read for Stephen who was too ill to undertake their delivery at Oxford.

and if these lectures by [δ the] *such* gentlemen *as* I have [δ named] suggested

F *I see here . . . a helper also* [contained in two sheets following marked **F** and *F 2*]

Ts. 1   *School*

academic training, while we are almost deploring too much of it—asks: "Why those who are more than boys at sixteen become less than men at thirty".[1] We, looking at the pasts of all English composers, alas, have to ask ourselves a further question: Why those who were according to their friendly critics more than men at thirty have invariably dwindled to nonentities between fifty and sixty. We feel that it is from want of inspiration—certainly not from want of technical ability, *and if these lectures by such gentlemen as I have suggested* can be brought to a hearing, I trust that we shall learn something from the poetical side of our art in a way which has not yet been attempted.

I see here many of my fellow musicians and I am complimented by their friendly interests in to-day's proceedings. I have wearied you by insisting on the indefinite nature of music in this University. One thing is *not* indefinite and that is my goodwill and I will say love of my fellow musicians. I hold very definite views as to our art, but I do not intend to use my position here in any other way than for the great, broad, open and let us say, peaceful advancement of the best. I therefore cordially invite the co-operation of all Birmingham musicians to this end; let us sink small differences and hold in view the good of our beloved art only.

As far as it is possible to help in any artistic work I will do so and like the whole of the members of the musical profession in this City to look upon me as a friend and, as far as my ability goes, a helper *also*.

I imagine to-day that I have here a number of students from the Institution with which I have been somewhat connected, the Midland Institute *School* of Music. To that Institution I look with affection and with hope. I feel that their destinies are in good hands, and I can only hope that some good for their future may come from the establishment of this Chair of Music. I will only say that no effort on my part shall be wanting. I would beg of them not to be led away by any of the small schools of thought that are so easily brought to the front and have their little day, and have their little coterie. One man admires another

---

[1] Reynolds was referring to the necessity for encouraging students to have intensive practice in drawing from living models in order to develop in exactness. "This scrupulous exactness is so contrary to the practice of the academies, that it is not without great deference that I beg leave to recommend it to the consideration of the visitors [of the Royal Academy] and submit it to them, whether the neglect of this method is not one of the reasons why students so often disappoint expectation, and being more than boys at sixteen, become less than men at thirty." *Seven Discourses on Art*, Cassell, 1888, p. 22 (*Discourse* of December 11, 1769). Elgar might have emended his statements on the Carracci had he read Reynolds's views on this subject, contained in this *Discourse*, more closely.

... a [δ Kensington] kitten ...
    G
    Let your inspiration ... confidence and faith"
    [on previous sheet (inserted), marked **G**]

Ts. 1   Hume *in another way and* in a sarcastic mood uses [δ the] *this*
simile [δ in another way] ... "We [δ have] [δ will] place[δ d]
our lever ...

and writes him up, and he says that So-and-so is the greatest composer living, and So-and-so says that the critic is the greatest critic alive. Believe me that has nothing to do with the movement of the world. The world revolves and the great things still go on, and the little clique is nothing more than a *kitten* playing with its own tail. You students have something—or should have—a higher ideal altogether. *Let* your inspiration be real and high. Listen to Hoffman.

1) "We speak a loftier language than mere human speech, in the wondrous accents of Music."

"It is as if we mortals were wafted upward in some condition of mystic consecration, on the pinions of the tones of the golden harps of the Cherubim and Seraphim, to the realms of light, where we learn the mystery of our existence".

2) "The morning light is breaking, and the inspired singers are soaring up in the sweet fresh morning air, PROCLAIMING the advent of the Divine, and celebrating it with hymns of praise".

"The golden gates are open, and art and knowledge (ART and KNOW-LEDGE) in one united ray, are kindling that flame of sacred effort which makes humanity one universal church. Therefore lift your eyes in courage, confidence and faith".[1]

Hume in another way and in a sarcastic mood uses this simile which I dare to transfer to us musicians: "We place our lever in Heaven and by it we can move the world".

[1] Ernst Theodor Wilhelm Hoffmann (1776–1822), music critic, composer, and romance writer, who exercised a considerable influence on Robert Schumann; in 1839 Schumann considered the possibility of composing an opera based on a story in *Die Serapions-Brüder, Gesammelte Erzählungen und Märchen*, 4 vol., with two supplementary volumes, published in Berlin, 1819–25. Elgar used *The Serapion Brethren*, trs. Major A. Ewing, published in two volumes by G. Bell, London, 1886–92.

After the lecture the Elgars went to the Peytons where a party of sixteen, including the Fiedlers and Lodges, were entertained to dinner. On the next day Elgar was back in London for a dinner in honour of Manuel Garcia's hundredth birthday. The day following he dined at Buckingham Palace with King Edward VII.

Meanwhile the citizens of Birmingham were digesting the lengthy report[1] of the inauguration of the Professorship of Music in their University:

> Sir Edward Elgar, as the "Richard Peyton" Professor of Music . . . made his first public appearance before a Birmingham audience yesterday; and the crowded state of the large lecture theatre of the Midland Institute bore eloquent testimony to the high appreciation in which he is held and to the popularity of his appointment. The new Professor was cordially introduced by the Principal, Sir Oliver Lodge, and he had the satisfaction of seeing present a distinguished party of his colleagues on the University staff; a large number of University students; many well known musical people in the city, and an evidently friendly assembly of the general public interested in all that concerns the prosperity of the University.

There followed a full and accurate summary of the lecture. At the end one point was amplified:

> Then the lecturer spoke of a library of musical literature. The Central Free Library, we believe, contains a good many works on musical subjects, but it may be doubted if much of what is there would suit Sir Edward, who was very severe on those who spent so much time in useless research. It is said that the future is read in the past. Sir Edward would have the student forget the past—or much of it—and devote himself to the present. Here, then, is the keynote of modernity which the new Professor of Music has so vigorously struck at the University of Birmingham. Whatever else may be said of Sir Edward Elgar's theories as they are further disclosed in future lectures, it may be said that he has already given the musical world something to think about.

In the April issue of the *Musical Opinion* the extent to which the feelings of the musical had already been aroused was thus exposed:

> It was only to be expected that Sir Edward Elgar's speech at Birmingham would arouse a deal of opposition. I hear of thunderbolts ready to be launched from South Kensington[2] and Tenterden Street.[3] It is generally held that a composer in the position of Sir Edward ought not to have made public such opinions. Many men in sympathy with what he said agree with this. But I cannot say that I am at one with them. Professional etiquette can be carried too far, and gives rise to the humbug which is uttered in public. And the chief humbug of our day is the tacit acceptance of the opinion so often uttered that the British composer has been neglected because he is

---

[1] *Birmingham Post*, March 17, 1905.
[2] Royal College of Music.
[3] Royal Academy of Music.

British. That is not what enlightened musicians and amateurs say among themselves; it is not what concert agents say when they are asked why they do not produce native compositions at their concerts.

After all, what did Sir Edward Elgar say that was so ill considered? He referred to the renascence of British composition, and placed the beginning of the movement in 1880,—a period which includes the efforts of all our living heads of music. He then went on to state that many lovers of music—accustomed to their Beethoven, their Weber and their Wagner (then the most modern of composers)—found much of the music they were asked to admire by a friendly press too dry. Well, is not that a fact? Have the works of the Brahmsites been really popular with the public? Sir Edward also expressed his pleasure that there is now some sign that the renascence is becoming vital, and he pointed to the fact that the most successful works at the recent festivals were from the pens of the younger school. All this may be very annoying to those who have borne the heat and burden of the day in advancing British composition; and naturally they do not relish being told that the fault of native composition has been that it is too white and commonplace. It may have been perfect in taste; but, in the lecturer's opinion, there is often more vitality in vulgarity, which can be toned down, whereas merely tasteful music cannot be given the breath of life.

Personally, I think that Sir Edward Elgar was quite justified in speaking out to his audience on this matter. What he said was not new, one or two of the younger school of critics have said the same thing in and out of season; but a critic is but a critic, and his opinions do not carry the same weight as those of a prominent composer. The critic is always held to be merely malicious (I have had recent experience of this fact). It was right and proper, too, that the Birmingham professor should have insisted that music must be written for the public and not for brother professionals. He did not say what he might have said, that our composers have not taken advantage of the one outlet for their talent,—the provincial musical festivals. For many years they have written choral works as if they were tradesmen. The chorus were supposed to like a certain style of composition, which had no higher aim than that of affording them some effective and easy music. All the choral works of the last twenty years—to go no further back—have been laid out on those lines. The orchestra was a mere instrument for accompanying the voices, and the suppositious love of robust choral effects have [sic] made our festival works inexpressibly wearisome to the amateur who is not a member of a chorus. The consequence has been that these festival works have been produced and then placed on the shelf. To such a pass has this state of things come, that the recognised publishers of festival choral works are by no means anxious to issue them.

In the domain of orchestral composition, our writers suffered from a want of outlet for their talent it is true; but it is strange that, when Elgar himself wrote his Enigma Variations, they were soon performed all over the country as well as abroad. The work may have its faults and its weaknesses; but it does aim at being music that will please and interest the public, and not at being admired by a few professors here and there who are in a position to grasp its technical exercises. And all the modern orchestral composition is on the same lines. At the last Palmer concert I heard at least two works which show that our native composition is no longer to be for the special public of a few professional musicians,—a suite by Mr. W. H. Bell and another by Mr. Balfour Gardiner were bright, glowing and picturesque.

The question of imitation on which Sir Edward Elgar touched is of great importance. For some reason or other we have had no music of our own for many a generation. In his little history of English music in the nineteenth century, Mr. Fuller Maitland assigns the cause to the idolatry of Handel at the end of the eighteenth century. But that was really an effect and not a cause. Handel was received with open arms because at the time there was [sic] no vital British compositions. The sudden popularity of Mendelssohn is not so easy to explain, unless it is considered that his "Elijah " appealed to the love of oratorio which Handel had aroused. But that does not explain the popularity of his instrumental works, his piano pieces, his chamber music and his symphonies. I am not at all sure that Mendelssohn did not embody much of the British feeling for art. In spite of our energy as a commercial nation and as a nation of fighters, our popular art has always been of a bright and sentimental nature. There must, at any rate, be a sound cause for the great influence that Mendelssohn exercised on our art. You cannot hear a composition of the period ending with the early Sullivan without being made to see that Mendelssohn had a very great influence indeed. I admit that it was most necessary that this influence should be put an end to. But the school of Stanford and Parry went the wrong way about their work. It was predestined that they should take Brahms as their model.

There were several reasons for this. In the first place, Sir Charles Stanford completed his musical education in Leipzig, then the hotbed of anti-Wagnerianism, just as at one time it had been the centre of Mendelssohn worship. Then, on his return to Cambridge, Stanford was naturally more taken up with chamber music than with any other form of composition. His early operas may be looked upon as his last offering at the shrine of Wagner. Now, in chamber music there is no doubt that Brahms was for a long time the only modern voice. There were no opportunities at either Oxford or Cambridge of hearing orchestras; nor are there any opportunities to this day. Consequently, you will find that all musicians educated at either of the universities, and all amateurs as well, have a particular love of chamber music and naturally of Brahms. But it is difficult to think of a composer whose spirit is more antipathetic to the British spirit that [sic] Brahms is. The works of the Parry-Stanford school could not be of a nature that would appeal to the public. In the meantime the public here had grown more and more acquainted with the music dramas of Wagner, in which, quite apart from their operatic significance, there was a new voice in harmony, polyphony and orchestration. The other composers such as Mackenzie tried to steer a middle course between Mendelssohn and Wagner with the conventional British choral writing thrown in. That could be no more a vital school than the school of the Brahms imitators.

And why did not the composers of the last twenty years attempt to break through all this sterile imitation? Sir Edward Elgar did address himself to this point, probably because it would raise a matter for discussion which could not come from his lips. It is so simple that it seems hardly worth mentioning: leaving Sullivan out of account, we have had no composers who can claim to possess genius. The first man with an inkling of it would soon have broken through the imitation which has made British composition so sterile. Elgar himself may not have genius, but he has something a great deal more than talent; and as a consequence his music, when once he had found his own voice, attracted the public. It has individuality in spite of what it owes to Wagner.

And Elgar's education and early environment have done much for him. He has never been the centre of a mutual admiration society; and, above all, he has not had to grind out the most creative years of his life as a professor or as head of a teaching institution. I verily believe that the Royal College and the Royal Academy of Music have been the death of the creative life of Parry, Stanford and Mackenzie. Only lately we have had an opportunity of hearing the early symphony of Parry (the work in F), and Stanford's "L'Allegro ed il Pensieroso" Symphony, and each work contains music of the utmost promise. In Parry's work, for instance, there is a slow movement which is in altogether a different vein from anything in the composer's later works. It is more dramatic in aim, more picturesque and more direct in emotional spirit. Had he continued to write in that style he would have been quite as popular as Elgar. Then, again, Mackenzie's early compositions display a real creative talent. None of these composers has developed as he should have developed, and I am firmly convinced that the dull life of professor has killed his talent. The future of British music, rests on no far fetched idea of looking to the literature of our country as an inspiration or to any real attempt to embody the spirit of the nation, but simply on our composers not being compelled to eke out their existence by undertaking the onerous duties of heads of teaching institutions. And it is in the nature of irony that Sir Edward Elgar himself is doing his best to dig his own grave at Birmingham. Hitherto, whatever the difficulty has been, he has been able to live without thus enchaining his gifts: and he should be thankful that this has been so.[1]

[1] No. 331, pp. 498-9.

CHAPTER 4

INTERLUDE

Sir Edward Elgar's "The Dream of Gerontius" was performed in French at the Brussels Concerts Populaires on Sunday, March 26. A critic, writing in the "Ménestrel", describes the work as beautiful, noble and grand. "He pays a tribute to its intense mysticism and profound sincerity, and thinks that the religious ardour of César Franck seems to live in its pages. The style is thought to be rather classical, but, at the same time, individual, in spite of some reminiscences of 'Parsifal'. The workmanship is irreproachable, especially that of the choral writing. In brief, Elgar is hailed as a truly remarkable personality, and we are told the English school of composition, so long silent that it could hardly be considered as existing, has the right to be proud of the composer.[1]

[Hereford]

March 28, 1905
Dear Professor Fiedler:
  Will this scrawl on the back of this do?
  I have been extremely unwell & am only just able to creep about
                                Yours sincerely
                                        Edward Elgar

[On reverse]

                                (word it as you please)
                        Music
Richard Peyton Professor: Sir E. E. Mus.D.(Oxon., Cantab. & Dunelm) LL.D.

————

  Lectures will be given on
   i English composers
   ii English executants,
        and
  iii English critics completing the subjects dealt with in the professor's inaugural address. These lectures will be given early in October; the dates of these & of two other lectures will be announced later.

[Hereford]
March 29   9 p.m.
Dear Mr. Peyton:
  Your card addressed to me at the University has just reached me here:

[1] *The Musical Standard*, April 8, 1905, p.221.

it must have been redirected in the secretary's office immediately on its arrival: this explains why I was in doubt.

It was a great pleasure to see you again. You may be interested to know that my interview with the oculist was satisfactory & there is no serious trouble.

Yours very sincerely
Edward Elgar

One of the prominent figures in music in Birmingham in the second part of the nineteenth century was Andrew Deakin (1823–1903). Self-taught as a musician, but with some skill as vocalist, organist, and violinist, Deakin learned the printing trade. In 1846 he printed the *Birmingham Musical Examiner*, edited by James Stimpson, organist of the Town Hall. Deakin, also organist at various churches, became music critic of the *Birmingham Morning News* and of the *Daily Gazette*. He was well known also as contributor of notes to concert programmes. He retired in 1895. Deakin was described as "one of the most estimable of the older school of musicians . . . whose art-judgements were invariably sound and impartial, though numbered among the musical prophets that knew not Wagner". He averred that "the two greatest choral works ever written were both by Mendelssohn: the 'Elijah' and the 'St. Paul' ". When asked about the B Minor Mass he replied, "I don't think much of it. There are many masses much better. I prefer any of Schubert's masses to Bach in B minor."[1]

The disposal of Deakin's library was a subject of discussion in the University. Excerpts from letters from Rupert Deakin, of the King Edward's School, Stourbridge:

(1) To Professor Heath (Vice Principal), March 23, 1905:

my father, Andrew Deakin, who died about fifteen months ago, left a considerable collection of Musical books, and I have been thinking whether the University would like to take them. Unfortunately I am not in a position to make a free gift of the books, nor is my mother to whom the books belong; but she would be very pleased to let the University have them for £50 . . . Altogether I reckon there are 2000 different works, or sets of works . . .

(2) To Professor Fiedler, April 2, 1905:

Many thanks for letter re Musical Library. Herewith I am sending you a catalogue, but I do not know whether it is complete. . . . (P.S.) We should like the library kept as the Andrew Deakin Library by the University.

[Hereford]

Ap. 3, 1905
Dear Professor Fiedler:

I am very glad to hear of the £500,[2] I think we should buy the Deakin

---

[1] See *Birmingham Post*, April 14, 1903, and *Birmingham Mail*, June 7, 1911.
[2] Allocated by University for Library.

library—on the report of Bantock and [Ernest] Newman but I have no idea what it contains.

Have they a library at the Music school? If so we ought to know what it contains don't you think and avoid duplicating unnecessarily?

I *hope* to be in on Thursday so don't write in answer to these questions: if I have to go [δ out] away I will wire at latest on Thursday early. I should like to see you to talk over how far we should consider the wants of the Institute students. I suppose our library is, or can be, at their disposal? or should it *not* be so?

I am better but a poor thing.

Kind regards
Yours sincerely
Edward Elgar

P.S. Very sorry! I see your letter says Thursday Ap *13th*. I shall be in Leeds that day[1] if well enough. I will try to come over to Birmingham.

[Hereford]

Ap. 3, 1905
Dear Mr. Peyton:

Very many thanks for your letter: I am very glad to hear of the commencement of the Library & will consult Professor Fiedler about it as soon as possible.

I am afraid my illness is not from overwork: thank you very much for your enquiries & good wishes. I am a little better but not fit for much

Believe me
Yours v. sincerely
Edward Elgar

From George Hookham, of Gilbertstone, near Birmingham, to Elgar, April 9, 1905:

I enclose my cheque for a 100 guineas as a donation for your Musical Library; & ask you to accept it as a mark of my appreciation of the views so admirably set forth in your inaugural lecture here.

[Hereford]

Ap 19/05
Dear Professor Fiedler:

If not too late could the enclosure[2] or something like it go into the Calendar?

Yes. I understand that Newman leaves Birmingham: he shd have been on the B. Post.[3] I have seen nothing of his about the address—all the

---

[1] To conduct *The Dream of Gerontius.*

[2] Missing.

[3] Having taught at the Midland Institute since 1903 Newman left to become music critic of *The Manchester Guardian,* but returned to Birmingham as music critic of *The Birmingham Post* in the next year.

remarks I have seen by others are absolutely beside the point & futile
to a degree more than ordinary even in musical criticism

Yrs sncly

Edward Elgar

[blot in margin of letter] unintentional "Bertillon"[1] caused by a recalcitrant
fountain pen.

[Hereford]

May 22. 1905
Dear Professor Fiedler:

I am returning the Index slip of Liepmannsohn's[2] to the Librarian:
enclosed I send to you the only books I have selected. I waited a long time
in hope of receiving the catalogue of the Deakin Library but it has not
reached me. We must have the full 'Bach Socy Edition' of J.S.B. of
course. But I hope to come over one day soon to talk things over with
you.

Bach & Beethoven (complete edn.) are both in this catalogue—but
they wd require binding. & of this question & various subscriptions to
editions now publishing (e.g. Purcell socy)[3] we must decide

Kind regards

Yours sincly

Edward Elgar

Hotel Touraine,
Boston. [U.S.A.]

July 3. 1905
Dear Professor Fiedler:

I ran over to Birmingham on my way here:[4] I am sorry I missed you.
We return soon (sailing from N. York on July 11th): will you let me hear
when & how we could meet? I want to talk over the library business.

I have been to Yale & have been going through the music department
there & may have found some useful ideas

Kindest regards

Yours sincery

Edward Elgar

July 3 1905   [Boston]
My dear Mr. Peyton:

I had hoped to have seen you when I passed through Birmingham on
my way here, but my time was too short. I am so sorry to have missed
seeing you.

---

[1] *Bertillonage*, "1892, f. name of Fr. criminologist. A system of identifying criminals
by measurements, finger prints etc." *S.O.E.D.*; *bertilloned*, "measured by the police for
identification", E. Partridge, *A Dictionary of the Underworld*, London, 1949.

[2] Leo Liepmannsohn, Berlin bookseller specialising in musical literature; whereabouts
unknown after *c*. 1935.

[3] Vol. 15, *Welcome Songs, Part I*, ed. R. Vaughan Williams, was published this year.

[4] Elgar was visiting the U.S.A. at the invitation of Professor S. S. Sanford, of Yale,
from June 9 to July 18.

I (with my wife) have been here a fortnight & I have been studying the music department in Yale University where my friend Prof. Sanford holds a post.

They gave me an Hon. degree which was picturesque & gratifying but I hope I may have found some useful ideas for practical use.

We return home on July 11th.

My wife joins me in kindest regards to Mrs Peyton & to you

Believe me

Very sincerely yours

Edward Elgar

Letter from Lady Elgar to Professor Fiedler, September 18, 1905:

My husband asked me to write to you at once & explain that he has gone for a short cruise in the Mediterranean.[1] He hesitated, and indeed all but declined, the invitation, but our Dr. who came over to Worcester & who has been attending him, so strongly urged him to go, feeling sure that it wd. greatly benefit his health to do so, that eventually he accepted & went. . . . I really do hope & feel that all his undertakings with you in Birmingham will be so greatly helped by this little absence . . . Please let me add that I helped to urge Sir Edward to go, knowing he had not been feeling very fit for work.

Letter from Lady Elgar to Professor Fiedler, September 24, 1905:

Very many thanks for your kind note. . . . Do you not think it wd. be best, if you wd. kindly make any announcement you think fit, pending his sending dates? He seems, as I thought he wd. be, *quite* amazed & delighted with the seas & sky & colours, "Everything a picture", & what especially gladdened me was to hear that so far as I have yet heard, had no headaches wh. had prostrated him so much this year!

C. W. Perkins to Professor Fiedler, September 26, 1905:

I don't know if you have had time to consider the possibility of providing an organ for the University, but it occurred to me that the organ of the R[oyal].C[ollege of].O[rganists].[2] (with a few additions which I have noted) is about the instrument required.

I hope the enclosed may be some guide to you. The cost, including Kinetic Blower would be about £1450.

[Hereford]

Oct 15 1905

My dear Professor:

I arrived home last night (in Norwich for rehearsal) & hasten to thank you for your letters to my wife.

I will not go into the question of thanks now for the kind consideration you & others have shewn.

[1] See "Diary of a Mediterranean Cruise" in *Letters of Edward Elgar*, pp. 146–62.
[2] Built in 1904 by Norman & Beard; Perkins enclosed the specification.

Now as to dates: will *Monday Oct 30th* do for the next address or lecture & Nov 6th (also Monday) for the next and (*possibly*) the 13th for the fourth: if these days are impossible please let me hear. I shd. think the lecture theatre in the University building wd. be best. I hope to come over very soon when you can give me an hour or two to settle the library. I trust the Librarian has had time to go thoroughly into the *Deakin* collection: if so we can then proceed

Kindest regards
Yours sincly
Edward Elgar

[on University note-paper]

Oct 22 1905
Dear Prof. Fiedler:
    I am sorry I could not call in at U[nion] Club. I found Mr. Hayes & subsequently Bantock & asked them to send someone to assist the U[niversity] Librarian so I hope that it is all going on.
    Let me have anything you can about the *most important* organ question —it will be awful if the architect has left no room.

Yr sncly
Edwd. Elgar

[on University note-paper]

Oct 29 1905
My dear Professor:
    I don't think you want a report from me (I had a circular letter) but in case you do I think something like the enclosed should do.
    I don't know if our donations have been noticed or if they are wanted. . . . You will see I have put a ? to that par.

Yrs scly
Ed. Elgar

[on University note-paper]

Oct 30 1905
Dear Fiedler:
    For Heaven's sake let us drop prefixes, life is so short!
    I am glad to hear about the organ but I can't help thinking that the specification sent by Mr. Perkins is far too small: is not the Hall to be as big as the Town Hall? The room in which the R.C.O. organ is placed is I believe quite an ordinary sort of large room.
    We must talk of this. In the meantime I return the letter & circular

Yrs sncy
Ed: Elgar

Meanwhile Elgar was in process of selecting books for the Music Library. On October 29 he sent a request to W. H. Cope, the University Librarian, for copies of Ernest Newman's *Gluck and the Opera* (Dobell, 1895) and *A Study of Wagner* (Dobell, 1899)—"*now remaindering*", observed Elgar, as well as the same author's *Wagner* ("Music of the Masters", P. Wellby, 1904), and *Musical Studies* (John Lane, 1905), *Wagner's Prose Works,* trs. by Ashton Ellis (8 vol. Kegan Paul, 1892–9), Otto Jahn's *Life of Mozart* (Novello, 1882), J. Stainer and W. A. Barrett's *Dictionary of Musical Terms* (Novello, 1876), Friedrich Niecks's *Programme Music in the Last Four Centuries* (Novello, 1906), and a copy of *The Musical Directory* for 1906 (Rudall, Carte & Co.). Subsequent orders during this year were for a subscription to *Die Musik* and the second edition of *Grove's Dictionary* (ed. J. A. Fuller-Maitland), while confirmation was sought for the ordering of the *Oxford History of Music*.

On December 11 Elgar received this letter:

> Curzon House,
> Mayfair.
> Dec. 10, 1905
>
> My dear Sir Edward,
>   Thank you very much for your letter, and for your most kind messages of enquiry about Lady Howe. I am thankful to be able to say that she is a little better, but she has been very seriously ill again, & her condition must be, for some time, a very anxious one.
>   It will give me great pleasure to do anything I can to help *you* in your work, and I am enclosing a little contribution, which please devote, in any way you like, to the purposes of the Musical Depart. of the University of Birmingham. Perhaps Schubert's edition would be a suitable gift? May I leave it to you, & also will you choose a suitable binding, which, if it should come to more than £5, please let me know. With all good wishes to Lady Elgar, & yourself,
> > Believe me,
> > > Yours most sincerely,
> > > > Howe.

He therefore wrote to Fiedler as follows:

> [Hereford]
>
> *1 Enclosure*
> My dear Fiedler:
>   Lord Howe has sent me a special donation to pay for a complete edition of *Schubert.*
>   Enclosed is his cheque: I am asking the Librarian to order the set.
>   If I come over early on Wedy is there anything to be done?
> > Yrs sncly
> > > Edward Elgar
>
> I send you the cheque £30 enclosed

On the same day he wrote to Cope:

> Dear Mr. Cope:
>   I have received a special donation to pay for the works of *Schubert*:

JAMES MILES.
Second-Hand Bookseller.

LIBRARIES PURCHASED. CATALOGUES FREE

Books sought for and reported free of charge.

Pd

"Ye Olde Boke Shoppe,"

32, Guildford Street,

LEEDS, ... 190

Dear Mr Cope:

Kindly order from this establishment a copy of British Violin Makers 4/6 for the Library. They are keeping a copy for you.

Yrs truly

Edward Elgar

will you kindly order the edition complete from Breitkopf & Hartel—
bound in cloth will do—that is to say like the Bach[1]

their usual style.
Yours truly
Edward Elgar

Franz Schubert
Complete Score Edition
£25
Bindings extra (as in the case of the Bach Edn.)

On the following day Cope received another letter:

Dear Mr. Cope:
    please enter the University as a member of the Purcell Society *via*
Mr. W. Barclay-Squire. British Museum & get all the volumes which
are ready.

Yrs sncy
Ed: Elgar

Sporadic notes concerning musical literature continued until 1907, by which
time, however, Elgar's interest in his Professorship had waned.

[1] See p. 69.

CHAPTER 5

ENGLISH COMPOSERS
(November 1, 1905)

DURING the summer Elgar had enjoyed the greatest respect both at the Three Choirs and Norwich Festivals. In respect of the former it was reported: "The dominating personality of the festival was undoubtedly Sir Edward Elgar." This notice tells in how many capacities he was actively engaged [librettist of Ivor Atkins's *Hymn of Faith*, conductor, composer]; his works drew the largest audiences of the week, 3,053 persons attending the performance of "Gerontius" and 2,933 that of "The Apostles" [1] At this time he was given the Freedom of the City of Worcester and soon he was to be invited to become Mayor of Hereford. This he refused on the day after the second of his lectures. Throughout this period the thought of delivering more lectures disturbed him. There were acrimonious sounds in the air. Noting the title of Elgar's lecture Frederick Corder sent a letter to *The Birmingham Post*, which was published on October 30:

Neglect of British Composers

With your kind assistance the Society of British Composers desires to direct the attention of the public to an instance of the grievances under which musical composers in this country labour.

The prospectus of a series of six orchestral concerts to be given shortly by the Sunday Concert Society has been issued, and an inspection of the complete programmes given, discloses the lamentable fact that it does not contain a single item emanating from the pen of a native composer.

In no other country could such a thing occur, and the Council of the Society of British Composers therefore desires to raise its voice in serious protest, and to express its regret that any body of music lovers should be thus regardless of the claims of native art.

F. Corder/Chairman

The next day saw a follow-up:

Mr. Corder's letter in your issue to-day encourages me to call your attention to another serious wrong which is at the present time being done to British composers. For twelve months most of the leading music publishers in London have combined together to refuse to publish any new song whatsoever, in the mistaken notion that they can by that means stop the trade of the music "pirates". To many struggling composers this has

---

[1] *Monthly Musical Record*, October 1, 1905.

meant starvation and ruin. To the sale of cheap music this policy has not made, and never will make, the slightest difference, since what the public requires the public will always find means of getting. And sometimes scores of good MSS. are going out of the country; for even composers must live, and if the market at home is closed to them they will find one elsewhere.

Oct. 30   ONE OF THEM

This second, anonymous, letter drew attention to a state of affairs that had long been exercising the minds of many musicians. The pirating of songs—especially of popular ballads—had for long gone unchecked simply because it was much more difficult to deal with infringement of musical than literary copyright. The only redress was for a copyright-holder to seize illegal issues. So far as publishers were concerned Messrs. Chappell & Co. took the lead in establishing a Musical Copyright Association. In 1902 an Amendment to the Copyright Act was introduced but it proved impracticable to administer it. A new Bill was brought before the House of Commons in 1903, but this was blocked by a Scottish Member. The Bill, none the less, won strong support and a meeting in its support was held in Queen's Hall at which were Stanford (the principal agitator for reform), Mackenzie, Parry (both of whom had been described by Stanford as no more than lukewarm), and Elgar. By this time certain publishers had declared their intention not to engage in publication, it being unprofitable. In August, 1906, however, a new Musical Copyright Bill, sponsored by T. P. O'Connor, was adopted, and on November 18 a Dinner to O'Connor, "in recognition of his untiring efforts in connection with the passing of the Musical Copyright Bill, now the Act", was held in the Hotel Cecil, London, with the Duke of Argyll in the Chair.[1]

As usual, as the manuscript shows, Elgar prepared his lecture in haste. When he arrived at the University to deliver the lecture he found an august assembly. Among those present were the Peytons, the Lord Mayor and Vice-Chancellor (Alderman Beale), the Pro-Vice-Chancellor (Alderman Clayton), the Vice-Principal (Dr. Heath), Professor Fiedler, Alderman the Right Honourable William Kenrick, Alderman Sir Hallewell Rogers, Alderman Bishop, Mr. M. Pollack, Dr. A. R. Gaul,[2] Dr. G. R. Sinclair, Mr. Granville Bantock, Mr. Max Mossel, and other Professors of the University.

[1] At this dinner Stanford exacerbated the feelings of the publishers present by contrasting the firm of Belaïeff (St. Petersburg and Leipzig) with English publishers: "How about England?" he asked. "With abundance of the finest material at hand, it is safe to say that at least nine-tenths of it is in manuscript, and procurable by nobody. The reputation of a country cannot be built on manuscripts. I am well outside the mark if I say that the list of such works published in England would not cover more than ten pages. Belaïeff's catalogue runs to 210 pages . . ."

[2] Alfred Robert Gaul (1837–1913), a former chorister of Norwich Cathedral and pupil of Zachariah Buck, was a prominent church organist in Birmingham. He also taught at the Midland Institute. He was widely known as a composer of oratorios, of which the merit was in inverse ratio to their popularity. The most celebrated of his works was *The Holy City* (Birmingham Festival, 1882).

As will be made clear, on this occasion Elgar leaned rather less than in the Inaugural Lecture on his prepared script. Partly because it was less complete; partly because his talent enabled him to achieve more in the way of verbal utterance when he felt free to improvise. The prelude to the lecture, although hinted at in the rough notes, does not appear in the final typescript at all, and is here gathered from the *Birmingham Post* of November 2, 1905:

By way of introduction he said:—The first thing they should do was to make Birmingham, musically, a place it was worth the while of a student to live in. They wanted primarily a library, and in response to that he thought he was justified in saying that by January 1 they would have in proper order a useful working library. He led the way by presenting a complete edition of the full score of Sebastian Bach's works as a mark of his reverence for the greatest musician that ever lived, and also as an inducement for other people to present full scores of the other great masters as soon as they possibly could. On the table of the library would be found periodical literature worth reading from Austria, France, Belgium, England, and so forth, so there would be something tangible to begin with.

He then proceeded to his main theme:

Rough Notes 2

Omit   In inaugural address: how are we preparing Birmingham for students?

———

Slow preparations: too much must not be expected.

———

I asked for a library
      response
Bach's works.
periodicals (Deakin collection)
Jany 1: 1906 will see us possessing a moderately fairly equipped working library for the use of musical students in Bir: & the first solid step towards making the music dept useful will have been accomplished.

TEXTUAL COMMENTARY

Ms.   *The present state . . . held in no respect"* written in pencil on facing page, marked * for incorporation in main text.

Birm.   "The present state of things might be pleasing to certain
Post   parochial musicians and to some well-established coteries, but in regard to higher forms of art he repeated that their serious art and serious compositions thus far produced had no hold on the affections of the people, and were held in no respect abroad."

Ms.   *but,* [δ *as I summed up the situation before*] *in regard to*

    & in [δ a certain] a larger degree

    The ground . . . one day written in pencil on facing page marked *

ENGLISH COMPOSERS

In my inaugural address I promised to continue the subject proposed 'A Future for English Music' in more or less definite divisions. From that much misquoted lecture I take the following:—

"What is meant by the young English school? I confess I do not know, and yet it is for that school that I stand here, and for which, in a certain sense, I plead."

The present state of things may be pleasing to certain parochial

musicians and to some well-established coteries, *but in regard* to serious forms of art, I repeat my former phrase, "Our art has no hold on the affections of the people and is held in no respect."

I need not go into the past history of music and composers; we have here in Birmingham to deal with the present, and *in a larger degree,* with the future. Much as I would like to trace the sequence of English composers, from our greatest, Purcell, down to his latest successors, and much as I would delight to give expression to the varying degrees of influence they have had in preparing the way for the present day (and future) composers, I refrain for the moment. *The ground* has been well covered and every scrap of literature, Elizabethan, Stuart, Georgian has been ransacked for anecdotes and amusing information. But I fear the serious side is sometimes overlooked; perhaps we can see to that *one day.*

In considering the present we are confronted with many difficulties at the outset. Our musical horizon has widened so much that we can hardly believe that we are in the same land of thirty—nay twenty—years ago; we have now an enlarged area in which compositions are

Ms.   . . . necessarily larger public [δ Halls suitable for Concerts]
[δ more Concert rooms are sometimes built;] Concert Halls
are not built in proportion and ([δ except] in our capital city
[δ where] they prefer to pull down such useless things.)
. . . day to day [δ ch] infants

★ [on facing page] [δ ★ *Numberless Compositions recd.*
*I feel like Beaumont & Fletcher's Captn· Bessus in 'A King &
no King'.*
*"I could make seven shillings a day o' tha' paper. Yet I learn
nothing by all these but a little skill in comparing of styles"*]
we know [δ that]

. . . how many, cases★ [to facing page]
           & the vast numbers of M.S.S. sent to me!
I sometimes . . . comparing of styles".

Ms.   Now the technical ability
                Young men
                   pay tribute to this
                     and
             teaching. R.A.M.
                „   R.C.M.

Birm.   "The technical ability of our youngest composers was very
Post   great, and the teaching in all the great schools, such as the
school in Birmingham, the Royal Academy of Music, and
the Royal College of Music, was as good as anything that
could be found in Europe. Amongst the composers were men
who were technically equipped as well as any that were living,
but the fact remained that they found a difficulty in obtaining
a publisher for their compositions".

produced—and *necessarily larger public* Concert Halls are not built in proportion and in our capital city they prefer to pull down such useless things.[1]

We have also a larger number of men (and boys) and, as Professor in this University I hear from *day to day* infants also) writing music: these it will be convenient for the present to call composers, the future will settle their right to the title.*

Our students have no lack of encouragement to compose, possibly there is too much help given in this direction in the earlier stages of musical education—too many scholarships for composition and too many outside inducements to put pen to paper: at *any rate we know*, so far as the higher branches of music are concerned, that unfortunately the supply of compositions is in excess of the demand.

Quartets, Symphonies, Operas, Symphonic poems are put forward in increasing numbers and the authors are anxious to get a hearing. But even amongst all the concerts now organised it is impossible for a tithe of the works to be heard. How do I know this? Well, since I have held the Professorship I have been consulted in I fear to say how *many—cases, and the vast numbers of M.S.S. sent to me! I sometimes* look round my heaped up study and say with Beaumont and Fletcher's Captain Bessus "I could make seven shillings a day of th' paper: yet I learn nothing from all these save a little skill in *comparing of styles*."[2]

(*Tribute to the technical ability* of these young men and to the R. A. M. and R. C. M.)

There is the Palmer Fund:[3] works are heard there and presented in good style.

---

[1] St. James's Hall, Piccadilly, was demolished during this year, the last concert having been given there on February 11.

[2] Captain Bessus, the unwilling recipient of a series of challenges, says: "If they would find mee Challenges thus thicke, as long as I liv'd, I would have no other lining; I can make seaven shillings a day o' th' paper to the Grocers: yet I learn nothing by all these but a little skill in comparing of stiles, I doe find evidently, that there is some one Scriven in this Towne, that haz a great hand in writing of Challenges for they are all of a cut, and sixe of 'em in a hand; and they all end, my reputation is deare to mee, and I must require satisfaction: Who's this? more paper I hope, no tis my Lord *Bacurius*, I feare all is not well betwixt us." *A King and no King*, Act III, 3rd ed., 1631, p. 44.

[3] This Fund was instituted by Ernest (later Lord) Palmer in 1903 with the intention of enabling young British composers to hear performances of their own orchestral works. There was an initial endowment of £20,000 and the management of the Fund was entrusted to the Royal College of Music. On May 30, 1904, William Wallace (1860–1940, Scottish composer) had drawn Elgar's attention to a letter from Wallace published in *The Times* on May 28, 1904 (p. 3). This letter occupied more than a column and was couched in blistering terms. Thus Wallace considered it unthinkable ". . . to set the Royal College of Music in a position to which it is scarcely entitled—namely, that of being the

Ms.   [pencil note] * *Ideal programme of English music*
on facing page
       [δ How we should]
        PROGRAMME
How we should . . . find the audience.

Ms.   Large executive *means* required

    . . . support [δ of] *of performances* of music

[Quotation detached from printed Prospectus of The Society
of British Composers and affixed to facing page.]

How many works produced under the auspices of the Fund have found their way into other programmes?

How we should like to see as a usual and everyday thing, a *programme*:— Overture

Symphony or Symphonic Poem

Concerto

all by Englishmen, as we see programmes by Germans, AND English people anxious to hear it. We could easily compile a dozen such programmes, but where should we find the audience? After what we have heard about the new enthusiasm for English music, how are we to account for the apathy of the public when English music is performed?

(Many causes: dull, learned, trite, frivolous, and we have had good. Perhaps there is a remedy.)

Music is not helped in performance like the other arts, a large *executive is required.*

Men willingly will finance picture exhibitions, and provide free libraries, being certain of a loss. Few instances of *support of performances* of music, although in this respect Birmingham must be excluded being one of the few places where much has been done by the munificence etc. Performances are what are required, answering to the exhibition of pictures.

I venture to read the prospectus of a new society:—

The present position of the British composer of high-class music is a very deplorable one. He is encouraged to educate himself well —scholarships even are offered to tempt him to undertake the production of work which, on the author's entry into the world, is declared on all hands to be a nonsaleable article. As a matter of fact, the number of new Symphonies, Concertos, Quartets and Sonatas published in London during the last ten years is quite insignificant. Other countries encourage and protect native work that is not directly remunerative. England alone does not. A few

authoritative body *par excellence* to be entrusted with the future of British music. . . . No musician can close his eyes to the fact that the Royal College of Music is associated with a certain phase of thought which is academically antagonistic, if not openly inimical, to every modern tendency. . . . We want British music, not Royal-College-of-Music-music." This campaign warmed up so that during the next year the *Musical Opinion*, (August 1905, p. 794) remarked that "the prevailing tone is critical, tinged with disappointment", and quoted *The Daily News*: "If the compositions performed really represented the best works that our composers have to show, the Palmer Fund might just as well be wound up and the money spent in other ways of encouraging live musicians."

Birm.
Post

"PLEA FOR AN ENGLISH PROGRAMME

Sir Edward wished to see English composers encouraged, and he was in favour of the programme at, say, an orchestral concert consisting of English works only. It would be possible to make dozens of programmes by Englishmen, but where were the audiences? There must be something wrong, some wane of interest. In France they had concert after concert without a German, English, or Italian name in the programme; in Germany, programme after programme with nothing but German names, except, perhaps, one Scandinavian: but in England we had not arrived at that yet. He hoped, however, in the future by steady endeavour we might arrive, at any rate, at having an art of our own which the people would love. The popular apathy was such that if English music only were performed the programme would not, as a rule, be commercially successful—in other words, the audience would not care to go. The remedy for that lay in the direction of helping English music forward more than had been the case hitherto. He reminded the meeting of the difficulty of publishing serious music which would bring a pecuniary return to the composer, who, unless some portion of his work was arrangeable for the piano would scarcely make sufficient bread and cheese for a week. We provided scholarships and the like, and incited young men to compose, and then gave them very little chance by taking very little interest in what they wrote. He felt that the solution of the difficulty lay in giving a larger public a chance of hearing music. He would not begin by giving symphonic poems and that sort of thing in a mining town, but what were wanted in many towns were larger concert rooms, where works might be produced in the same style as now, but to a larger public and at a small fee."

Ms.   * *I fear however . . . product of Variations* [on facing page, marked *]

years ago even a hearing was denied to most, and poor, indeed, would the prospect have been without the noble efforts of Sir August Manns to brighten it. Even now, as a rule, only one performance of a new work can be obtained—thus treating it as a mere curiosity instead of a thing requiring time and attention to appreciate.

The number of talented young composers is nevertheless—strange to say—very large at the present time; so large, in fact, that it is felt that some effort must be made to put matters on a better footing. Accordingly a number of the most energetic among them have held meetings to discuss the situation, and as a preliminary step towards the desired ends have founded THE SOCIETY OF BRITISH COMPOSERS, to which they invite all their fellow-musicians to seek election. The immediate aims of the Society are;

1. To facilitate the publication of such high-class works as the ordinary publisher cannot or will not undertake.

2. The protection of the British composer's interests in the matters of publishing agreements. This is a great need, as a young musician is seldom a good man of business.

Protection against pirates of the ordinary sort does not at present enter into the Society's scheme.

The Society consists of members (composers) and Associates (friends of music and musicians other than composers).[1] The subscription is one guinea annually, for both classes, and subscribers will have the privilege of obtaining the Society's publications upon specially favourable terms.

It is sad, in a measure that this, which I will venture to call dignified preface, should be necessary. Attached are the names of some forty young composers, some very well-known—others who have not been very prominently before us.

The scheme, I may scarcely say, has my warm sympathy and I trust some good may come of it. *I fear however* that any pecuniary result cannot be looked for.

---

[1] Within two years the total of members and associates of The Society of British Composers had risen to 254. Publications (undertaken at the cost of the Society, or the composers, or both) numbered forty-four, mostly chamber music and songs. The Chairman of the Society throughout its existence was Frederic Corder (see p. 75). In 1918 the Society was wound up and its funds transferred to the Manns Memorial Fund.

[δ we] all

Birm. "Sir Edward wished to see in every town a large hall
Post   capable of accommodating a large sixpenny audience, for
the working classes, with their education, should be provided
for as they were in Germany. He looked forward to a great
increase in the real musical public of the future. It was
coming. Concerts now could not be given without loss, and
yet the vast mass of the people remained untouched. From
these the audiences in the future would be drawn."

Ms.   ... audiences. [δ *And too much stress cannot be laid on the
Music tests sometimes called competitions.]
But. I am ...

         ... for better things.
                competition (festivals)
                educating listeners

[*ital.*] *gauche*
        unfortunately [in pencil]
                ★ *The man ... same shock* [on facing page, marked ★]

(I will dare to give an instance:—
3 scores and sets of parts will set the whole of the musical country up.
Piano arrangements refer to later.
Net *product of Variations*.)
But all who are interested in the welfare of our art, should consider
many points raised by this announcement. What we build up on one
hand do we not destroy with the other? (Amplify) I feel that the
solution of the difficulty is in creating a larger public: we must not
depend on the audience—the amateurs now existing. We encourage
composers and have no halls—or few, and these small. We ask for
Operas to be written and have no means of performing them—we
have Royal foundations for the culture of music on the one hand and
the Government allows organised piracy on the other.

I would like to see in every town—a large hall capable of accommodating a large *sixpenny audience*.

Concerts cannot be given without loss and the vast mass of the
people are untouched. From these we must draw our future *audiences*.
But I am sometimes dubious about the real feeling for music in the
middle classes,—it exists but fitfully and easily expires.

(Instance Crystal Palace Concerts, History. Vanish and leave no
trace among the large 'Villadom'. We must hope however for *better
things*. Competition festivals. Educating listeners. Our present young
men are well equipped. R.A.M. R.C.M. Teaching good, and our
own school of Music the choice of subjects to be illustrated is no longer
limited by popular prejudice—the freedom of choice allowed to
painters and sculptors and authors is open to composers.

The Art cannot be narrowed.

Some sacred subjects are still thought to be out of place. This idea
only lurks in the minds of those who remember the time when music
was an amusement only. It is unfortunate that the Englishman is
always rather *gauche* in a crowd.)

(Audiences necessary *unfortunately*.)

The man who will gladly and reverentially look at a picture, a sacred
picture—when he can choose his own time and not be jostled—is
horrified of the meeting simultaneously of a number of people to hear
some music. Imagine a picture—veiled—and at a given moment
uncovered—same *shock*.

In the Cathedral performances, to me it is a glorious sight to see the
building FULL: the sight seems so unusual to people who do not attend
regularly that they see in the necessary movement of the crowd—

The objector [in pencil] mistak[δ ing] *es*

★ *we ask for intellectual works* [δ *to compare with other nations*] *we
expect to be able to compare with foreigners* [in pencil]

Ms.   [Marginal note] (W. C. Kent)
                              1823   *? Feltham*[1] [in pencil]
                          Dreamland

Now, how far has the [δ *modern*] *youthful* English composer
                                        his own strength [in pencil]

to the occasion.★ [On facing page, in pencil, without parentheses, marked ★]
                    Gruesome subjects . . . the young school.

modern scope & tendencies.★ [On facing page, in pencil,
marked ★]
                    Imitation of Strauss . . . Heldenleben (Eroica).

---

[1] Probable reference to Owen Feltham (1602?–1668), author of a famous series of
essays—*Resolves, Divine, Moral, Political* (1623)—which ran into twelve editions by 1709
and were reissued in the "Temple Classics" in 1904. Essays LII, *Of Dreams*, and LXXXVIII,
Of Music, would have attracted Elgar. In the former we read: ". . . In sleep, we have the
naked and natural thoughts of our own souls: outward objects interfere not either to
shuffle in occasional cogitations, or hale out the included fancy."
    In the latter: ". . . For as the notes are framed, it [music] can draw, and incline the mind.
Lively tunes do lighten the mind: grave ones give it melancholy. Lofty ones raise it, and
advance it to above. . . . And I think he hath not a mind well tempered, whose zeal is
not influenced by a heavenly anthem. So that indeed Music is good, or bad, as the end to
which it tendeth."

irreverence. *The objector mistakes his own uneasy feeling and his own awkwardness for misbehaviour in others.*

To resume:— We set a lofty ideal before our composers *we ask for intellectual* works and expect to be able to compare him with foreigners and in addition we expect them [*sic*] to be sober citizens (useful) etc. and we give them nothing on which to subsist; it is impossible to obtain a performing fee for any orchestral work.

(Dominion of the Piano. Everything must be arranged for pf.)

Now I know that men do not write for profit but because they must: we may have our Schubert amongst us and our duty will be to see that he does not starve. How many disappointed a composer, a weaver of pure sounds, has gone sadly through this life, his only reward being to take his tribute above and lay it

> Before the builded throne of symphonies,
> Himself a fragile instrument of strains immortal
> (*W. C. Kent. Dreamland. 1822*)[1]

Well, how far has the youthful English composer stood in his own light? In many ways. In misjudging *his own strength*—the public his works are to meet: I mean, of course, not that he should compose with a view to please a certain audience, but he should, on the rare occasions of a performance, choose a work suited *to the occasion.*

(*Gruesome* subjects, ransacking old poems for these. My wish for a short brilliant piece—10 minutes—something cheerful and uplifting. Could not find it amongst the music I knew of the *young school.*)

Also old forms have in many cases been needlessly thrown aside without, it seems in my poor opinion, correspondingly good results.

(*Modern scope* and tendencies. *Imitation of Strauss* adding to the orchestra when he adds. Ransacking for new titles or forgotten poems. The old re-illustrated will serve. Don Juan. Don Quixote. Heldenleben. (*Eroica.*))

[1] *Dreamland, with other poems,* W. Charles Kent, barrister-at-law, London, 1862. The volume was dedicated to Bulwer Lytton, and comprised ". . . a series of Poems delineating the Great Masters of English Song, each in the locality haunted by his memory . . . that simply is the one design I have hoped to realise while writing DREAMLAND . . . I have ventured, in several instances, to write of each Poet in the manner familiar to himself." Elgar quotes from "Milton at Cripplegate", p. 31.

The book has a certain inspirational significance in respect of Elgar's obsession with dreams (cf. William Beckford's *Dreams, Waking Thoughts and incidents,* p. 257, and see *Elgar O.M.,* p. 277). There is also interest in Kent's phrase ". . . to write of each Poet in the manner most familiar to himself", in comparison with Elgar's remark to Jaeger, of October 24, 1898, that in the "Enigma" Variations "I have written what I think *they* would have written . . ."

writing of poetry [in pencil. Quotation extracted from book and affixed to following page.]

Ms.   I should like [δ but to] *to sketch*

Abhorrence of form, needless alarm on the part of theorists: music will exist when the stuff (material) is good. It matters not if it is in classical 'form' but use proportion (explain).

Listen to Charles Kingsley:—

the utterance must be the expression, the outward and visible autotype, of the spirit which animates it. But the thought is defined by no limits, it cannot express itself in form, for form is that which has limits. Where it has no inward unity it cannot have any outward one. If the spirit be impatient of all moral rule, its utterance will be equally impatient of all artistic rule; and thus, as we are now beginning to discover from experience, the poetry of doubt will find itself unable to use those forms of verse which have always been held to be the highest; tragedy, epic, the ballad, and lastly even the subjective lyrical ode, for they too, to judge by every great lyric which remains to us require a groundwork of consistent, self-coherent belief; and they require also an appreciation of melody even more delicate, and a verbal polish even more complete, than any other form of poetic utterance. But where there is no melody within, there will be no melody without. It is in vain to attempt the setting of spiritual discords to physical music. The mere practical patience and self-restraint requisite to work out rhythm when fixed on, will be wanting; nay, the fitting rhythm will never be found, the subject itself being arhythmic; and thus we shall have, a wider and wider divorce of sound and sense, a greater and greater carelessness for polish, and for the charm of musical utterance, and watch the clear and spirit-stirring melodies of the older poets swept away by a deluge of half-metrical prose—run-mad diffuse, unfinished, unmusical, to[o], which any other metre than that in which it happens to have been written would have been equally appropriate, because all are equally inappropriate and where men have nothing to sing, it is not of the slightest consequence how they sing it.

Now:—if an incoherent composition fails to attract even the people it was designed to please, I fear the composer too often poses as a martyr and perhaps thinks of Tarpander who improved the lyre—according to one account, the Spartans nailed the new instrument to a tree.

I would like to sketch an education necessary for a musician in case he

*I fear it wd. be only an enumeration of suggested helpful surround-
ings &*
[in pencil] a bit of
Literature
[δ Art] *the study of Art* [in pencil]
& *last* of all music
Some day [δ this may be done] we will consider the early
training of the child musician.

several of the men *Walford Davies, Holbrooke, Bantock*
[in pencil] are making their [δ mark] *way sturdily* [in pencil] &
opening the doors for the *more* juvenile composers [δ from]
upon whom . . .
But I would ask [δ them] *what I will call the coming men not
those I have named* [in pencil] to consider . . .

* *Let them think . . . does not occur in our own day* [on facing
page in pencil]

Continuing the quotation already read [in pencil]
C. Kingsley referring to poetry
*Kingsley was rather unnecessarily afraid of the new school in
poetry* [in pencil]
But cannot we have simplicity manhood etc. *clearness &
melody* in [δ the] *our* new school. I believe [δ so] and hope so &
[δ in] indeed . . .
young composers works [δ works I have no] who . . .

End note   *At the request of several* [in pencil]
N.B. I shall leave this subject next week
Brahms' Symph. in F No. 3

should develop (or dwindle) into a composer but *I fear it would* only be an enumeration of suggested helpful *surroundings*.

(Literature, the study of Art, and LAST of all music. Some day we will consider the early training of the child musician. In the meantime

several of these men, Walford Davies, Holbrooke, Bantock are making their way sturdily and opening the doors for the more juvenile com-

posers upon whom we expect the burden to fall next. But I would ask what I will call the coming men, not those I have named, to consider many things at the outset of their careers. I do not ask them to give up any sane modern idea: by no means, let us progress. *Let them think* seriously of the words which they set: if they cannot heighten the expression, give more force to the meaning, give a wider application, let the words alone: they must no longer be treated as mere pegs on which to hang musical exercises. It is easy to laugh at fugal choruses and the vain repetition of words but let us beware that worse maltreatment of words *does not occur in our own day* but amongst all the unnecessary complications and amongst the neurotic rubbish with which they are surrounded I beg to think of Charles Kingsley's words again and again.

Continuing the quotation already read:—

"Simplicity, manhood, clearness and finished melody, the very opposite, in a word, of our new school?"

Kingsley was rather unnecessarily afraid of the new school in poetry.

But *cannot we have* simplicity, manhood, clearness and melody in our new school, *I believe* and hope so and indeed these qualities are not wholly absent from some of the young composers' *works* who will have the making of "A Future for English Music".

[on University note-paper]

Nov 2 1905
Dear Fiedler:
   Please give this gown houseroom.
   Will you put my name up for the U[nion]. Club?

Yours ever

Ed: Elgar

on reverse

   Could we not start a men's choir in the U.—(as at Yale & other places)
   I should like to begin it even if we can't carry it thro'.—
   The way to begin wd. be to put up a notice: but where? Will you ask
   the Principal & think over [δ if] the whole thing.
   It would be a jolly thing to do.

E. E.

On November 3, 1905, a "thunderbolt from South Kensington" in the form of a letter from Stanford struck *The Times*.

If [said Stanford] Sir Edward Elgar is correctly reported as saying from the professorial chair at Birmingham that 'English music is held in no respect abroad—that was to say, the serious compositions which up to the present time had been turned out'—he is stating what a little investigation at such musical centres as Berlin, Vienna, Leipzig, Hamburg, Amsterdam and the Rhineland will prove to be an undeserved aspersion upon the taste, judgement and perspicacity of foreigners and an unjust disparagement of the influence which has long been exerted by the music of his own country. In fairness to foreign taste, to my colleagues at home and to the reputation for accuracy which our universities have so deservedly earned, I traverse a statement—which Sir Edward himself, even within the radius of his own experience could hardly endorse—in loyalty to his friends abroad.

This letter was reprinted in the *Musical Opinion* for December, 1905,[1] which also observed, under the heading of "Musical Gossip":

Some people have a genius for misunderstanding the simplest statement. When Sir Edward Elgar recently delivered his first lecture as the Birmingham professor of music, he expressed a hope that the day would come when concert programmes would consist entirely of British compositions; he also thought that even now there should be orchestral concerts of native music. Immediately, a number of correspondents wrote to the papers to protest against his Chauvinism. The composer of "The Apostles" is not a narrowly national musician in any sense; and it should have struck those who objected to his lecture that he could not mean that works of genius by foreigners should be omitted from programmes or that he wanted to see any kind of blind protectionism in music.
   All that Sir Edward Elgar meant to say was no doubt that, while it is

[1] No. 339, p. 177.

quite common to have concerts of German, French or Russian music in England, it is seldom that an all-British concert is given; and that, when it is given, the event is considered very exceptional.

The point of view is surely reasonable enough. Just as Richter will often direct a concert composed of music by Brahms, Beethoven and Wagner, so an English conductor in the future will be able to make his programme entirely of British compositions,—not as an exceptional thing but because the works are of the proper artistic value. But I join issue with Sir Edward's implication that even now this might be done. In a few spare moments, after reading a report of his lecture, I took the trouble to draw up a series of programmes for orchestral concerts in which nothing but British compositions were included. It would be possible to give a series of about three concerts, of which the music would be well worth hearing for its own sake; and there the *répertoire* ends. And (how shall one put it?) the programmes of those three concerts did not contain a single work of undoubted genius, if you omit Elgar's own "Enigma" Variations and his "In the South" Overture. We are, I was forced to recognise, singularly lacking in the big forms of composition. We have not a single symphony of our own which the amateur could be expected to accept in the place of works by Brahms or by Tschaïkowsky. I purposely do not mention the great classical masters. In their early days, both Parry and Stanford wrote symphonies of promise, of which even now some of the movements are worth hearing. But the compositions as a whole are not of the very first rank.

I am not at all sure that the fuss made about British music is altogether advisable. For many years we neglected it entirely, mainly because the British school of the period had nothing to say to the amateur which he wished to hear. Then came a kind of *renaissance*, and concert goers—thanks largely to Elgar's own compositions—began to see that it was possible for an Englishman to write music which was not an imitation of Brahms. With that discovery a kind of madness has come over the musical world. Every day the press publishes letters deploring the neglect of British compositions, and the composers themselves—especially the younger men— have joined in the fray. Now, the public does not care a brass farthing who writes the music to which it listens, so long as the music is worth hearing. The public had some experience of the average British composition at the Promenade Concerts and elsewhere and it is by no means keen on hearing too much of it. Exaggerated championship always does harm; and I am inclined to think that the protests made against Sir Edward Elgar's lecture are proofs that the admirers of British music have already gone too far in their enthusiasm.[1]

[1] Ibid., p. 181.

CHAPTER 6

BRAHMS'S SYMPHONY NO. 3
(November 8, 1905)

A most interesting and instructive lesson in Brahms' music was given last night at the University of Birmingham by Sir Edward Elgar, the Richard Peyton Professor of Music. It formed the second of the special series of lectures which Sir Edward has arranged to deliver, and on this occasion he took for his subject 'Brahms' Third Symphony'. The large lecture theatre of the University was well filled with ladies and gentlemen, who attended with their music so that they might more easily follow the professor's details and explanations of a practical and technical lesson. The reason Sir Edward selected Brahms' Third Symphony was because it was included in the concert to be given by the London Symphony Orchestra on Monday next, and he was asked by letter by several persons if it would be possible for him to give some description of it.[1]

Among those present at this lecture was the Worcestershire composer Julius Harrison, who, many years later, recalled the deep impression it had made on him.[2]

The twenty-one years that intervened between the first London performance of Brahms's Third Symphony in 1884 and the delivery of Elgar's lecture were years of great change in musical attitudes. The degree of change is best recognised by noting that during these years the works of Tchaikovsky and Dvořák were popularised in England, and that in 1904 the first English performance of Debussy's *L'Après-midi d'un faune*, conducted by Henry Wood, took place. Hence the disorders of dialectic revealed in this chapter, which also emphasise a reluctance on the part of some to contemplate change.

---

[1] *Birmingham Post*, November 9, 1905.
[2] B.B.C. talk, *The 15th Variation, Recollections of Elgar*, May 12, 1957; repeated August 3, 1966.

Philharmonische Concerte.

Sonntag den 2. Dezember 1883,

Mittags präcise halb 1 Uhr,

im grossen Saale der Gesellschaft der Musikfreunde:

2tes Abonnement-Concert

veranstaltet von den

Mitgliedern des k. k. Hofopern-Orchesters

unter der Leitung des Herrn

HANS RICHTER,

k. k. Hofopern-Kapellmeister.

PROGRAMM:

F. Mendelssohn . . Ouverture zu „Die Hebriden".

F. Dvorák . . . . . . Violin-Concert (NEU) vorgetragen von
Herrn **F. ONDŘÍČEK.**

J. Brahms . . . . . . Symphonie Nr. 3, F-dur (1. Aufführung)

Streichinstrumente: Lemböck. — Programme unentgeltlich.

Das 3. Philharmonische Concert findet am 16. Dezember statt.

Wallishausser's Buchdruckerei.

TEXTUAL COMMENTARY

The typescript of this Lecture represents no more than what elsewhere is shown as "rough notes". The report given in *The Birmingham Post* on November 9, 1905, however, amplifies the basic material. It also places the contention-stirring term *absolute music* in its context.

Birm.   ". . . of that year, and it was played by Dr. Richter at his
Post   concerts from manuscript or proof copies in May, 1884.[1] The production in Vienna evoked a scene of tremendous enthusiasm, and Brahms a most reticent man, was called forward several times. In London the third movement was encored, which was a very unusual thing".

ibid.   "The form of the Symphony was strictly orthodox, and it was a piece of absolute music. There was no clue to what was meant, but, as Sir Hubert Parry said, it was a piece of music which called up certain sets of emotions in each individual hearer. That was the height of music. . . ."

---

[1] "By courtesy of its publishers, Messrs. N. Simrock, of Berlin, copies of the score and parts were supplied to Dr. Richter in advance of their publication, and thus he was enabled to bring the work before an English audience at a much earlier date than would otherwise have been possible." Programme note by C. A. B[arry]., St. James's Hall Richter Concert, May 12, 1884. The programme printed Hanslick's article as in *The Musical World*. The symphony was repeated some days later. Another performance was given on November 4, and other early performances were at Liverpool (Charles Hallé), Crystal Palace (Manns), and a London Symphony Concert (George Henschel).

BRAHMS'S SYMPHONY No. 3

Composed in 1883. First heard in Vienna on the 2nd of December of that year. First produced in England at the Richter Concerts on May 12, 1884.[1] Third movement encored.

In what is known as orthodox form.

A curious sort of 'motto' theme: introducing the first subject, running through the whole first movement and knitting it together:—

The movements are 'related' to each other in the following way. The 'motto' theme reappears in the last movement twelve bars from

[1] ". . . As now advised, we place the opening Allegro amongst the best things Brahms has done. The themes, striking in themselves, are happily contrasted, and worked out not only according to art, but in an interesting manner. There is, moreover, an absence of the mere verbiage which so disfigures modern music. The 'argument' is concise and it is complete—two cardinal virtues. As to the style of the movement, the word noble best describes it. Not once does the composer come down from the lofty height proper to a symphonist. The Andante is of less value. Its theme, repeated in the 'song form' so often adopted by Haydn, falls on the ear 'like a tale that is told', and only the ingenuity of an accomplished orchestral writer sustains the connoisseur's interest. But the public will take to this movement, despite a passage which has been greatly praised by amateurs who confound the uncommon with the beautiful. The Scherzo, if so we may call the third movement, will also be popular, thanks to its engaging and easily appreciated qualities. We cannot but think, however, that both here and in the Andante Brahms gains the public voice at the expense of symphonic character. He affects 'prettiness', which is all very well in its place. The Finale balances the opening Allegro, and lifts the work again to the highest level. It is a remarkable movement, very characteristic of the author, and elaborated in a masterly manner. The soft ending has a particularly happy effect. On the whole, the new Symphony deserves to rank with its predecessors, but its exact place, we repeat, must be decided later on. It was most admirably played and loudly applauded, the third movement having to be repeated." *Musical Times*, June 1, 1884, p. 336.

ibid.   ". . . ended either piano or pianissimo. When the Symphony was produced everyone was talking about reminiscences, and it would be very easy to pick out several phrases which suggested other masters. When it was produced in England the critics had not quite settled down to their Brahms, and two or three endeavoured to say rather small things about one or two of the themes, and Sir Edward referred with satisfaction to a little sketch which he wrote of Brahms at Malvern when he was an obscure violinist. In that sketch he said it was to be hoped that Malvern, which had shown itself so ready to appreciate pieces bearing well-known names, would do itself honour by duly appreciating the classical composer par excellence of the present day, who, free from any provincialism of expression or national dialect, wrote for the whole world and for all time—a giant, lofty and unapproachable. It was not exactly a prophecy, but it was a feeling that the power of such a great man was coming right down amongst all musicians."

[Continuation of *Birm. Post* report on p. 105]

the end—the first subject proper of the first movement reappears in the last nine bars from the end.

The second theme of the second movement reappears as a subsidiary theme in the finale.[1]

The Form.

4 movements.

Contrasted Keys.

Curious, all end *p or pp.*

In spite of reminiscent phrases the whole work is by Brahms and no other.

If criticised as Whately's[2] tutor, Dr. Copleston,[3] criticised in burlesque fashion 'L'Allegro' of Milton, several of the themes would be severely handled, and I can imagine the severity with which a critic would point out the resemblance of the Andante to a tune in a well-known Overture, etc. etc.

The opening theme (first movement) of course suggests Men-

---

[1] "To Sir Edward Elgar I owe the remark that this is the tragic outcome of the wistful theme in the middle of the slow movement." D. F. Tovey, *Essays in Musical Analysis*, London, 1935, I, p. 112.

[2] Richard Whateley (1787–1863), sometime Fellow of Oriel College, Oxford, and Archbishop of Dublin.

[3] Edward Copleston (1776–1849), sometime Fellow and Tutor of Oriel College, Bishop of Llandaff, and Dean of St. Paul's Cathedral. More interesting than Copleston's views on Milton is his reference to music in *A Sermon preached at Usk, July 20, 1848, at the First Annual Meeting of the Society for the Improvement of Church Music in the Archdeaconry of Monmouth* (pub. London/Usk [1848]): ". . . but as Music is confessedly the most powerful of those agents which awaken past sensation, with a kind of magical force, I cannot dismiss the argument for its close cultivation in connection with religion, without adverting to one instance often related as a fact . . . that the soldiers of Switzerland when enlisted in foreign [French] service, were debarred from hearing the music of their native land, because of the longing to return to the country they had left, which these wild and simple notes created . . . from the power they had of calling up images of things they loved, and with which their tenderest affections were entwined." This legend appears in Crotch's *Specimens*, where the forbidden *Le Rans des Vaches* is given (no. 296).

Mus.   "Sir Edward said there were fine orchestral effects and
Standard beautiful music into the bargain, and all orchestral effects did
not come into the category of beautiful music (a statement
that evoked laughter)."   [Nov. 25, 1905, p. 336]

delssohn —the passage which links it to the 2nd subject suggests Wagner. The Andante suggests, momentarily, Zampa.

The 'echoing' of the Wind by the strings recalls the 9th Symphony, as also does the triplet passage for Violins.

Orchestration—noble and restrained: but there are curiously 'casual' passages—ending pp fiendishly difficult to get 'level'—doubling the third—where special effects are intended—such as 'solo' passages for any instruments—we must not cavil but accept what is given us, but where we see a Tutti—full force and the effect is thin we may enquire where the disappointment lies.

Similarly, when we see a chord, and know that this chord employs every instrument, and know also that a pp is required, we may enquire why the instruments are so arranged as to make it almost impossible to obtain a real pp.

Final chords 1st movement, the third appears *nine* times, dull, heavy effect,—the clearer you want to sound omit the third.

Tonic eleven times.

Dominant eight times.

Third might be cut out of four or six places.

Compare last chord of all.

Trumpet parts—cruel.

Second Trumpet—long skips—open notes only.

The newspaper report of the lecture ended thus:

Going to the piano, Sir Edward played a number of passages from the symphony, pointing out the principles on which the movements were constructed and the themes by which they were knit together. In this he was closely followed by the audience with the aid of their music. The whole work, he told them, was very reticent, very broad, very noble. There was no cheap effect, and it had a sweep, a breadth, and elasticity which was not always to be found in Brahms. It is interesting to learn from Sir Edward that he will follow this precedent and call attention to some of the principal works done at the Halford Concerts, and also, if anything new is done, at the Choral Society's concerts, he will devote some time to their works. By that means, he says, a little light will be thrown on the enterprise which is being carried on in the city. He is, moreover, anxious to see established a choral society or male voice choir, and if possible a ladies' choir, or a combination of the two, so that they may have instruction as well as amusement.

Immediately the lecture was over Max Mossel returned to his room in the Midland Hotel and wrote

Wednesday
7.30 p.m.

My dear Sir Edward,
I'v just got home from your lecture, and feel that I must just tell you how very much I enjoyed your most interesting and original analises (I hope I'v written the word all right!) of that glorious work. I loves every word you said and felt when I came out that I had learned something. I really thought I knew the work, and really I think I could play it by memory but you'v clearly shown me (and many others with me) that I *did not* know it. "Herzlichen dank" and do please take the others in hand at your future lectures. I intend to come to every one of them. I send you herewith the photo and do so want you to see the original. If you can manage it I should be so glad if you would be my guest and stay with me on Monday. I promise you I won't worry you and wont come near you till after the Concert. You could have a nice room just opposite my rooms, which I would have well warmed for you and use my sitting room during the day as I am at the Institute till 5.45, and I do so want you to see the original of the photo. Do say yes.

With my kindest regards also to Lady & Miss Elgar,
believe me
Yours very sincerely
Max Mossel

I need not say how delighted I shall be if Lady Elgar will be with you.

It was agreeable to have such an open-hearted reaction. Not least of all because this lecture—like almost every other—set off detonations. This time it was the question of the "absolute".

On the day following the lecture Newman went off in *The Manchester Guardian* at full blast, soon afterwards rewriting what was printed as a leading article for the last chapter of his book on Elgar.[1]

If Sir EDWARD ELGAR's lecture on BRAHMS at the Birmingham University yesterday is fairly represented by a brief report, some of us may well sit up and rub our eyes in astonishment at his championship of "absolute" music. He protests first of all against people, when they hear a BEETHOVEN symphony, "calling up all sorts of pictures, which might or might not have existed in the composer's mind." But did not BEETHOVEN himself tell NEATE on one occasion that whenever he wrote he had a picture in his mind? And even if we set that aside as an exaggeration, is it not beyond dispute that BEETHOVEN very frequently worked upon a "picture"? Sir EDWARD ELGAR lays it down that music is at its height when it merely "calls up a set of emotions in each individual hearer," and that when music is "simply a description of something else it is carrying a large art somewhat further then he cared for," music, "as a simple art," being at its best "when it was simple, without description," as in the case of BRAHMS's Third Symphony. If this means anything at all it means that absolute music—in which themes that are purely self-existent, not springing from the desire to "describe something else," are taken and woven into a tonal pattern—is by far the highest form of musical art. That much of the greatest music of the world is of this kind no one will deny. But does not Sir EDWARD ELGAR blunder when he denies the rank of first-rate to music in which the composer gives us a "clue to what was meant," as he expresses it? Did not BEETHOVEN give us a clue to what he meant when he called his Sixth Symphony the "Pastoral"; when he called the Third the "Eroica" and bade us see in it his own reflections upon NAPOLEON; when he said of the opening theme of the Fifth, "Thus Fate knocks at the door"; when he calls one great overture "Leonora No. 3" and shows us in it Florestan and Leonora, and "paints" by means of a trumpet-call the arrival of the governor; when he calls another overture "Coriolanus" and "describes" therein the various characters of the drama so clearly that any ordinarily attentive reader of SHAKSPERE can pick them out at once? If all this is not "giving us a clue to what was meant," if this is not making music "a description of something else," by what appropriate name shall we call it?

But the case against Sir EDWARD ELGAR may be pressed still further. Look once more at the sentence "He thought music, as a simple art, was at its best when it was simple, without description," as in the case of BRAHMS's Third Symphony. Well, in the first place, it really does not do to assume that even the most "absolute" of musicians has not been "descriptive" merely because he himself has not told us so at once. BRAHMS, for example, probably worked upon "pictures" a great deal oftener than we imagine. It is quite easy to enumerate compositions of his, ostensibly non-descriptive, that are now known—from KALBECK's "Life"—to have had a poetic or pictorial basis. These works do "mean"

[1] See review in *Musical Standard*, May 26, 1906.

something external to the notes themselves; and if the composer did not give the "clue to what was meant" to every purchaser of a copy, he certainly gave the clue to private friends. But if Sir EDWARD ELGAR's thesis is rickety here, what are we to say when we apply it to his own case? How many pages has he himself written that are frankly descriptive? What is the prelude to "Gerontius," for example, or the "Cockaigne" Overture, or "In the South" but a series of musical "descriptions"? If he really believes now that music is at its height only when it concerns itself with nothing but purely tonal pattern-weaving, he is condemning all his own best work *en masse*. Nay, not only his published but his unpublished work; for the symphony upon which he has been engaged so long, has *it* not a title? Has he not already given his friends the "clue" to it? If the music is not descriptive, in some way or other, of the character whose name is affixed to it, what is the use of the title—the "clue"? And if the title really applies, if the music really answers to it, why does Sir EDWARD choose to work in a medium that his judgment condemns?

But Elgar had his champions, and the Editor of *The Manchester Guardian* was hard put to it to accommodate their views. This appeared on November 10:

Sir: With regard to Sir Edward Elgar's own music, it is of course true that it is chiefly written according to "programme": but it is equally true that as music it is often supremely beautiful. The prelude to 'Gerontius', referred to in your article, is an instance in point. This movement could stand on its merits as an independent composition without the aid of any description as to what was happening to the body or soul of Gerontius—

A. F. Walker
29, Mosley-street, Manchester,
November 9, 1905

Three days later two more letters—the first from a distinguished Manchester critic—were published:

ABSOLUTE MUSIC
To the Editor of the Manchester Guardian.

Sir,—It is reassuring to find in Sir Edward Elgar a champion of absolute music who cannot be derided as a Philistine, as old or old-fashioned, or even as the fossil product of an academy. When in your article you venture to paraphrase Sir Edward's views and say, "If this means anything at all it means that absolute music—in which themes that are purely self-existent, not springing from the desire to describe something else, are taken and woven into a tonal pattern—is by far the highest form of musical art," we feel that Sir Edward is forced into an extreme position which he would probably not care to defend. When you add, "That much of the greatest music of the world is of this kind no one will deny," the feelings of every musician with a spark of poetry in him must rise in revolt. Such words are an adequate description of no good music, least of all of the great music to which you intend them to be applied.

It is the distinction of music that it alone among the arts is primarily an expression of transcendental feeling, the feeling which accompanies us through all our experiences. Other arts are doomed to begin in imitations of or thoughts about particular things or experiences, and yet only attain distinction and rise "to their height" by a clear infusion of this feeling. In music no such fusion is necessary—it is born free and unfettered, and so it is a "simple" art in a sense that other arts are not, and can be "at its height" without description.

It is possible for a listener to understand the connection between the programme and the music of a symphonic poem without being far on his way towards understanding the music. No programme, unless it is poetical itself, can give any idea of the transcendental feeling in music, and so there is no wonder that composers often wish to hide rather than reveal the effect of actual experience on their works. That such experiences have their effect there is no doubt, but they are rarely the main matter. Let us respect the mystery of our art.—Yours, &c.,

SAMUEL LANGFORD.

Burton Road, Withington.

To the Editor of the Manchester Guardian.

Sir,—Sir Edward Elgar in his statement that "music is at its height when it merely calls up a set of emotions in each individual hearer" expresses the limits of not only absolute music but programme music also. Music itself is incapable of giving definite expression to anything, except a few too realistic imitations of sounds, as in the cuckoo and nightingale passages in the "Pastoral" Symphony. But will any serious musician say that such passages touch his feelings, except so far as to raise a smile?

In your leader you say that Beethoven "calls another overture 'Coriolanus' and 'describes' therein the characters of the drama so clearly that any ordinarily attentive reader of Shakspere can pick them out at once." Can they? I defy any reader to pick out any passage and say that this expresses "Coriolanus," this "Virgilia," expressing them with such definition as to make it impossible to mistake such a passage for anything else. I do not say that the first subject in C minor is not vastly different from the lovely E flat subject generally associated with Virgilia. What I do say is that it no more expresses Virgilia than it might express Francesca da Rimini.

Music is less definite than painting, and much less so than literature. It can give no outlines which shall suggest Coriolanus and Coriolanus alone. But its limits in this respect are more than counterbalanced by the depth of expression it can give. Without being capable of indicating scenes in the life of Coriolanus, it arouses our feelings so that we experience a series of emotions parallel to those suggested in reading the play, and as the last bars sob themselves away we have, without having had a single definite idea of the hero, had our emotions touched with a profound sympathy. In this sense only is programme justifiably applied to music.

If we consider "Also sprach Zarathustra," our programmes tell us that a certain theme suggests Nature. I say again, Does it? There is no man living who, hearing this work without knowing what it was about, could safely say that that theme suggested Nature and nothing else. Music is not a kind of riddle in which we are to puzzle our brains to find out something which we can only say is there when we have put it there ourselves. Yet according to the canons of programme music we must be able to say that such a passage represents Nature, another Science, another Gargantua.

If the work is intended to kindle in our minds feelings identical with or parallel to those aroused by the perusal of a poem, we replace a definite poetical emotion by an indefinite musical feeling. A definite act such as Coriolanus addressing the mob cannot by any stretch of normal imagination be depicted in music even as a riddle.

I maintain that Sir Edward Elgar was justified in his statements, and that his views on programme music are sound. Beethoven expressed this in an immortal phrase heading the Sixth Symphony. It is a misfortune that the same term should be used to express two such different things as a programme suggesting a desire to kindle certain feelings similar to those aroused in reading a poem and a programme which records certain incidents that a composer thinks he may suggest in music, but which no amount of intelligence can solve without calling in the assistance of another art, literature. All art is self-contained.—Yours, &c.

O. HOOLE.

Douglas Villas, Clifton Road, Prestwich,
8th November, 1905.

From the south there was a letter to Elgar from Vernon Blackburn (d. 1907), sometime Rome Correspondent of *The Tablet*, a member of the staff of *The National Observer*, and Music Critic of the *Pall Mall Gazette*. He had, he said on November 11, "just read an article in a London paper, commenting upon your recent lecture on Brahms. 'This,' says the writer, 'when we remember all that Sir Edward has written, is indeed surprising.' He refers of course to your praise of 'absolute music'. I am sure you will not mind if I send on to you my musical opinions on this point . . ." He did, at great length, in what amounted to an unqualified eulogy of *The Apostles*.

In connection with this controversy, the reverberations of which went on for a long time, a programme note (Queen's Hall Concert, November 8, 1902), by E. F. Jacques, but evidently inspired by Elgar, makes a convenient summing-up: "The Variations are put forward simply as music, and if they also make their due effect as 'mood-pictures' on hearers accustomed to receive impressions of that kind from music, well and good. But knowledge of the personalities illustrated forms no necessary part of the listener's equipment."

Meanwhile the performance of the symphony duly took place on November 13, and the next day's report of the concert in the *Birmingham Post*, in addition to showing that the Welsh antecedents of the *Introduction and Allegro* were generally known at that time, gives a picture of Elgar as conductor:

The enterprise shown by the director of these concerts remains unabated. More than thirty years ago the Hallé Orchestra was introduced to Birmingham through the Harrison Concerts; other organisations have been heard since, and last night the latest professional combination paid us a visit under the same auspices. When the Queen's Hall Orchestra was reconstituted a few years back the conditions were not acceptable to a number of performers, and the seceders formed themselves into a corporate body, for the purpose of giving concerts, and also for taking engagements in the metropolis or the provinces. The association became known as "The London Symphony Orchestra." There is no permanent conductor, but the management engage conductors for their own concerts, and the members play under any conductor appointed by the society or individual engaging the band. As there is nothing new under the sun, it is not difficult to find precedents for the course pursued by the London Symphony Orchestra. In 1853, a society, with precisely similar objects, was started in London, and it had some local interest inasmuch as the well known Birmingham musician, Alfred Mellon, was its conductor. It was in existence for some years, and its provincial engagements extended to Yorkshire. In 1854 the London Orchestra was formed, but it was a short-lived institution.

The London Symphony Orchestra consists of a number of our best instrumentalists. Of the 74 names in the band-list of last night's concert, exactly one-half belong to the London Philharmonic Orchestra, admittedly the finest in this country. The violins numbered twenty-six, against eight violas, and six each of violoncellos and basses. The proportion was unusual, but the effect was decidedly good, especially in the fully-scored works of Elgar and Dvořák. The programme stood as follows:—

Overture, "Le Nozze di Figaro".................Mozart
Symphony, No. 3, in F, Op. 90.................Brahms
Concert Overture, "In the South"....................Elgar
Introduction and Allegro, for strings.................Elgar
Two Slavonic Dances...........................Dvořák

Sir Edward Elgar, the conductor of the concert, had a great reception when he appeared upon the platform. Hitherto his reputation has been greater as a composer than as a conductor. We do not wish his star to wane in the first of these capacities, but we must record his advance in the second. He had his forces well in hand throughout, and though sparing in gesture, and entirely without fussiness, he obtained every shade of tone he wished, and every variety of expression. He certainly had magnificent material to deal with, but tone and animation do not always imply artistry; it was this last feature that was so conspicuous in all the performances. The merry little overture of Mozart went absolutely to perfection, and the crescendo of the strings toward the close was one of the finest effects of the evening—because it was so purely musical. The Symphony of Brahms was introduced at the Festival of 1891, the first of the composer's symphonies heard in this city. It was given at the Halford concerts in November, 1901, and cannot be strange to the musical public. Interest attached to last night's performance through the lecture given on the work by Sir Edward Elgar last week, a lecture that has provoked discussion in at least one important provincial journal. Curiously, last night the "absolute music" of Brahms was contrasted with the "programme music" of Elgar. With Sir Edward's expressed opinion on the subject, and his practice in framing the programme, we can have nothing to do here. We have to record a fine—even a great performance of the Symphony, though we thought the Andante taken rather too slowly—its "peace and contentment" seemingly too greatly insisted upon. The first and last movements were magnificently played, and so prolonged was the applause at the close that Sir Edward motioned to the band to rise in response to the compliment. The overture "In the South," savours more of the vigour of ancient Rome than of the dolce far niente associated with modern Italy. There are fine things in the overture, but there are passages that are dangerously similar to the noisy effects of Richard Strauss. It was curious that the Art Gallery clock should strike while the "Canto Popolare" was being played, the first phrase resembling the chime of the first quarter. The climax worked up by side-drum and brass struck us as inferior to Mozart's string crescendo. The performance was very fine, every artist working with a will; and the audience gave the composer and his forces every evidence of appreciation. The Introduction and Allegro for strings gave unqualified delight. The quartet of solo players sat on the conductor's left; the "chorus" strings played standing. Effects exceedingly clever, and themes that lent themselves to every variety of treatment were alternated with lyric simplicity when the "Welsh time" [tune][1] was introduced. We attempted a description of this piece when it was performed at the Worcester festival, and need only add that last night's performance deepened the good impression already formed. For displaying the ability of the string orchestra few things could surpass it, and for light and shade, the hue being the same throughout, the variety is remarkable. The Slavonic Dances of Dvořák, No. 2 from the first, and No. 1 from the second set, were brilliantly played, Sir Edward Elgar being in thorough sympathy with the Slavonic temperament.

Miss Edna Thornton was the vocalist, and she gave most artistic interpretations of Elgar's Song-cycle "Sea-Pictures." Of these, three: "Sea Slumber," "In Haven," and "Sabbath Morning at Sea," were in the first part of the programme, and "Where Corals Lie" and "The Swimmer" in the second. Special praise must be awarded the rendering of "In Haven," "Sabbath Morning," and "The Swimmer." The band accompaniments were superb. Altogether a notable concert.

Elgar's talents as conductor, here generously applauded, were treated elsewhere (see p. 111) with greater reserve. No doubt he found food for thought for his next two lectures.

---

[1] See *Letters to Nimrod*, p. 142, and illustrations facing pp. 108, 109.

CHAPTER 7

ENGLISH EXECUTANTS
(November 29, 1905)

THE Birmingham concert was one of a series arranged for the London
Symphony Orchestra, with Elgar conducting, in the provinces. From Birmingham Elgar went to Liverpool, Manchester—where Brodsky "came in weeping
saying oh if Brahms cd. have heard yr. rendering",[1] Sheffield, Glasgow,
Newcastle, and Bradford. Regarding the Manchester and Sheffield performances
one critic at least wrote with muted enthusiasm.

Manchester, November 15
    This visit of the London Symphony Orchestra to Manchester for the
first time was an event of uncommon interest and it was anticipated that
this "invasion" would draw together as great an audience as had been
met with on the previous day at Birmingham and Liverpool, but hopes
were not fully realised and there was only a moderate audience not over
enthusiastic either. Various reasons contributed to this lukewarm reception both of Elgar and his music which predominated. The programme
was not altogether well chosen. It was too advanced for the generality
of the listeners, and nothing found place therein sufficiently strong
enough to display the varied qualities of the excellent body of instrumentalists engaged. Sir Edward Elgar as a conductor does not inspire his
players with enthusiasm, and this absence of magnetic power dwarfed
some of the beauties of the Brahms Symphony. It was obvious he was
heart and soul in his work and felt it within him as a whole, but, he
unfortunately does not possess the actuosity necessary to bring home the
message in a potent and living manner. In one place towards the close of
the first movement his beat was behind the tempi of the players. The
most successful section of the work was the Andante and the beauties
enshrined in every page were revealed with rare clearness by each
department of orchestra. It was in similar quieter passages in the other
movements that the wood wind and brass were telling and effective.
With the exception of the tricky fugato, the Introduction and Allegro in G
minor and major, Op. 47, for strings, hardly went as well as it did at
Norwich a few weeks back. The "Alassio" Overture is by far the finest
piece of work Elgar has yet given us for the orchestra. Here it was that
the audience first warmed to enthusiasm, and deservedly so, for it was
also an excellent performance. Of the song-cycle, "Sea Pictures," No. 3,

[1] Diary, November 15, 1905.

"Sabbath Morning at Sea" and No. 4, "Where Corals lie" are the most attractive. Miss Edna Thornton, who was the vocalist, possesses a good contralto voice and might with advantage cultivate more of the expressive side of the same. The other orchestral items do not call for mention being well known.

Sheffield, November 16

There was a good audience on the occasion of the visit of the London Symphony Orchestra, conducted by Sir Edward Elgar. The programme seems to have produced the same impression as at Manchester the night before. It was too advanced for an "Harrison" audience fully to be appreciated. One hopes the experiment will be repeated by Mr. Percy Harrison in the future, with a great conductor and a more varied choice of works.[1]

On the evening that Elgar was conducting in Sheffield his international reputation was taking a further step forward, with the first Viennese performance of *The Dream of Gerontius*, directed by Franz Schalk, under the auspices of the Gesellschaft der Musikfreunde. The biographical note on the Vienna programme shows the interest awoken both in Austria and Germany by his works.[2]

The concert tour finished, Elgar returned to Birmingham for the Jubilee Celebrations of the Midland Institute, held on November 22. The programme of the concert which followed the speeches included Elgar's version of *God save the King* and the first of the *Pomp and Circumstance* Marches, which Elgar, who was "warmly received", conducted. But he was in "wretched spirits".[3] Lady Elgar was greatly disturbed when he came home "very tired & depressed. Dreadfully worried"[4] and she telegraphed for Dr. East, the family doctor, to come over from Worcester. She had a long talk with the doctor about Edward and his work; his condition was such that doubts were entertained as to whether he would be able to complete *The Apostles*. On November 28 he turned again to his University responsibilities, busied himself with his forthcoming lecture, and wrote to Peyton:

Nov 28 1905   [Hereford]
Dear Mr Peyton:

Very many thanks for your letter & kind invitation to dine & sleep tomorrow night. My wife will be accompanying me & if quite convenient to you & Mrs. Peyton to have us both we should be delighted to come. I am not sure which train we shall be able to take but *unless* I telegraph to you tomorrow we should arrive at Snow Hill at 4.22. I shall have to go straight to the University & my lecture will be over about 5.30.

Please arrange anything most convenient about meeting us: you might

[1] *The Musical Standard* (articles by W. H. C.), November 25, 1905, p. 346.
[2] See reproduction of programme facing |
[3] Diary, November 22.
[4] Ibid., November 24.

Gesellschaft der Musikfreunde in Wien

dem Protektorate Sr. k. u. k. Hoheit des hochwürdigst-durchlauchtigsten Herrn **Erzherzog Eugen.**

Donnerstag, den 16. November 1905, abends halb 8 Uhr:

Erstes ordentliches

esellschafts-Konzert

unter der Leitung des Konzert-Direktors, Herrn

FRANZ SCHALK.

Mitwirkende:

Frau **Rosa Stwertka**, Konzertsängerin.
Herr **Felix Senius**, Konzertsänger (Petersburg).
Herr **Richard Mayr**, k. k. Hof-Opernsänger.
Herr **Georg Valker**, Mitglied der k. k. Hof-Musikkapelle (Orgel).
Der **Singverein.**
Das **Orchester des Wiener Konzertvereines.**

Zur Aufführung gelangt:

Edward Elgar:

er Traum des Gerontius."

Oratorium für Soli, Chor, Orchester und Orgel. **I. Aufführung in Wien.**

Donnerstag, den 7. Dezember 1905, abends halb 8 Uhr:

Erstes ausserordentliches Konzert.

PROGRAMM:

Gustav Mahler . . . . . V. Sinfonie (unter persönlicher Leitung des Komponisten).
(Neu, I. Aufführung in Wien.)

J. S. Bach . . . . . Motette (a capella) „Singet dem Herrn" (149. Psalm).

Sitz-Billette à 10, 6, 5, 4, 3 und 2 Kronen, Entrées à 2 Kronen

Wochentagen täglich von 9—1 und von 3—5 Uhr in der Kanzlei der Gesellschaft der Musikfreunde
und am Tage der Aufführung an der Vestibul-Kassa zu haben.

Edward William Elgar

geboren am 2. Juni 1857 zu Broadheath bei Worcester, Sohn eines Organisten, in s
Jugend als Violinspieler Mitglied des Orchesters zu Birmingham, 1882 Konzertm«
zu Worcester, 1885 Nachfolger seines Vaters als Organist an der katholischen St. Ge
kirche, gab 1889 beide Stellungen aus Gesundheitsrücksichten auf und zog nach Lo»
aber schon 1891 nach Malvern, nur noch der Komposition lebend. Im Verlauf
letzten zehn Jahre haben ihm seine Erfolge immer entschiedener die erste Stelle »
den modernen englischen Komponisten angewiesen. Seine Hauptwerke sind die Orat
„Lux Christi" (Musikfest zu Worcester 1896), „Der Traum des Gerontius" (Birmingham 1!
„Die Apostel" (Birmingham 1903) und die Cantaten „Der schwarze Ritter" (
Uhland 1893), „Szenen aus der Sage von König Olaf" (nach Longfellow 1896)
„Caractacus" (Musikfest zu Leeds 1898). In Deutschland ist er zuerst durch
Aufführung des „Gerontius" bekannter geworden, die Musikdirektor Julius Buths
in Düsseldorf veranstaltet hat. Hier machte das Werk so tiefe Wirkung, daß es
zu einer zweiten Aufführung kam. Inzwischen wurde es auch in Darmstadt
Amsterdam, und in französischer Sprache in Brüssel aufgeführt. Aufführunge
Crefeld und Breslau stehen noch in diesem Jahre bevor, während gleichzeitig in E
und in Düsseldorf das neuere, erst vor Kurzem ins Deutsche übersetzte Oratorium
Apostel" studiert wird.

In Wien waren zuerst Instrumentalwerke von Elgar zu hören. Der Konzertv
machte vor zwei Jahren den Anfang mit den originellen Orchestervariationen, in d
der Komponist seine Freunde musikalisch zu charakterisieren versucht, und brachte
darauf die das Londoner Straßenleben ausmalende Konzertouverture „Cockaigne".
Philharmoniker folgten im vorigen Jahre mit der breiter angelegten Ouverture „Aus
Süden", und vor einigen Tagen erst war im Konzertverein das glänzende Streichorch«
stück „Introduktion und Allegro" zu hören.

Mit dem „Traum des Gerontius" erscheint zum erstenmal ein großes Chor
Elgars in Wien. Der Text rührt vom Kardinal John Henry Newman her, dem ber
ten Führer des Anglokatholizismus im neunzehnten Jahrhundert, der erst im Laufe s
Lebens und seiner Tätigkeit als anglikanischer Pfarrer nach und nach immer meh
streng katholischen Anschauungen kam, endlich zum Katholizismus übertrat, 1853 R
der neugegründeten röm.-kath. Universität zu Dublin war und 1879 von Papst Leo :
zum Kardinal erhoben wurde. Er hat eine Anzahl historischer, theologischer
poetischer Schriften veröffentlicht, darunter einen Band „Verses on varions occass
(Gelegenheitsdichtungen verschiedener Art), worin der „Traum des Gerontius" zu f
ist. Näheres darüber in der Einleitung zum Textbuch von Elgars Oratorium.

find it best to pick up the luggage from the cloakroom soon after five for instance & 'collect' us at the University—but I leave all in your very kind hands. I am delighted to have this opportunity of seeing you again & will talk over the prospects of the boy about whom you wrote when I was away in the North.

With my kind regards
Believe me
Yrs most sincery
Edward Elgar

The next day Lady Elgar wrote: "E. frantically busy with lecture, A [Lady Elgar] & May [Grafton, Elgar's niece] frantically writing it out till time to start. Worked all the way in train." It is not surprising that the notes, drafts, and emendations thereto, are in a considerable state of disorder: more so than usual. To some extent, however, Elgar was drawing on previous exercises:

SIR EDWARD ELGAR AND CONDUCTORS

Sir Edward Elgar attended the annual meeting of conductors of choirs and orchestras connected with the Morecambe Musical Festival, and in the course of his address referred to his practical acquaintance with the various forms of musical work.

Considering that I (said Sir Edward) started life as second violin player in an amateur orchestra, I do not see why I should be supposed to look down on such orchestras. I conducted one for many years. If one's judgment was worth anything one must have been brought up in the things one was judging. I have taught an amateur choir—very badly, I admit; they sang very well, but that was in spite of me. About the demeanour of a conductor before the audience and the choir I have a word to say. It seems to me there is room, I will not say for improvement, but for alteration, in a great many cases. Take the greatest conductor in England, Dr. Richter. Dr. Richter conducted an orchestra of artists, and consequently he had only to give them a lead, explain a piece to them, and they followed him, and you saw in his case absolute dignity in gesticulation, no exuberance of gesture, or anything of that sort. That is what conductors should aim at—the absolute purity of a rendering without any (I would use the word) humbug. In playing in an orchestra or singing in a choir you soon find your level, but a conductor is allowed to do pretty much as he likes, and some people seem to think the more he jumped about and exerted himself the more the public were impressed. There is no school for conducting. It is a thing that could not be taught, but the man who arrives at the greatest result with the simplest methods must be the artist. I have known instances where the simpler the music was the wilder the conductor became. I cannot see the relation between the two. Of course, in judging, the judges went only by what they heard; they did not see the singers and conductors, and judged simply by the result. But I would like to see a little more dignity and restraint and more usefulness in the conductor. There is, I know, a great difference in choirs. Many of the members are not artists, and in the early stages of

training a good deal was required to keep them in order, but for all that
I wish that conductors would avoid exaggeration, and study how to get
the best results with the least possible exertion, and make the position a
little more dignified. Again, the conductors in many cases have to deal
with persons who have not much of a literary culture, and in that event
the singer is apt to see only the mere surface of the words he used; he did
not discern their meaning. Expression made all the difference, and it is
their mission as conductors and as educated men to bring home to their
choirs something more than the mere fact that it was music they were
singing; it was theirs, in short, as someone had said, to make romance
into reality, and to give to their musical realities a great deal of romance.
I wish them to aim more and more at the cultured and refined in music.
By persistent effort they would no doubt get more of that sort of
expression into their singing to which I have referred. I wish my hearers
to remember that I am not speaking now from my experiences at
Morecambe, for the singing there I have praised, and I stick to what I
have said; but behind the mere rendering of music it seems to me that
there is room for a great deal to be done.[1]

In respect of singing there was to hand the Preface contributed to *The Singing
of the Future*, David Ffrangcon-Davies (John Lane, 1904).

"The soul which has seen most of truth shall come to the birth as a
philosopher, or artist, or some musical and loving nature." I do not now
follow Socrates[2] into his subsequent divisions; for the moment it is
enough that, as one who "has seen most of truth," he has included the
Musician: and in this rich-sounding word I include all—composers,
executants and critics alike—who labour, not for any selfish ends, but for
the good of the art of music.

But musicians have not always shewn to the world, when their
works have come to the birth, that they have seen the most of truth.
The art easily lends itself to make passing amusement for the frivolous
and the unthinking; in this there is nothing to deplore: we should rather
rejoice in knowing that music can be an amusement, for it, in itself, is
never ignoble; this it can only be when allied to unworthy words or to
degrading spectacle. The manysidedness of an art is a chief joy to its
possessors, but the ineptitudes, and worse, of the creators of the material
on which executants and critics live, have too frequently tended to
degrade the two last-named in the exercise of their duties in their
branches of the complete art. But with composers and critics and instrumental executants we need not now concern ourselves; although it may
be profitably read by all musicians, this book is mainly for singers. I will
add, for all singers; certainly for all those proposing to sing, and certainly for many who have already embarked upon their professional
careers.

With the march of time, and with it the improvement of musical
education, a new desire has possessed us,—the desire to *understand*. The

[1] *The Musical Standard*, July 30, 1904, p. 70.
[2] Phaedrus,—(Jowett). [Elgar's footnote]

desire has brought with it the interpreters we need. True, they are few in number and their array is meagre compared with the ample numbers and amiable affluence of the popular vocalists; but those who have "the most of truth" are with us all the same, working, striving, and above all, singing. Where in former days the vocalist entered upon his task with a lighthearted assurance that all the old "points" would meet with unquestioning acceptance, the singer of the present day has to think as behoves a responsible artist. In circles of lesser value the modern ballad, with its unanalysable inanities, is still accepted as a recognisable form of art, but our better singers,—our real interpreters and our teachers—have long ceased to affront their own intelligence by presenting the rubbish demanded by the uneducated for their pleasant degradation.

This book is a serious appeal to the singer, especially to the English-speaking singer, and I welcome it and hope for much real and lasting good from its dissemination. Written with complete knowledge by a singer who is also an artist it forms a worthy portion, or it may be at this date a commencement, of that long desired new edifice of English music which will some day be raised by those, and by those only, who have seen the "most of truth."

EDWARD ELGAR.

HEREFORD, December, 1904.

Rough Notes

Ms.
1 page

	Notes	III
III	English executants	
	a) Singers	
	b) Actors	
	c) Conductors	

? should lecturers be here or in IV critics

Ts. (blue ribbon)   [Whole page cancelled, and marked K=copied]
Ms. emendations   matter such as the first performance of a graet [*sic*]
1 page   symphony, the perfunctory performance [δ for the] [δ 3] 50th thime [*sic*] of Mr. Somebody's three dances[1]

of a popular piece

(go on now finishing the paragraph abt singers)
as the laughing jackass is from the mere hee-hawing [δ fraternity]. creature
B [δ But w] *W*ith the march of time, and with it [intellect and] the *improvement of musical* education [δ the positions of

[1] Edward German, Three Dances from *Henry VIII*, 1892; Three Dances from *Nell Gwynn*, 1900.

which should be reversed] a new genius *desire* has possessed
us,—the desire to understand. The desire brings with it the
interpreters we need. True they are few in numbers and their
array is meagre compared with the ample numbers and
affluent presence of the popular vocalists: [δ But they] *who
have 'seen the light of truth'* are with us all the same, working,
striving and, above all, singing. Where in former times the
vocalist entered in with a lighthearted assurance that all
[δ his] *the* old 'points' [δ (oh, how cheap they were!)] would
meet with [δ rapturous] acceptance, [δ now] the singer has
now to think as behoves the responsible artist, [δ the descen-
dant of Apollo and the heir of Israfel]. In circles of lesser value
the unanalyzable inanities of the modern ballad [δ still are] *is
still* accepted as a recognisable form of art; but our better
singers have long [δ ago] ceased to affront their own intelligence by [δ singing] *presenting* the rubbish demanded by the
uneducated [δ mob] for their pleasant degradation B [cf. p. 117]

C *This book is a serious appeal to the singer,* ESPECIALLY THE
ENGLISH SINGER [δ *of English especially*] *of the present day &
is a serious work, I welcome it & hope for its dissemination.* [cf. p. 137]

Ms. (in   [1] Stratonicus[1]
pencil)   visited Rhodes a town in [?] people looked
2 pages   very bilious he remarked this is what Homer meant when he
compared "man to leaves in autumn".
      On their remonstrating against his calling *inference that* their
city was unhealthy—he rejoined no city could be really
unhealthy where even dead men could walk about
                                                        (Strabo)[2]

---

[1] Stratonicus, a musician living (it is supposed) in the time of Alexander the Great, was
famed for his rebuke to Philotus when he boasted of victory over Timotheus: see William
Smith, *Dictionary of Greek and Roman Biography and Mythology*, London, 1849.

[2] "And indeed little tales of the following kind are repeated over and over, that
Stratonicus the citharist, seeing that the Caunians were pitiably pale, said that this was
the thought of the poet in the verses, 'Even as is the generation of leaves, such is that also
of men;' and when people complained that he was jeering at the city as though it were
sickly, he replied, 'Would I be so bold as to call this city sickly, when even the corpses
walk about?'." *The Geography of Strabo*, Book 13; trs. H. C. Jones, Loeb Classical Library,
Vol. 6, p. 267.

Strabo (b. *c.* 63 B.C.), a Stoic, was the author of the first famous geography book, which,
deriving from Polybius and other writers but based on the author's extensive travels,
was regarded as a classic by the sixth century.

ital.

[2] *Stratonicus*

An amateur boasted that he had in his house several performers on flutes & the like *a family orchestra* "Hm" said S. "You will want a family audience"

Visited Rhodes. sang in public. no applause after the first solo. he left the Theatre—saying 'If they wont give what costs them nothing I am not likely to collect much [δ beside] else'. [See p. 118.]

TEXTUAL COMMENTARY

Ms. 1 Marginal note in pencil
        Work thro'
        The lesson of discouragement
        The lesson of sorrow
        & the best, perhaps, of all & the
        most difficult to bear
        the lesson of success & triumph [cf. p. 135]
    But [δ the composer] *we* ignores not only the friendly aid
    of [end of page]
    But (I refer principally to '*large*' music only—

Ms. 2 [δ But] *As usual* I refer principally   ⎡part C.A.E.⎤
Ms. 1 composer himself) Before we   ⎣part M.G. ⎦
        the *a large musical* work [δ of a composer]
Ms. 2 ['call' misread as 'ask' by C.A.E., corrected to 'call' by E.]
Ms. 1 [δ prototypes] *counterpart*
        [δ depend] *rely*

        . . . we have [δ nothing to do] at present nothing to do
        . . . upon the [δ glorious] past
Ms. 2 . . . upon *it may be recent or* long gone by performance

Ms. 1 To take soloists [δ who] first
Ms. 2 [δ To take soloists first]
Ms. 1 . . . the tone[δ s] of Clara Novello & Tietjens [δ Sims Reeves]
Ms. 2   Titiens
Ms. 1 :— [δ later] or [δ F] Sims Reeves or Joseph Maas [δ and
        Edward] [δ name another artist not having] [δ Edward Lloyd]
        —to name only a few singers who have . . .
Ms. 2 *and the voices of* Sims Reeves or Joseph Maas, *are not forgotten*—
        to name only a few singers who have . . .
Ms. 1 not only given pleasure
Ms. 2 not [δ only] merely given *supreme* pleasure
Ms. 1/2   we are grateful

ENGLISH EXECUTANTS

We now approach the side of music wherein it differs from the other arts.

As I said on a former occasion—the painter requires no vehicle; the author requires a printer and a publisher, (except dramatic authors who are dependent on actors).

As usual I refer to LARGE music principally—not to solo work which in many cases can be given and given most effectively by the composer *himself. But,* before we can appreciate to the full value, *a large musical work,* we must *call* in the aid of a number of people who have no *counterpart* in the other arts:— we must have executants.

Upon these we *rely* for a proper presentment: and upon these the proper understanding of a work mainly depends. The position of the actor is very similar but with the drama except incidentally, we have at *present nothing to do.* One of the pleasantest things in music is to look *back upon,* it may be recent or long by, performances and to hear again in memory, noble and worthy presentations by great and worthy artists of great and elevating works.

Who is there who does not find pleasure in contemplating the singers of a generation ago:— *the tones of Clara Novello and* Tietjens still linger in some ears—a precious possession, and the voices of Sims Reeves and Joseph Maas[1] are not forgotten to name only a few singers

who *have, in their distinguished way, not merely given supreme pleasure* by their actual moment of singing but by the memory of something great, for which we *were grateful,* and which will only pass away with

[1] Joseph Maas (1847–86), a chorister of Rochester Cathedral, trained in Milan and became one of the leading English operatic and oratorio tenors of the day. His last important appearance was at the Birmingham Festival of 1885, where he took part in the first performances of Dvořák's *Spectre's Bride,* and Stanford's *Three Holy Children.*

Ms. 1   next page
[δ Naturally the executant has in all ages been the subject of much pleasant comment not to say ridicule, as well as of unbounded adulation.] We need only [cf. p. 123, l. 18]

Ms. 2   *and if music . . . of the next* [inserted in pencil at foot of page and continued on facing page]

Ms. 1   . . . are merely memories

Ms. 2   [δ merely]

Ms. 1   . . . to be content with [δ merely] meagre . . .

Ms. 1   of the [δ executive singer per] actual *singing of* a song

Ms. 1   the Art withers with the artist [*caret*]

Ms. 2   the Art [δ perishes] withers with the artist [in pencil]

Ms. 1   [δ bows] *arrows*

Ms. 1   . . . performances of our own day. Let us see what we expect of them.

Ms. 2   [δ Let us see what we expect of them.]

Ms. 1   [cf. page 125] Next page
[δ These are [δ our] the darlings we of the public]

Ms. 1   It wd. [δ be] not [δ unamusing] *be unamusing*

Ms. 2   *Now let me see what we expect from our artists.* [In pencil]

Ms. 1   Oratorio—neither

Ms. 2   Oratorio—neither [Marginal note in pencil] *enlarge*

Ms. 2   *all honour to them* [in pencil]   *In Handel* [in pencil]

Ms. 1   . . . and utterly wanting

Ms. 2   . . . and [δ utterly] wanting

Ms. 1   position of singers
adulation. worship
& pleasant sarcastic comment

conceit
not always conceit
nervousness . . .

life itself, and if music is really seriously taken, it may be the glorified sounds will come to us again. With all reverence we can look for music in the next world—the divine art is divine in this way that it does not seem mean or poor in the most sacred surroundings. We cannot well think of painting or drama in Heaven but music we may. Let us fit ourselves by our music in this world for that of the next.

But these after all *are memories*, and it is *impossible to be content* with meagre hearsay accounts of bygone glories: the works of composers live—in print at least—and we can reconstruct in a measure the effect of them for ourselves; "the written outlives and outdazzles the spoken word". But the *life of the actual singing* of a song perishes with the singer—the Art withers *with the artist*: "It darkens with his eye, stiffens with his hand, freezes with his tongue". *The arrows of* song are buried with the archers.

We then, with a due respect for the past and its hallowed memories, are more concerned with the present and with those artists into whose hands are committed the performances of our *own day*.

Naturally the performer has in all ages been the subject of much pleasant comment, not to say ridicule, as well as of unbounded adulation. *It would not be unamusing*, or uninstructive, to collect these sarcastic comments—but, in all ages, there have been some artists capable and willing to make equally witty retorts from the days of Demosthenes that arch-wit Stratonicus, the harp player.

Now *let me see what we expect from our* artists. We require our solo singers principally (almost entirely) for the Concert room. *Oratorio is neither* Opera nor church service but originally something between the two. Music in the eighteenth century was kept alive in the country by the organists, *all honour to them*, and a church style was introduced into Oratorio. *In Handel* there was not much difference except so far as the heavy choruses etc. between his Oratorios and his Operas—the church style prevailed—oratorio singing became dull and heavy *and wanting* in elasticity, this affected very generally the whole of our national art.

The position is one of adulation and worship. They are accused of

Ms. 2   Position of singers—
                         Adulation—worship—
                    [δ & pleasant sarcastic comment]
                    They are accused of conceit *but* not always

Ms. 2   [Marginal note in pencil] *enlarge*

Ms. 1   . . . are our *the* pets
                    they are praised & reviled like a savage to his god, when
                    they do not exactly do what is expected. They are worried—
                    if they read papers—they are reproached for their want of
                    intellect etc. etc. & if he lifts up . . . of his art he is reviled
                    by the professional scribblers, etc. etc.

Ms. 2   they are praised *when they please* & reviled [δ like a savage to
                    his god]. When [δ he does not] *they do not* exactly do what is
                    expected * *take in* [facing page *] *This is the reward or penalty
                    of being gods or goddesses to unthinking but enthusiastic savages.
                    They* SOLOISTS *are worried if they read papers—they are*
                    SOMETIMES *reproached . . . of his art, he is reviled* [δ reproached]
                    (*over*) *by the professional* [δ scrib] *writer.*

Birm. Post   . . . savages (laughter)

Ms. 1   . . . but we have amongst us as earnest a band of workers . . .
                    as ever existed

Ms. 2   . . . but we *know we* have amongst us [δ no] *a more* earnest
                    band of [δ worthies] workers educated men & *women* more-
                    over [δ as] than ever *before* existed.

Ms. 1   . . . too many brainless singers are amongst us still & even
                    the elevating influence of our great colleges has [δ have] been
                    unable to raise the standard all round.

Ms. 2   * [facing page *] We have . . . institutions for [δ the improve-
                    ment] their great influence . . . singing; but in [δ amongst] the
                    younger generation
                    [δ too many brainless singers are amongst us still] & even . . .
                    standard all round, *& some brainless singers are amongst us still*

Birm.   We had also too many brainless singers with us still
Post   (laughter).

Ms. 2   [Marginal note] *Self sacrifice in attending rehearsals beyond praise
                                    & beyond thanks*

Ms. 1   . . . without much understanding
Ms. 2   . . . without [δ much] *adequate* understanding

Stratonicus

An amateur boasted that
he had in his house
several performers on flute,
family orchestra
"So" said S.
"You want a family
audience"

visited Rhodes. Sang
in public - no applause
after the first ~~person~~. he left
the theatre — saying "If they won't
give what costs them nothing I
am not likely to collect ~~beside~~ much
else".

English Executants: (a) Rough notes

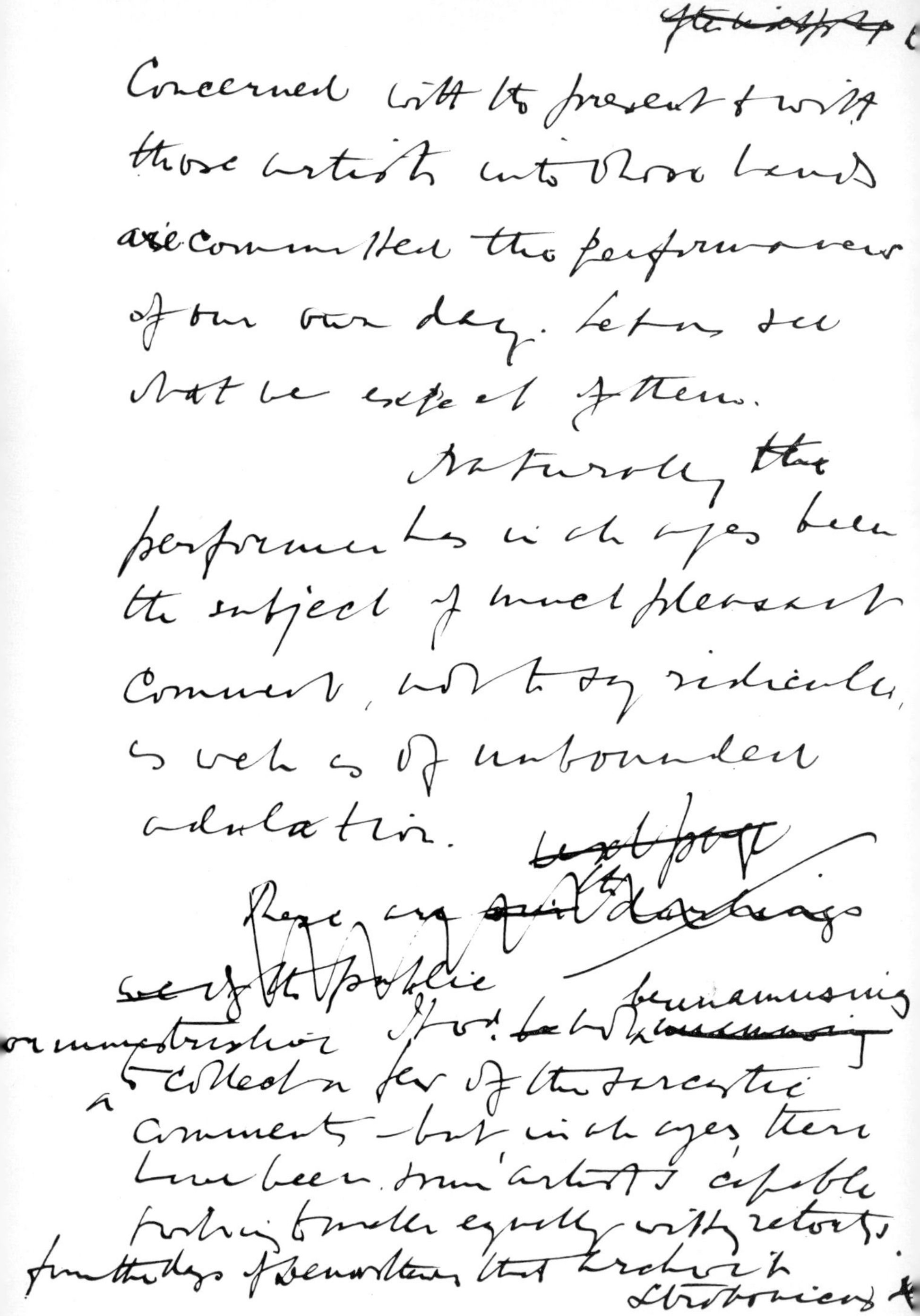

~~[illegible]~~

Concerned with the present & with those artists into whose hands are committed the performances of our own day. Let us see what we expect of them.

Naturally the performers in all ages been the subject of much pleasant comment, not to say ridicule, as well as of unbounded adulation. ~~next page~~

There are ~~[illegible]~~ the days ~~[illegible]~~ ~~seen~~ of the public or unmusical ... It would be ~~[illegible]~~ amusing to collect a few of the sarcastic comments — but in all ages there have been some artists capable of making equally witty retorts. From the days of Benedetto that Archbishop [illegible] Strobonicus [illegible]

(b) First manuscript in Elgar's hand

7

It wd not be unamusing, or uninstructive, to collect [~~a few of~~] these sarcastic comments.

Cent, in all ages, there have been some artists capable & willing to make equally witty retorts, from the [days of] Demosthenes that arch-wit Stratonicus, the harp player —

~~Now, let us see~~ that ^we ^Not ~~but~~ ex-pect ~~from such artists.~~

We require our Solo Singers principally (almost entirely) for the Concert Room:

// Oratorio — ~~written~~ neither Opera

large nor Church Service ~~between~~ originally something ^the two //

(c) Second manuscript, Alice Elgar, with corrections by Edward

given supreme pleasure by their actual moment of singing
but by the memory of something great, for which we were
grateful, and which will only pass away with life itself,
and if music is really seriously taken, it may be the
glorified sounds will come to us again.   With all reverence
we can look for music in the next world - the divine art is
divine in this way that it does not seem mean or poor in the
most sacred surroundings.   We cannot well think of painting
or drama in Heaven but music we may.   Let us fit ourselves
by our music in this world for that of the next.

But these after all are memories, and it is
impossible to be content with with meagre hearsay accounts of
bygone glories: the works of composers live - in print at least
- and we can reconstruct in a measure the effect of them for
ourselves; "the written outlives and outdazzles the spoken
word".   But the life of the actual singing of a song perishes
with the singer - the Art withers with the artist: - "It darkens
with his eye, stiffens with his hand, freezes with his tongue."
The arrows of song are buried with the archers.

We then, with a due respect for the past and its
hallowed memories, are more concerned with the present and
with those artists into whose hands are committed the
performances of our own day.

Naturally the performer has in all ages been the
subject of much pleasant comment, not to say ridicule, as well
as of unbounded adulation.   It would not be unamusing, or
uninstructive to collect these sarcastic comments - but,
in all ages, there have been some artists capable and willing
to make equally witty retorts from the days of Demosthenes
that arch-wit Stratonicus, the harp player.

Now let me see what we expect from our artists.

conceit, but it is not always conceit but nervousness. *Let us consider*: at one moment the artist has to do his best or his future suffers. Let us

forgive nervous self-consciousness under the circumstances. Have we to do this sort of thing? After all, *they are the pets* and darlings of the public, they are praised when they please and reviled when they do not exactly do what is expected. This is the reward or penalty of being god or goddess to unthinking but enthusiastic, educated *savages*.

Soloists are worried if they read papers—they are sometimes reproached for their want of intellect etc. etc, and if one lifts his voice seriously in defence or explanation, or glorification of his art, he is reproached by the professional writer.

We have, we are told, not the voices, the superb voices of a bygone day, but know we have *amongst us a more earnest band of* workers, educated men and women moreover, than ever before *existed*. We have, once more to thank our great teaching institutions for their great influence on the serious side of singing; but in the younger generation, even the elevating influence of our great colleges has been unable to raise the standard all round and some brainless singers *are amongst us still*.

Our chorus singers have long been our great insular wonder and pride: and so much has been said on the choral work of this country that it will be immaterial for me to go into detail. In the last few years we have had choruses trained—perhaps over-trained in some instances — to a perfection of finish and attack never before attempted. Much derision has been poured upon foreign choruses, without *adequate understanding*, it would seem, on the part of the fault finders. In

(*d*) Typescript used for delivery of lecture
10—AFFEM

Ms. 1   is studied, but too often
Ms. 2   [δ too] often
Ms. 1/2   a COMPLETE understanding

Ms. 1   "Blest pair of Sirens'
                                    Jarr'd
                                            quote [verse ?]
                                            (see over)
Ms. 2   [page inserted by E.]
                            Milton wrote
                                "That we on earth . . .
                                    Jarr'd . . .
                                        . . . HARSH DIN . . .
                                        . . . no more etc etc
        The word 'Jarr'd' far too strongly accented—anticipating
        the 'harsh din' which comes two bars later
                            go back
                                [to passage, "This sort of thing . . .]
Ms. 1   . . . on the whole they have a superior education—actual
        number not studied—power of voice etc. subordinate to real
        musical knowledge. Hence to disproportionate numbers. So
        we see . . . general education.
Ms. 2   . . . superior education, accustomed to hear . . .
        personalities. *The* actual numbers . . . Hence [δ ? to] *the*
        disproportionate numbers.
                    [Marginal note by E.] PAYMENT *of singers in Germany.
        T. & B. difficulty, in getting men to your mixed choruses owing to
        men's vocations.*
Ms. 1   [δ To proceed] Next in turn

Ms. 1   The same nervousness etc.
Ms. 2   „   „   „   „   *tension*
Ms. 1   . . . & we may assume
Ms. 2   . . . it is [δ we may] assumed
Ms. 1   . . . characteristics which are
Ms. 2   . . . character[δ istics] which [δ are] is
Ms. 1   [δ Here] When

England, in the north, chorus singers are plentiful—it is possible to pick voices—to balance the numbers accurately and to turn out a machine as regular as a steam engine and perhaps as explosive. Every detail, every syllable is studied, *but often* there is something wanting—that something is *an understanding of* the subject sung about. I have heard an effect in an otherwise fine performance of that English masterpiece, 'Blest *Pair of Sirens*'. Milton wrote:—

> "That we on earth, with undiscording voice,
>   May rightly answer that melodious noise;
>   As once we did,
>   Till disproportioned sin
>   Jarr'd against nature's chime and with harsh din
>   Broke the fair music" etc.

The word JARR'D was far too strongly accented—anticipating the 'harsh din' which comes two bars later.

This sort of thing would be impossible in a good German Chorus: *on the whole*, they have superior education, accustomed to hear classics in their theatres in every town and to become acquainted familiarly with subjects and personalities. The actual numbers, not studied, the power of voice subordinate to real musical knowledge, hence the disproportionate numbers. So we see where improvement may be: and I have said so many times—it must come from general education.

Next in turn come our instrumental soloists. Much that has been said concerning vocalists naturally applies to instrumental soloists *The same nervousness* and tension. I am not going through the whole list of instruments used for solo purposes. It is worthy of note that we do not shine as solo players of stringed instruments, have never done so and *it is assumed* that there is something in our national *character* which is repugnant to the highest form of virtuosity in string playing: certain it is that we have never had string soloists of such standing as other countries or equal to our pianists. *When we come* to piano playing, the case is different: a series of great names is immediately called to

Birm.	. . . Leonard Borwick (Applause).
Post	. . . I have no sympathy (Applause).
	. . . pianola (Applause).

. . . commendation or blame (Hear, hear)

Ms. 1   . . . are known & their performances [δ noted] balanced & criticised.

Ms. 2   . . . are known & their performances ————→ balanced & criticised. *This is pleasing etc. etc.*

Ms. 2   . . . many of the *best of* modern orch. players

Ms. 1   . . . admit that we [δ are] *can*
         . . . [δ satisfied] *contented*

Ms. 1   . . . dwell with affection on . . .

Ms. 2   . . . dwell with *reverence and* affection on . . .

Ms. 1   Dr. Hans Richter & before him Sir August Manns

Ms. 2   ,,   ,,   ,, [δ & before him] *an earlier pioneer* Sir August Manns

Ms. 1   It would seem that we have up to the present produced only one conductor—himself a giant—Henry J. Wood.

Ms. 2   . . . up to the present [δ produced] *had room for* only one conductor—*i.e. a conductor who does nothing but conduct*—himself a giant. [Following sentence added by E.]

Ms. 2   Fagge Op. 35[1]

[1] Arthur Fagge (1864–1943), formerly conductor of the Dulwich Philharmonic Society.

mind; not of the Herculean school, but real artists—restrained and capable of the highest things; one name occurs to me here in Birmingham, Fanny Davies, a name known all over Europe and I will add one more—the player who gives me, among Englishmen the greatest and highest satisfaction, *Leonard Borwick*. For the firework soloist, I have no *sympathy*—I feel it is only a passing phase and all that is done in the way of mere execution is better done by a *pianola*: and we can leave it to those who enjoy it without a word of commendation *or of blame*.

Luckily there is one department in which we can all join hands, over which we can all be as patriotic as we please without fear of reproof; our orchestral players, the finest in the world. Time was when no interest was taken in the PERSONNEL of the orchestra, the names of few except the principals were ever mentioned.

The spread of orchestral music has changed all this and the names of most of the strings and of all the wind instrument players are known *balanced and criticised*. We have to thank our music schools for producing *many of the best* orchestral players, but since, at least the visit of Berlioz, all foreign conductors have been unanimous in their praise of best English orchestras. But when we leave this very satisfactory department and turn to the chief of all—the Conductor—we must admit that *we can in no* way indulge in very *contented* feelings. We have heard of snakes in Ireland and we have heard of English conductors. True, gossips talk of Sir George Smart and several others of a bygone day; I have talked with many players who have worked under that brilliant and capable man Alfred Mellon,[1] and we pass from the sixties to our own day.

It will be remembered that I speak of English artists—otherwise I would dwell with *reverence and affection* on the name of Dr. Hans Richter and *an earlier pioneer*, Sir August Manns—but to keep to our nation. *It would seem that we* have, up to the present, had room for only one conductor, i.e., a conductor who does nothing but conduct—himself a giant—*Henry J. Wood*—. Other countries have Colonne, Lamoureux, Nikisch, Seidl, Richter, etc. True we have many composer conductors and to these I am coming:— Dr. F. H. Cowen of Glasgow, Liverpool and London; Dr. Riseley of Bristol; Allen Gill of Alexandra Palace—capable choral men; we had also the conductors of the Three Choirs, and Halford and Godfrey.

---

[1] Mellon, Alfred 1821–67. Violinist in opera orchestras in Birmingham and later leader of Ballet at Covent Garden—and Conductor of the Liverpool Philharmonic. [E.]

Ms. 1   To arrive . . . happily over. [*caret*]

Ms. 2   *To arrive . . . happily passed.* [inserted in margin]

Ms. 1   But we have also unfortunately the mere pedantic mechanics, respectable men who would be equally successful as school-masters, or [δ time] better, as time keepers in a factory yard.

Ms. 2   [on facing page ★] ★ *Thirty or forty years ago we had* [δ *some*] *enlightened conductors but* (continue) But we [δ have] had also . . . equally respectable men who would *have been* equally successful as schoolmasters or [δ better as timekeepers in a factory yard if they must keep time they would figure] *take in* ★ [on facing page ★] *or, if they must keep time for others they would figure more usefully as timekeepers in a factory yard. Those were* the Men who [δ treat ed *ing*] treat[δ ing]*ed* an orchestral work . . .

Birm.   . . . timekeepers in factory yards (Laughter)

Post

Manc.   „   „   a factory yard (Laughter)

Guard.

Ms. 1   without emotion

Ms. 2   without [δ emotion] sympathy

Ms. 1   [on reverse of page, inverted]

                    [δ *Memo*]

               Education

          Nerves—having to appear at a certain moment.

               future depending upon it.

                    Excuses for conceit [cf. p. 125]

Ms. 1   . . . the boy who was so [δ carried away] delighted with

Ms. 1   [Marginal note] from Art of Thinking

Ms. 1   a deadly cold performance of [δ Brahms by a standa[?]] every-
                                        thing . . .

Ms. 2   [δ a] „   „   performance*s* of Brahms everything . . .

---

founded the London Choral Society in 1903: Op. 35 = *Caractacus*; Elgar probably intended Op. 45.

The first concert of the London Choral Society took place on October 26, 1903, when *Gerontius* was given. This work was repeated on February 15, 1904, and on October 24, 1904. On April 25, 1904, *King Olaf* and the Op. 45 part-songs were presented. On February 13, 1905, Fagge, assisted also by the Dulwich Philharmonic Society and members of Mr. James Bates's School of Choristers, conducted the second London performance of *The Apostles.* The soloists were Ffrangcon-Davies, Plunket Greene, Madame de Vere, Marie Brema, Gregory Hast, and Francis Braun.

To arrive at this we have 'won through' times of darkness now *happily over*. Thirty or forty years ago we had enlightened conductors but we had also unfortunately the mere pedantic mechanics; respectable men who would have been equally successful as schoolmasters or, if they must keep time for others they would figure more usefully as time-keepers in a factory yard. Those were the men who treated an orchestral work like a problem of Euclid and thrashed it out *without sympathy*, without love and without hate.

We have heard of the boy *who was so delighted* with the reasoning of Euclid that he used to peruse the argument with considerable warmth of feeling, the teacher reproved him saying, "Euclid knows no emotion". This is quite right, but, when applied to music is quite wrong. *I* HAVE *heard deadly cold* performances, everything flattened out to a cold and bare proportion: any attempt at expression sternly repressed by the icy pedagogue who directed. Think of this system applied to a living work of art—a work so alive that if you cut it it would bleed[1]—*but, as* I said, all that is changed; pioneers have arisen in many places. In Birmingham, Mr. Stockley paved the way for the

---

[1] cf. Letter from Elgar to Jaeger, August 6, 1897 (*Letters to Nimrod*, p. 3), "I always say to my wife (over any piece or passage of my work that pleases me): 'if you cut that it would bleed!' "

Ms. 1   but, as I said . . . stagnant state of music [*caret*]
Ms. 2   [on facing page ⋆] ⋆ *But, as I said . . . stagnant state of music.*

Ms. 2   we are *numerically* weakest
Ms. 1   It is to be hoped . . . expected and hoped [*caret*]
Ms. 2   [on facing page ⋆] ⋆ *It is to be hoped . . . expected and hoped.*

Ms. 1   . . . and we will see . . .
Ms. 2   . . . and [δ we will] *incidentally* see

Birm. Post. . . conductors exists (Hear, hear)
Ms. 1   opportunities; they . . .
Ms. 2   opportunities; [δ They] *These*
Ms. 2   [Marginal note] *Prof Dr Fritz*
Ms. 2   *Parsifal*
         [Marginal note in pencil] *selection Enrico Bossi important works*

. . . if *musical* degrees

Birm. Post   . . . to make them? (Hear, hear)
Ms. 2   [Marginal note] *enlarge*
Manc.   As to the education of orchestral players, everything should
Guard. be done to encourage fire and virtuosity. He was aware that
         experts differed on these points, but in schools they should
         be allowed to 'bash' at a thing as much as possible. The only
         drawback to pupils turned out from our schools was that
         they lacked fire. It was much easier for a conductor to restrain
         the ardour and bring down too much fire than to excite a
         player, dulled by his tuition, up to the necessary level.

present orchestra's work and it would be easy to name many who made noble efforts to improve the stagnant state of *music*.

It will be seen then that taking the English musical world as a whole *we are numerically* weakest in the department of conductors. *It is* to be hoped that proportionately more conductors will be found among our coming men; much good is done by importing conductors from a distance—men periodically visiting a town in the way that Sir Charles Stanford visits Leeds or Dr. Cowen visits Liverpool, must do good bringing with them the most modern views from the capital, but it is in the increase of resident conductors that development *may be expected and hoped*.

I will now go backwards through my sections *and incidentally see* what may be done to improve the position of things.

It is to be regretted that no system for the training of *conductors exists*; young musicians sadly want *opportunities*; *these* are given, I believe, as far as possible, at our own music schools. I was struck at Mayence; *Professor Fritz Volbach* the conductor took the piano and his pupil conducted *Parsifal—selection—Enrico* Bossi,[1] important works—here you have a great man not afraid. In England the conductor would be timid about laying down his stick—it would affect the chorus—the poor chorus; it is so easy to assume they know nothing and are easily put off. The real thing is, it would affect the conductor.

Now in the future, *if musical degrees* are ever granted in this University, conducting will become one of the main points to be considered and form an important part in the examination; facilities for practice will be provided. It is all very well to say 'conductors are born not made'—but have we ever seriously attempted *to make them*? or to assist them seriously in acquiring practical knowledge.

To quote Protagoras:[2]— "Art without practice avails as little as practice without art".

As in the education of our orchestral players everything should be done to encourage fire and virtuosity, I am aware that this view is opposed to the feelings of some experts. But the only drawback to the players turned out of our institutions is that they lack fire; they have to be whipped to enthusiasm in many cases. This is the fault of studying

---

[1] Enrico Bossi, 1861–1925, Italian organist. [E.]

[2] Protagoras (c. 490 B.C.- after 421 B.C.) the first and most famous Greek sophist (see Plato, *Protagoras*), an agnostic (*Concerning the Gods*), a friend of Pericles, and a teacher of the art (science?) of politics, was the source of many aphorisms, the most celebrated being the first sentence of *Truth*: "Man is the measure of all things." See E. Dupréel, *Les Sophistes*, Neuchatel, 1948.

Ms. 1 under the wooden Capellmeister conductor
Ms. 2 under [δ the] an [δ inefficient] uninspiring [δ wooden Capell-
       meister] conductor:
Ms. 1 ... we admire in some foreign orchestras
Ms. 2 „   „   „ our [δ foreign] adult orchestras
Ms. 1 too great ardour
Ms. 2 „   „ [δ enthusiasm] ardour
Ms. 1 ... it is difficult to say much.
Ms. 2 „ „   „   „   „ little I was going to say much

Ms. 1 And to them ... success and triumph [caret]
Ms. 2 And to them ... success and triumph [on facing page in pencil]

Ms. 1 As to the improvement of Chorus singing. I feel much may
       be done perhaps not in the way of tone production, finish ...
Ms. 2 As to the improvement of Chorus singing [δ I feel much]
       something may be done; [δ perhaps] not in the way of tone
       production, finish ...

Ms. 2 ... the rule adopted generally which I [δ introduced in a
       Choral Society I once conducted] proposed long ago; that
       no member should join for more than three years two years
       wᵈ probably be better
Ms. 2 [δ had] should to undergo
Ms. 1/   This should [δ kept] keep [δ t] the [δ thing] chorus alive &
Ms. 2 [δ it was] make it impossible that [δ the chorus] it should ever
       become inept from the increase of age or [δ honest] diminution
       of ability of its members.

under *an uninspiring conductor*; everything should be done to make the players appreciate to the full the nuances and general 'sweep' which we

admire *in our adult orchestras*; it is easier to restrain *too great an ardour* and bring it to an artistic level than to excite a dulled—not dull— player—dulled by his tuition—to the same feeling.

In the education of soloists it *is difficult to say little*, I was going to say much. Most of our soloists on instruments other than the piano have studied with a view to being capable musicians as orchestral players— (ladies always excepted). Some few prodigies—or monsters—have blossomed forth at once into virtuosity but these are naturally excep- tions and our serious players pass through proper tuition and education and become soloists in a reasonable and satisfactory manner. *And to them,* as to all true artists, singers and what not comes the time of trial by which we arrive at the supreme mastery, the true interpretation, the carrying home to the hearer the inner meaning of the composer. They work through the sour lesson of sorrow,—and the last, perhaps the most difficult to bear, the sweet and final lesson of success *and triumph.*

As to the improvement of Chorus singing something may be done: not in the way of *tone production, finish,* and in one sense, expression; but I would ask, for a more general study of the SUBJECT—the literary side of the composition. I know one town where immediately a work is announced, every book bearing on the subject is taken from the Free Library and eagerly devoured—this makes for the understanding and the performance of well-read chorus singers is more intelligent and gratifying, more 'EXPLANATORY', more vivifying, and carries its message better than a more highly trained chorus can do without such—well, education. I have spoken of the false accentuation, and this point is one which requires more serious consideration than any other concerning chorus training.

I should like to see, for the general improvement of Choral Societies, *the rule adopted generally* which I proposed long ago:— that no member should join for more than three years, two would probably be better; in other words each member should undergo an examination every third year.[1] This should keep the Chorus alive and make it impossible that it should ever become inept from the increase of age or diminution of ability of its members; if the triennial examination was not success-

[1] A resolution restricting performing membership of the Worcestershire Philharmonic Society to an initial period of three years was passed in 1901. A year later Elgar resigned the post of conductor (see *Letters of Edward Elgar,* p. 106 f.).

Ms. 1/   . . . tasks have been set [δ & they] choirs have *triumphantly*
Ms. 2   surmounted them
Ms. 1/   . . . justifying the [δ present spread] *increase* of
Ms. 2   musical education.
Ms. 2   *Fagge* [in pencil; see p. 128]
Ms. 1   Now as to the training etc. education of solo[δ ists] singers: we
            cannot amongst the multitude of voice doctors . . . pursue—
            we cannot, I repeat, in the compass . . .
Ms. 2   . . . education & training of solo singers. [δ We cannot
            amongst the] *We have amongst us the best teachers &* we cannot
            . . . pursue—we cannot—[δ I repeat],
Ms. 1   we must allow
Ms. 2   „   „   [δ show] *allow*
Ms. 2   *& the physical ability also* [in pencil]
Ms. 1   appearance
Ms. 2   [δ performance] *appearance*
Birm. Post . . . to their future (Hear, hear).
Ms. 2   . . . opera *stage* for them [δ to sing in]
Ms. 2   . . . in some singers is [δ painfully] wanting . . .

Ms. 1/2   . . . less satisfied. [δ they] *These people* . . .
Ms. 2   [on facing page in pencil] *West end theatres—leading actresses*
                                                            so called
Ms. 2   . . . or *the drama* [in pencil]

Ms. 2   . . . English [δ actor or actre] player

Ms. 2   *Ed Lloyd, Ben Davies, A. Black, Muriel* [Foster], *Kirkby Lunn*
                                                            [in pencil]

Ms. 1   . . . there is [δ more] *something*

Birm.   . . . had to deliver (Hear, hear). [The report ends at this point;
Post   that in the *Manchester Guardian* continues to the end.]

fully passed the candidate ceased to be a member. But the whole status of the Chorus has improved during the last few years—more difficult *tasks have been set*; choirs have triumphantly surmounted them; justifying the confidence placed in them by modern writers and *justifying the increase* of musical education.

Coward, Wilson, Gill, Dr. Sinclair, *Fagge*.

Now as to all the education and training of solo singers. We have amongst us the best teachers and we cannot amongst the multitude of voice doctors—or whatever name they prefer—voice producers and the thousand and one methods they pursue—we cannot in the compass of a few minutes, decide upon the rival merits of varied teaching. We can however judge by results: and in doing this *we must allow* much for the idiosyncrasy of the pupil *and the physical ability also*. Many of our young singers make their first *public appearances* too early:— detrimental to their physical well-being and detrimental to their *future*. We lack dramatic singers—the national characteristic again—we lack opera singers because primarily we have no particular *opera stage for them*. But the dramatic instinct which we admire so much in some singers *is painfully wanting* in the majority. I account for this by the fact that we have no drama in England. That is to say we have no real dramatic (stage) art; we have in the whole ranks of the theatrical profession enough good actors to properly cast one play—and NO MORE: dressed-up dolls and dummies fill the stage at most of our theatres and the public seem more or less *satisfied*. *These people* cannot act—as acting is an art—they only dress up and pretend to be somebody else—which is a very different thing. I have said at another time that the effect of one great dominating spirit in literature or painting *or the drama etc.*, has the vivifying effect we want in England now: one art helps the other,—but it is, I venture to say, more felt in the want of a definite great *English player* and a definite school of English acting: this has effect on our concert singers, they lack drama as a whole, although we have great exceptions:— Santley, *Edward Lloyd, Plunket Green[e]*, *Ffrangcon* Davies, Andrew Black, John Coates, Muriel Foster and Kirkby Lunn.

You will have gathered from my remarks that although we have much to be thankful for, *there is something* to regret in our executants:— we certainly want voices—the training is apparently ready for them if they will come. We also want general education for our aspirants: we want them to understand the message they *have to deliver*. A book has been written by Ffrangcon Davies—a thoughtful suggestive book,

Ms. 1   . . . ideals [δ set forth] held up

Ms. 1   . . . [δ and it cannot . . . their responsibilities.]
Ms. 2   ends at this point
Ms. 1   . . . young people, *or their teachers for them*, to find . . .

Ms. 1   . . . perishes in the attempt.* *back* [Marginal note in pencil]
             When I see a fragile young singer who at
Ms. 2   ⎡reverse of last page⎤ *When I see a fragile . . . Ford's night-*
             ⎣   in pencil   ⎦ *ingale the*
Ms. 1   . . . like the nightingale in Ford's 'Lover's Melancholy'.

             She "would vie for mastery—the bird ordained . . .

Ms. 1   [δ dropped] down dropped

as far removed from ordinary dry-as-dust 'tuition' as it is possible to
conceive—on the 'Art of Singing'. I advise you to read it. I do not say
that I endorse all the views set forth but I do heartily approve of tone,
style, and noble *ideals held up* for examples. Our singers are by critics
often lectured for their want of brains, they must think:— well here
is something for them to think over *and it cannot but help* them to better
understanding of their art and their *responsibilities*.

One is tempted to ask *young people, or their teachers* for them, to find
their limitations and to sing or play things suited to their capabilities—
this is a very general remark, but many are spoiled by taking up branches
of work for which they are in no way fitted—the naturally idyllic
singer WILL attempt the heroic and perishes in the attempt. When I see
a fragile young singer who at best should attempt Fifine's song or
Lakme audibly expiring in 'Ocean, thou mighty monster' or 'Ah,
perfido'[1] I think of Ford's nightingale (Lover's Melancholy). She
"would vie for mastery".

The bird ordained to be Music's first martyr, strove to imitate

> "These several sounds: which when her warbling throat
> Failed in, for grief down dropped she on his lute,
> And brake her heart."[2]

[1] "Fifine's song", ? *Fifinella, Florentine Love Song* (no. 6 of 6 Romances, Op. 38)
Tchaikowsky; cf. Elgar's own waltz-song *The Blue-Eyes Fairy: Ah! où va la jeune Indoue*
(*Légende de Clochette*) from *Lakmé*, Delibes, which was performed by Florence Schmidt at
Queen's Hall Concert, October 26, 1901, at which *Pomp and Circumstance Marches* nos. 1
and 2 were played for the first time in London: "Ocean, thou mighty monster", *Oberon*,
Weber, Act II, Sc. 3: *Ah, perfido! Scena* (Op. 65), Beethoven.

[2] Elgar hit on one of the most informative passages concerning music in the drama of
the early seventeenth century; in its entirety it runs:
Menaphon:

> ... A sound of musicke toucht mine eare, or rather
> Indeed intranc'd my soule: as I stole nearer,
> Invited by the melody, I saw
> This Youth, this fair-fac'd Youth, upon his lute
> With straines of strange variety and harmony,
> Proclaiming (as it seem'd) so bold a challenge
> To the cleare *Quiristers* of the Woods, the Birds,
> That as they flockt about him, all stood silent,
> Wondring at what they hears. I wondred too.
> Amethus:
> And so doe I, good, —on
> Menaphon:
> A Nightingale
> Natures best skill'd Musicion undertakes
> The challenge, and for every severall straine

. . . drama on our [δ stage] platform-singers
. . . better stage [δ presence] *manner.*
the *old* Spectator *approvingly* remarks [pencil insertions]

Also, returning to the effect of drama on our platform-singers, we want frequently a better stage manner. This has been noticed ever since concerts have been given in England—the old Spectator approvingly remarks on a singer:— (Spectator No. 231)

"Whose more than ordinary concern on her first Appearance, recommended her no less than her agreeable Voice and just Performance. Mere bashfulness without Merit is awkward; and Merit without Modesty, insolent. But modest Merit has a double claim to Acceptance, and generally meets with as many Patrons as Beholders".[1]

The wel-shapt Youth could touch, she sung her down;
He cou'd not run Division with more Art
Upon his quaking Instrument, then she,
The Nightingale did with her various notes
Reply too, for a voyce, and for a sound,
Amethus, 'tis much easier to beleeve
That such they were, then hope to heare againe.
Amethus:
How did the Rivals part?
Menaphon:
You terme them rightly,
For they were Rivals, and their Mistris *harmony*.
Some time thus spent, the young man grew at last
Into a pretty anger, that a bird
Whom Art had never taught Cliffs, Moods, or Notes,
Should vie with him for mastery, whose study
Had busied many houres to perfit practise:
To end the controversie, in a rapture,
Upon his Instrument he playes so swiftly,
So many voluntaries, and so quicke,
That there was curiositie and cunning,
Concord in discord, lines of diffring method
Meeting in one full center of delight.
Amethus:
Now for the bird.
Menaphon:
The bird ordain'd to be
Musicks first Martyr, strove to imitate
These severall sounds which, when her warbling Throat
Fail'd in, for griefe, downe dropt she on his lute,
And brake her heart; it was the quaintest sadnesse,
To see the Conquerour upon her Hearse,
To weepe a funerall Elegy of teares
That trust me (my *Amethus*) I coo'd chide
Mine owne unmanly weaknesse, that made me
A fellow-mourner with him.
Amethus:
I beleeve thee.

John Ford, *Lover's Melancholy*, Act I, sc. I.
[1] See Everyman Edition, 4 vol., II, p. 186.

Ms. 1   . . . remains [δ the same] *pretty much where it was.* (A below)
[followed by] **B** To sum up . . . but brains **C**
[followed by] **A** I have purposely . . . church music (back **B**)
[After deletions there follows section **C** We hope [to end of lecture.]
. . . among the best [δ althoug]
church music. so for the present I [δ leave them] pass on

we [δ could do with] have room & ample room . . .
. . . *more* conductors . . . *more* singers [pencil insertions]
[deleted passage noted above]
                                  I would passing hastily over the
[δ groups] main divisions: we require our solo singers principally, almost wholly for the concert room—someday we
    We require oratorio singers with some dramatic feeling we
C *We* hope we may *some day* find . . . operatic performers—but *we* want . . .

[δ mostly] *mainly*
. . . real good of music [δ not as Carlyle says] dependant on [δ 'Weltering like] one another . . .

Ms. 1   . . . suggest [δ some] alteration
I [δ at the present moment] I leave
with regret [pencil insertion] only saying, *and my last words shall be* [pencil insertion]

English Executants
               End

So we see that times change but manners do not move so much and human nature *remains pretty* much where it was.

I have purposely left till last my reference to our organists; here we may rest satisfied in many ways. Our leading church organists are among *the best and we* have concert performers able to hold their own anywhere—we need not go out of Birmingham for a shining example.[1] But organists will be dealt with more fittingly on some future occasion when I shall hope to make a special reference to church *music*.

To sum up—we have reason to be proud of our English Executants; *we have room and ample* room for more of the highest rank—especially we *want more conductors and we want more singers*—singers with not only hearts but brains. *We hope we may some* day find more opening for operatic performers—but we want to see more alertness—less attention to pronunciation of UNimportant words and more appreciation of the important ones.

I want more intelligence from our Chorus singers—they should read up everything possible which bears upon the subject—the plot or story—of which they sing. A great objection made to our heavy choirs is that they sing flat—many foreign musicians find this; unavoidable perhaps with so little rehearsal with orchestra. I speak of selected choirs for festivals; but the drawback to the great northern choirs is this tendency.

On surveying the whole of the earnest body of workers and artists who form the English Executants it is a happiness to see the unselfishness of the artistic brotherhood—*mainly* working together for the real good of music—*dependent on one another* and helping each other—not quarrelling as is sometimes supposed, not (in Carlyle's words) "weltering like an Egyptian pitcher of vipers each struggling to get its head above the others" which is the view taken by the minority.

Some day we may *suggest alteration* or it may be improvement in the training of our executants but *I leave* the subject *with regret and my last words shall be* that the greatest happiness to me—who came into the active musical world somewhat later in life than many—my greatest happiness has been to see and feel the whole-hearted generosity—the unending charity—the chivalry and goodwill of the best of our English Executants.

[1] C. W. Perkins, Birmingham City Organist.

The reverberations from the explosions caused by such plain speaking took a long time to die away. December, with two more lectures to prepare (and the first on another prickly subject), was a wretched month, even though supporters rushed into what by now was a regular, if small-scale, *guerre des bouffons*. Two days after the lecture R. J. Buckley came to Hereford "to write an interview re storm raised by misleading quotations from E's lecture". On December 5 Lady Elgar, helpless, watched the "storm going on over his lectures". Whoever was at fault in saying what Elgar had or had not said it was not the local reporters, despite the fact that they must have wished to have been elsewhere.

The Musical Standard of December 9, apparently intent on keeping hostilities going, reprinted Stanford's letter to *The Times* of November 3. The *Standard*'s own report of *English Executants* was prefaced by:

> The lectures of the Peyton Professor of Music at the Birmingham University, Sir Edward Elgar, are creating quite a stir in the musical world, and are eagerly awaited. Many knew that Sir Edward is not in the habit of mincing matters, and his address at Birmingham University of November 29 is even more remarkable than the others that preceded it. We give below some of Sir Edward's more important observations as they appeared in the course of a lengthy report in "The Manchester Guardian" of November 30, which we advise our readers to purchase.

and was ended with this comment:

> At the Leipzig Conservatoire, as is fairly well known, Nikisch, its director, has instituted a class for conducting, and we believe several students have shown considerable talent. The class is open to foreigners, who, if musicians in other respects, need not go through the regular curriculum. At the Royal College of Music Patron Fund Concerts the scholar-composers have conducted their own works, but how little they had learnt the business of conducting was patent in every case. Sir Edward is very—but rightly—severe on the English composer-conductor, and, of course, he is a composer-conductor himself, one of his latest achievements being a tour with the London Symphony Orchestra. We do not know very much of his conducting in London, but it has been possible to note improvement from time to time; and, happily, he is having plenty of experience. Time will show whether Sir Edward will prove he is a "real conductor" or otherwise—that is to say, in the sense that Mr. Henry Wood is. Much might be taught at our musical institutions—but the "real conductor" is a product of a long practical experience. Mr. Wood to-day is very different from the Mr. Wood of—say—five years ago. He showed talent at the very beginning, but his talent would have been useless without opportunity. A man feeling he would do well as a conductor could hardly do better, for a beginning, than become conductor of an amateur orchestral society and attend as many concert rehearsals as possible; rehearsals, of course, directed by conductors of acknowledged greatness. If gifted and industrious, he would secure, in the end, a post as

conductor of a professional band—or, at any rate, as assistant conductor. We fancy that where there's a will there's a way. Talent will out.

We do not think that, speaking in a general way, it is easy to dispute this statement of Sir Edward's: "The only drawback to pupils turned out from our schools is that they lack fire." But we do not think that that "lack of fire" is necessarily permanent.[1]

On December 12, Josef Holbrooke wrote to *The Birmingham Post*:

SIR EDWARD ELGAR AND CONDUCTORS

I quite agree with Sir Edward Elgar that we have at present only one conductor of eminence, viz., Mr. Henry J. Wood, but I do not agree that there are not many clever conductors in our midst, though, unfortunately, of native origin. The pity is that some conductors cling blandly to office, and never invite composers to conduct their own works. We should find that we had conductors if this was done. Is this the way to encourage our conductors, if they are not given every possible chance of conducting their own works? As for the contention about conductors pure and simple—I have not the least belief in anything of the kind. There have been many magnificent composer-conductors, as fine as any other conductors, witness Franz Liszt, von Bulow, Mottl, Berlioz, and many others. I, for many reasons, prefer the sympathetic composer-conductor before all others. It is only a crank which exists about the "pure" conductor.

Dec. 11   Josef Holbrooke

The next day this prompted:

SIR EDWARD ELGAR AND CONDUCTORS.
To the Editor of the Daily Post.

Sir,—Mr. Josef Holbrooke's letter on the above subject is hardly convincing. He appears to think that the best way of discovering conductors is to let composers conduct their own works. Would he always expect composers for the violin or piano to play their own compositions on the instrument for which they are written? Because, after all, the orchestra is an instrument in its way, and requires an adequate training in the knowledge of how to play upon it like any other instrument. The reason we have so few great conductors in this country is because the opportunities of conducting are, comparatively speaking, so few, and also because we make those opportunities fewer by importing conductors of foreign origin. This is, however, a national peculiarity which shows that our so-called musical leaders are still in leading-strings.

Mr. Holbrooke gives the names of Liszt, Bu[e]low, Mottl, and Berlioz as composers who were distinguished as conductors. He is curiously unfortunate in his choice of examples. When were Bulow and Mottl composers? I am sure I do not know, nor, do I think, does he. Why did he not quote Wagner and Mendelssohn? On the other hand, he forgets to

[1] pp. 370-1.

mention that Beethoven and Schumann, who were, I fancy, composers of some standing, were failures as conductors. I frankly do not understand Mr. Holbrooke's last sentence: "It is only a crank which exists about the pure conductor." If he means that a musician who gives the whole of his time to conducting is not to be preferred to one who only conducts occasionally, and that the contrary opinion is only a craze—this statement sounds to me like nonsense, but perhaps this is not Mr. Holbrooke's meaning.

By the way, I rather fancy that Sir Edward Elgar was himself at fault in saying that Mr. Wood was our only conductor in the sense that he was the only conductor in Great Britain who gained his livelihood by conducting, because I believe he teaches. Mr. Cowen is, I understand, our only musician who restricts himself to conducting; but then he is a composer as well, so I suppose we have no conductor in the strict sense of the word as Sir Edward employs it, and more's the pity.

December 12.   A MUSIC LOVER.

At the week-end the army went into action:

MILITARY BAND MUSIC

Lieutenant J. Mackenzie Rogan, bandmaster of the Coldstream Guards, lectured before the Manchester section of the Incorporated Society of Musicians on Saturday night on military bands and music. The meeting was held in the Grand Hotel, and Mr. Wilhelm Schroder presided.

Mr. Rogan said that the best military bands now played works of a far higher class than they were accustomed to attempt in former days. This was largely due to the lively interest in music shown by the King and other members of the Royal Family. British bandmasters had been reproached with a preference for works of foreign origin. The fault, however, lay mainly with British composers, who neither wrote directly for military bands, nor superintended the arrangement of their works for military bands by others. Sir Edward Elgar had recently said that England was "especially weak in wind instruments." Mr. Rogan strongly disputed this. This country excelled, he thought, in wind instrumentation, and in no foreign country of which he had experience would wind soloists be found better or even so good as those in Great Britain. To this some of the greatest foreign conductors had themselves borne testimony. Sir Edward had also said, speaking of English conductors, that we had far too many "pedantic mechanics." It was to be remembered that in this country there were no schools for teaching the art of conducting, and in these circumstances we realised excellent and even surprisingly good results. Perhaps the conductor was born and not made, but even the born conductor might be improved by reasonable tuition in the days of his youth. He did not gather that Sir Edward considered that his own works had suffered at the hands of the "pedantic mechanics." Sir Edward had often conducted his own works, but Mr. Rogan did not hesitate to say that he had heard better orchestral performances of Sir Edward's music when directed by other hands than when directed by Sir Edward's own.

No composer had received a larger measure of justice from British conductors.[1]

In another report[2] Rogan was allowed one more sentence: "In return for this justice I would respectfully bespeak from Sir Edward Elgar the exercise of the sister virtue of 'Charity'."

On New Year's Day, 1906, the *Musical Opinion*[3] had its say. First, editorially

Sir Edward Elgar is perhaps just a trifle too outspoken. Lecturing recently at Birmingham University on the subject of "English Musical Executants," he deplored the existence of "too many brainless singers" and declared that even the influence of the teaching in our colleges had been unable to raise the standard all round. Mr. Wood, he says, is our one and only conductor. We have plenty of "pedantic mechanics, respectable men who would be equally successful as schoolmasters; but, if they must keep time for somebody, they would be more useful as timekeepers in a factory." Again, in England "there are only enough actors and actresses in the ranks of the profession to cast properly one drama, and no more." An eminent organist has made perhaps the most decided answer to all that, and he does it so: "My opinion of such language is simply this: the statements are unworthy of a professional chair."

But there are two sides to every shield; so some days ago Dr. Cowen forwarded to Sir Edward Elgar a newspaper cutting in which reference was made to certain alleged remarks of the Birmingham professor on the subject of conductors and singers. Sir Edward replied to his friend in a letter expressly made open to publication, and a copy of it has reached us. We quote the more important passages. Having characterised the cutting as "absurd," Sir Edward goes on to say with regard to Dr. Cowen himself: "In my letter I made a special, wholly friendly and laudatory reference to you and to the splendid work that you do in London, Liverpool and Glasgow." The writer adds, touching his allusion to Mr. Henry J. Wood: "My reference to Henry Wood was to the effect that we had only found work for one conductor—a conductor who did nothing else but conduct—this with a view to point out a possible opening for young men in the future, if music proceeds to grow as it has done. The telegraphic reports of my lecture are, so far as I know, wholly misleading." It is manifestly important, in order to remove misapprehension, that a faithful report of Sir Edward's lectures should appear as soon as may be, and we are glad to know that arrangements to that end are in progress.

and then, under "Musical Gossip":

Sir Edward Elgar has managed to set the musical world by the ears. It must be admitted that his speeches at Birmingham have not been characterised by the kind of discretion that one expects from a professor

---

[1] *Manchester Guardian*, December 18, 1905.
[2] *The Musical Standard*, December 23, 1905, p. 410.
[3] January 1, 1906, no. 340, pp. 257 and 260.

of music. He might have been a militant critic bent upon making a sensation. But, personally, I must confess that I have some admiration for his courage. As a rule, our professional musicians are the soul of professional discretion; if they utter an opinion at all, it is harmless and colourless. Sir Edward was quite right in his attack on English conductors: there are none except Wood and Cowen. As the composer of "The Apostles" has been conducting a tour of the London Symphony Orchestra, he of course includes himself among the number of composer-conductors who cannot conduct,—a piece of broadmindedness which has escaped the general notice.

There is also a great deal too much of the wooden unemotional view of music in England. Professors of that sort with their sham profundity have done much to keep British music unpopular. There has always been a gulf between the practice of the art by our professors and the taste of our amateurs, so that it has been very difficult to make the latter take any interest in native music.

The Birmingham professor also attacked the drama, and he has been told that a cobbler should stick to his last. His opinions (as reported) were not, it is true, very valuable; because it was evident that he did not know the real cause of much of our poor artificial acting. But I must protest against the implication that a man who is clever in one walk of life has no right to have or to utter opinions on any but his own special subject. Sir Edward Elgar's opinions on Protection would be of interest, for he is a clever man.

As a matter of fact, we really have a number of talented actors and actresses. What is wrong is the tradition of our stage: there is no real school of acting. Mr. Tree's academy, as far as one can judge from the appearances made by its most promising pupils, is devoted to teaching all the stale old tricks of the profession; and not long ago, when a kind of exhibition was given, a gold medal was presented to the young man who had most of the faults of the English stage. No one teaches our young players; and the stage manager has most conventional ideas of *ensemble*— ideas which are mainly based on the necessity of giving as much prominence as possible to the antics of the leading gentleman and the leading lady. When there is an intelligent stage manager and no leading players to consult, our actors and actresses can do well enough.

CHAPTER 8

CRITICS
(December 6, 1905)

THE critical years in Elgar's early career as a composer were 1882 and 1883 when he first came fully to recognise the significance of the musical language of Wagner and Brahms. Two essays of that period in particular affected him, and, as will be seen, these were also fundamental to this lecture. The first of these essays (in fact a review of the vocal score followed by notices of the first two performances of *Parsifal*) was by Ebenezer Prout (1835–1909). The review of the score (an English translation of the libretto was simultaneously issued by Schott) appeared in *The Athenaeum* on July 29, 1882 (pp. 151–3). In it he wrote:

> With regard to the music, it is so difficult to judge any of Wagner's scores from a pianoforte arrangement, that we prefer to reserve a final opinion till we have heard it at Bayreuth, simply saying now that while a few passages are unquestionably very beautiful, a great part of the music seems, at least on the piano, excruciatingly ugly. . . .
>
> We are quite prepared, bearing in mind our previous experiences with Wagner's works, to find that many portions of the music which are unendurable on the piano prove most appropriate on the stage . . . and it is only by being submitted to the test of actual performance that such music can be fairly judged.

On August 5 his despatches regarding the performances given on July 27 and July 29 appeared (pp. 183–5).

> (July 27) . . . Wagner's art creations, however, are of so complex a character and depend so entirely for their total effect on the blending of the various factors into a homogeneous whole, that any description founded merely on a study of the printed music must necessarily be incomplete, and requires to be supplemented by a record of the impressions produced in performances if any adequate notion of the work in its entirety is to be conveyed to those who are unable themselves to witness its representation. . . . In no other work of Wagner's is the music so singularly unequal in merit. While we find many passages of unsurpassable beauty and charm, there is also much that must be pronounced harsh, nay, even positively ugly. The composer's resolute avoidance of everything that is in the least commonplace leads him at times to overstep the line of musical beauty . . .

Prout agonised over his task of appraisal. After the second performance he was overcome by the effect of the work not only on himself but on the entire audience; the experience, he said, was akin to that he had known at the Passion Play at Oberammergau: "... it will be seen that I have considerably modified my views since writing the preliminary notice of the work. I admit the fact at once. My first article was founded solely on the knowledge of the published score. I could not have believed it possible that so solemn, so devotional an impression could have been produced by a stage performance. As my object is not to take sides either with or against Wagner, but simply to arrive at the truth, I believe it to be my only honest and straightforward course to say candidly that I was altogether mistaken in my first estimate of the general character and tendency of the work . . . E. P."

At the beginning of 1883 Elgar paid his first visit to Leipzig—the effect of this visit has already been made apparent—and his enthusiasm for Wagner, Schumann, and Brahms was greatly increased. It was at the end of that year that he read Hanslick's account of the first performance of Brahms's Third Symphony.[1] This, translated from the original version in the *Neue freie Presse*, of Vienna, was published in *The Musical World* of December 22, 1883[2]. It was as follows:

BRAHMS AND DVOŘÁK.

The 2nd December will probably be the great day in our present season, and shine as doubly red-lettered in the calendar of the "Philharmonicans." On that day Hans Richter gave us, in addition to Mendelssohn's "Hebrides Overture," which served as an admirable introduction, two grand novelties: a "Violin Concerto" by Dvořák (played by Ondriček) and the as yet unpublished Third Symphony of Brahms. A perfect feast—but rather for the delighted man and musician in us than for the critic, who had afterwards to say what Brahms' new Symphony was like and describe its various beauties. Now it is nothing either uncommon or incapable of explanation for the critic's eloquence to sink the deeper, the higher the composer has soared. Spoken language is not so much a poorer language as no language at all, with regard to music, for it cannot render the latter. This was, perhaps, felt less in former and more easily satisfied times. But if, at the present day, we read the best criticisms, which appeared immediately after the first performance of Beethoven's Symphonies and place ourselves mentally in the place of the first readers, we are compelled to confess that we have seen the announcement of some grand and beautiful music, but have gained no definite idea of its individual physiognomy. It was not till Beethoven's Symphonies had spread far and wide, and subsequent critics were able to connect what they said with something the reader knew, to assume that the reader had himself heard and felt, that we were really taught anything by the admirable Beethoven criticisms of modern times. Brahms' Third Sym-

[1] See reproduction of programme, p. 97.

[2] It was reprinted in the programme for the Richter Concert of May 1st, 1884, at which the Symphony was given its first English performance (see pp. 98–9).

phony in F major, performed on the 2nd December for the very first time, and still unpublished, has as yet no such bridge between the great mass of the public and criticism, and so the latter has to rely principally upon comparison with earlier and known works by the same master.

The Imperial *Capellmeister*, Hans Richter, when lately proposing a clever toast, gave the new Symphony the name of "Eroica." And, in truth, if we characterize Brahms' Symphony in C minor as "Pathetic" or "Appassionata," and the Second in D as a "Pastoral Symphony," the new Symphony, in F major, may aptly be styled "Eroica." But the epithet does not quite meet the case, for only the first movement and the third strike us as "heroic." In his C minor Symphony Brahms plunged, with the very first dissonant bars, into despairing passion and gloomy Faust-like speculation; the Finale, reminding us of the concluding movement of Beethoven's "Ninth," in no way changes, with its tardily achieved reconciliation, the essentially pathetic, nay, pathological, character of the composition, in which a suffering, morbidly-excited individuality finds expression. The Second Symphony, in D major, is a quiet and almost pastoral contrast to the first; while in the latter the thunder of the old Beethoven still rolls, we hear, in the former, from out the pleasing distance, the voices of Mozart and Haydn. Brahms' Third Symphony is really another new one. It repeats neither the mournful song of fate of the First nor the joyous idyll of the Second; its fundamental tone is conscious, deed-loving strength. The Heroic element in it has nothing warlike about it, and leads up to nothing tragic, such as the Funeral March in the *Eroica*. By its musical character it reminds us of the healthy energy of Beethoven's second period, and never of the singularities of his last; while, through everything else, there occasionally vibrates the dim romantic light of Schumann and Mendelssohn. The first movement (F major, *Allegro vivace*, 6/4) is one of the most important and most perfect things Brahms has ever given us. Magnificently, after two vigorous, dull chords of the wind instruments, does the theme of the violins energetically shoot down from above, to rise again on high immediately in its proud course. The entire movement was created in a happy hour and in one piece. His second motive, in A flat, simultaneously tender and impellent, blends in an incomparable manner with the whole. This movement, in its development, reaches a lofty and vigorous height; but, when nearing the end, surprises the hearer by making way for a gradually tranquil[l]ized tone, which dies out in gentle beauty. The two middle movements have no powerfully startling effects in store for the hearer, but invite him to peaceful repose. The slow movement is not "sad unto death," nor is the quicker one "exultant, heaven-high;" both move forward with easy moderation, and on a middle level of feeling, allowing the Tender and Graceful to be calmly developed. The "Andante con moto" (C major 4/4)—a very simple alternate strain for the wind instruments and the deeper strings, which latter take up, as it were, the refrain—might stand in one of Brahms' Serenades. The movement is short, without, properly speaking, rise or development, but surprises us in the middle by a succession of magical harmonies, sound-effects reminding us of the alternate play of softly sounding and differently tuned bells. The place of the Scherzo is taken up by an Allegretto in C minor (3/8), which has a passing touch of Mendelssohn about it, and which subsides with easy grace into that hybrid mood Brahms is so fond of introducing into his middle movements. The piece is very simply scored (without trumpets, trombones, or kettle-drums), being rendered effective more especially by the incisive grace of its middle part in A flat major. Despite all their radical difference, Brahms' First Symphony and his Third resemble each other in one point: their two middle movements appear, in purport and extent, somewhat small compared to the mighty pieces between which they are enclosed. The Finale (F minor, Allegro, alla breve) is another piece of the very first order, equal, if not superior, to the first movement. A low sound rolls towards us with a quick sultry figure of the deep stringed-instruments. This theme, which in subsequent performances will, probably, be taken somewhat more quickly, is by no means imposing at first, but very soon is developed in the most grandiose manner. The weird-like sultriness of the commencement finds an outlet in a magnificent tempest, which elevates and refreshes us. The music rises higher and higher; the second theme, in C major, brayed out in mighty notes by the horn, soon makes way for a third vigorous motive in C minor, which storms onward with even greater power. When the movement has reached the height of this imposing development, everyone probably expects a brilliant and triumphant ending. But with Brahms we must always be prepared for something unexpected. His Finale glides imperceptibly from the key of F minor into that of D major; the high-heaving ocean-waves calm down to a mysterious murmur—muted violins and tenors break, in lightly rippling passages of thirds and sixths, on the long sustained chords of the wind instruments, the whole sounding strange and mysterious, but wonderfully beautiful.

All this is, properly speaking, idle talk—the Symphony must be heard and not described; heard, but not read. The Aulic Counsellor in Immermann's *Epigonen* is not quite wrong, when he confesses that there is only one kind of conversation which he finds more wearisome than that about painting: conversation about music. It is certain that a few short examples in musical notation of the principal themes in the new Symphony would tell the reader more about it than all our description. As, however, Brahms runs over with surprises, and as what he develops from the motives is often a great deal more important than the motives themselves, a musical paper—and only such a paper can indulge in the luxury of examples in musical notation—would have gradually to print half the score and then refer us, after all, to the entire work. Another method, the poetically-pictorial, which renders the impressions received into a series of finished pictures, subjects for ballads, and chapters of romance, is repugnant to my conviction of the purely musical significance of an instrumental work; besides, I do not possess the "talent for sound-pictures," of which the otherwise unmusical Heine could boast, and which, a poet by the grace of God, he proved practically, in many a genial description of music, he possessed. Thus, nothing is left for me save simply to express my delight at the new Symphony, in which we have gained one of the most beautiful and ripest creations of modern instrumental music. Many persons may prefer the Titanic power of the First Symphony, and many the muffled grace of the Second—each of the three most certainly contains certain special beauties of its own—but the Third strikes me as artistically the most perfect. It is the most compact in form, the clearest in the details, and the most plastic in the leading themes. The instrumentation is richer in new and charming colour-combinations than it was in the two former Symphonies. For genial modulation, the Third Symphony is not inferior to the best works of its composer, and, in the art, most peculiarly his own, of most freely connecting different tempi and rhythms it possesses the recommendation of not achieving this at the cost of intelligibility. Clear and direct in its effect on the first hearing, it will pour forth, on the second, third, and tenth, from still more delicate and deeper sources, yet richer enjoyment for every musical ear. Once again have we come to the joyful conviction that Brahms' creative power is still unimpaired and full of life, and still putting forth fresh branches. What a picture of rich abundance is that presented by his labours for the last six years! Three grand Symphonies, the two Overtures, the Violin-Concerto, the second Pianoforte Concerto, the incomparable Stringed Quartet, and the C major Trio, the Pianoforte Rhapsodies, the "Nänie," the "Song of the Fates," and a blooming wreath of songs, in the intervals —is not the blonde Johannes one of the benefactors of the human race? The success of the new Symphony at the Philharmonic Concert was, also, in a material sense, most brilliant. The very first movement so excited the audience that Brahms was compelled to appear twice in answer to the calls for him, which seemed as though they would never end. Anybody who knows what exertions are needed to get him out only *once*, may imagine what must have been the impression made by the first movement. After the third movement he had to show himself once more, and after the Finale again and again. I could not get rid of the one idea, which I will not suppress here: If Schumann were only alive now!

Dvořák's new Violin Concerto (dedicated to Joachim), a work of fresh fancy delicately carried out, and entrancingly played by Ondriček, met with the warmest approbation. Its reception would, probably have been still warmer, had not Brahms' Symphony, which was awaited with the greatest interest, cast, as it were, its shadows before. Herr Ondriček, who by his execution of it proved himself a great master, has done well in repeating the work at his farewell concert, which will shortly take place. The first movement (A minor, allegro, 4/4) begins with a pithy theme, but becomes rather colourless and lengthy as it progresses, passing much too imperceptibly into the Adagio (F major 3/8), a beautiful piece, of a soft and dreamy character. The finale (A major, 3/8) pleases by its fresh and naïve joyousness; there is something of a Bohemian church-wake about it. Dvořák unites in the most happy manner national Sclavonian touches with eminently German art. His music is the best "Policy of Reconciliation;" it is accepted unreservedly by Germans and Czechs. Herr Hans Richter, who, the Sunday before, on appearing at the conductor's desk, was received with long continued demonstrations of satisfaction, was rewarded on the present occasion, also, with the loudest marks of approbation. In the performance of Brahms' extraordinarily difficult Symphony, he once more proved his eminent talent as a conductor. Everything was so clearly set forth and rhythmically graduated with such delicacy, while, at the same time, it was accented with such warmth and spirit, that the composer himself could not wish to have his work better performed, and probably will never hear it performed better anywhere else.

EDUARD HANSLICK.

In view of the spasmodic character of his own musical education Elgar was keenly interested in the Festival movement, in which he rightly saw a great potential for widening the general musical horizon. He resented the fact that the festivals, particularly those with which he was personally concerned, were not considered newsworthy. This fact he ascribed to metropolitan ignorance and indifference. His closest connections were with the Festivals at Madresfield (Malvern) and Morecambe, the former inspired by Lady Mary Lygon, the latter by Canon C. V. Gorton.

The Morecambe Festival that took place between April 29 and May 2, 1903 (for which he composed *Weary wind of the west*) made a deep impression. *The Banner of St. George* was also among the works given on this occasion, and if the daily press ignored the event *The Musical Times* (June 1, 1903, p. 403) at least did it justice:

> . . . But the standard of the orchestral playing on the whole could well be considered astonishingly high, for one remembered that the performers were mostly working men from small manufacturing towns in North Lancashire.
>
> In rehearsing and performing his cantata Dr. Elgar did not find it necessary to make much allowance for the amateur status of the instrumentalists. . . . The behaviour of the enormous masses of competitors and listeners was in accord with the excellent record of former years . . .

There were some 4,000 competitors and the sum of the audiences was in the region of 6,000.

From Morecambe Elgar went on to Madresfield, where the *Coronation Ode* was the central work. Elgar, who conducted this, "also publicly stated that in his opinion the standard was higher than it had been" (*Musical Times*, ibid.).

On May 26 he wrote to Gorton. His letter was quoted in the July issue of *The Musical Times* (p. 461) under the heading of SOMEWHERE FARTHER NORTH:

> . . . I cannot [he said] well express what I feel as to the immense influence your Festival must exert in spreading the love of music: it is rather a shock to find Brahms's part-songs appreciated and among the daily fare of a district apparently unknown to the sleepy London Press: people who talk of the spread of music in England and the increasing love

of it rarely seem to know where the growth of the art is really strong and properly fostered. Some day the Press will awake to the fact, already known abroad and to some few of us in England, that the living centre of music in Great Britain is not London, but somewhere further [*sic*] North.

During that summer there were other festivals in the north, particularly at Carlisle, Kendal, Spilsby, York, and Pontefract. Their special value was attested in later years by Havergal Brian in a passage that suggests that Elgar was justified in his warmth of utterance. Brian wrote that ". . . the most remarkable movement in English music for several centuries was that of *a cappella* choral singing at the Northern Musical Competition festivals".[1]

Rough Notes

Sheet

[1]   *Notes*   IV
                            IV   English Critics
                          mema. see Leslie Stephen

[2]   [cancelled]
                It is said to be to his credit that He is never vulgar: that
                is true; but he is much worse, he is *commonplace*: vulgarity
                may in the course of time be refined; it is often inventive
                & at times it *can* take the initiative,[?] in a rude & mis-
                guided way no doubt; but often it does *something*, & as I
                have said can be & has been refined. But the common-
                place mind can never be anything but commonplace—
                & no amount of education no amount of the polish of
                a university, can eradicate the stain from the low type
                of mind we call commonplace— & the commonplace
                mind is represented in its fullest & most debased way in
                J.A.F[roude?] can have no useful place in our art, [See
                Inaugural Lecture, p. 47.]
                [cf. Elgar's Introduction to Hubert Leicester's *Forgotten
                Worcester* (1930): "From among the crudities which one of
                the many—why are there so many?—unbrilliant university
                men has used in reference to myself, the following comes to
                mind. I am said to have 'left the humdrum atmosphere of
                Worcester for'—etc."

[3]   The first critic was the devil & he criticised with little
                effect except to himself, it seems, the creation [cf. pp. 24, 157]

[1] *Foreword*, Bantock Memorial Concert, Midland Institute, November 12, 1946.

Leslie Stephen, "English Literature and Society in the xviii century"[1] (Duckworth) [cf. p. 57]

Lecture I

(see this)

"Critics in an earlier day conceived their function to be judicial. They were administering a fixed code of laws applicable in all times & places"

(The fixed 'code' was *Aristotle's* canon)

"I will not say that the modern critic has abandoned altogether that conception of his duty. He seems to me not unfrequently to place himself on the judgement seat with a touch of his old confidence, and to sentence poor authors with sufficient airs of infallibility. Sometimes, unless the reflection that he is representing not an invariable tradition but the last new aesthetic doctrine, seems even to give additional keenness to his opinions and to suggest no doubts of his infallibility".

[4]   L. Stephen. p. 5

"When the critics

assumed that the forms familiar to themselves were the only possible embodiment of those principles, and condemned all others as barbarous, they were led to pass judgement, such, for example, as Voltaire's view of Dante & Shakespeare, which strike us as strangely crude and unappreciative"

[following passage cancelled]

We must begin by asking impartially what pleased men, and then again why it pleased them. We must not decide dogmatically that it ought to have pleased or displeased on the simple ground that it is or is not congenial to ourselves

[See p. 57.]

[5
reverse]

p. 308[2]

"An original idea (of hell) was the result of the speculative inquiries of Jean Hardouin.* This "most learned fool", as he has been somewhat impolitely called by Peignot

* 1646–1729.

[1] The Ford Lectures of 1903, pub., Duckworth, 1904.
[2] This refers to Mew, *op. cit.*; see p. 47.

among the Jesuits was a contemporary of Pinamonti.[1] He
maintained that rotation of the earth was due to the efforts of
the damned to escape from their central fire. Climbing up the
walls of hell, they caused the earth to revolve as a squirrel
its cage, or a dog the spit."

　　　possibly this erudite Jesuit was mistaken as is the lot
etc. etc. etc. (See p. 47.]

[6]　　　* Critics **B**

Critics of music have, in this country, a difficult task,
inasmuch as their work has to be hurriedly displayed or, in
the opinion of newspaper editors, its value ceases: possibly I
should more correctly have said 'subeditor' as musical news
is considered to be utterly unimportant its fate regarding its
position & the time of appearance is left to the cultured
ignorance of the last named official.

On the whole the art is well served by the critics & their
advice is welcome when based upon experience.* I do not
forget that the first critic the world ever saw was Lucifer (the
devil) & he criticised—with little effect except to himself it
seems,—the creation [See pp. 24, 155.]
[in pencil]

　　* but sometimes they follow *the example of* [δ their first
predecessor] the first critic the world ever saw & speak boldly
without experience & [δ the] here they fail.

[7]　　*Notes*　　　　　　　Notes last lecture
　　　　　　　　　　　　　　　　　　A　　　　　　　[δ **B**]
　　　　　　　　　　　　　Critics
　　　　　　　　"Somewhere farther north"

[1] Giovanni Pietro Pinamonti (1632–1703), an Italian Jesuit, was the author of a work
which was published in London in 1715 as *Hell opened to Christians, to caution them from
entering into it; or, considerations of the infernal pains, propos'd to our meditation to avoid them;
and distributed for every day of the week.* Effectively illustrated with discouraging steel
engravings this work bears more signs of the Enlightenment, perhaps, than the writings
of Hardouin; e.g. "The exposing of our selves to such evident Danger of Burning for the
space of a Thousand years, on Account of some vile and transitory *Pleasure*, would
undoubtedly be a very great Madness: 'Twould be a much greater to expose one self to
the Danger of continuing Ten Thousand Years: 'Twould still be greater and greater, to
expose one self to burn for a Hundred Thousand Years: Will not then the exposing our
selves to burn for ever, for so small a Trifle, be an infinite Madness?" See Mew, *op. cit.,*
pp. 298–9, and 357–8.

[illegible deletion] less than their usual modesty etc. could
not wish them & expect them to do more than they do.
                    this remarkable information
"Another lovely day. It compares with a [passage ?] earlier
[on ?]
                    10,000 people engaged in following music. not
a word
papers pretend to give the news of England.
[heavily deleted] :
getting [*Standardisch* ?] [?] when people got their money's
worth they only get their [?]
M.M.R. Delibes suite c.f. *Wagner*. [See p. 175.]
Hanslick. Language is less than language' etc. etc. [See pp. 150,
169, 173.]
                    [?] programme book

[8]   [in pencil]
                    Begin
                    Man learns
                        teachers
                    Harmony Counterpoint
                    Orchestrt^n·—Communion with nature etc. in-
spiration
                        He finds his last teacher the critic.
                    Repetition.
                        [?]
                    Not in [Newman ?]

[9]   [in pencil]
                    use of words. English '*piece*' not morceau
                    ⎯⎯
                    too many versed in piano literature only. pt. song
                    ⎯⎯
                        naive announcement
[illegible line]
                    It sometimes makes us pause when we read Analyses.
                    omissions
                        Brahms 3$^{rd.}$ Sym
                            motto omitted
                        Tovey's analysis is correct [last two words added
                        in ink] [See p. 101.]

[10]   Critics
Anything ungenerous, ungentlemanly, illiberal, mean & con-
temptible comes happily out from our journalistic quarter ?
i.e. the Times
It is the fashion nowadays to [δ deny] question the teaching of
the O.T. or at least to discredit many of the allegories which
were once [δ formerly?] believed as absolute facts by some
of our ancestors: I have no desire to enter into this question
[δ although I may possess some knowledge of the subject],
but leaving debatable matter on one side it is patent to
everyone that in the ancient words are embedded [δ in a]
some tremendous truth, which,* although their first surroundings & prime reason for [δ existence creation] their
enunciation have passed away. Still shine like a strong light

[11]

through the gloom & mist which even now encompasses us
in some [δ matter] matters other than religion*
Ours is a high & holy art & we who really serve it [δ must be]
are *men*: far away in the law of the temple we read the terrible
words in Lev. 21, 20; these have a real significance to us still;
service in our temple is the desire of many; the *useful* &
acceptable service is given to few: the [δ use men] creature
incompletely equipped [δ ?] only mars what they he wd
make. [δ They] He brings to the service an incomplete
intellect, an emasculated mind— & [δ they] he can have no
part in the service of the Lord—"he hath a blemish".
We may leave to his own impotence.
    See the '*A* character' Tennyson Stanza 5.[1]

[12]

mem:
    writing for festivals not necessarily a bad thing
    everything almost has failed—this gives a chance—
    gratefully

        [1] With lips depress'd as he were meek,
        Himself unto himself he sold:
        Upon himself himself did feed:
        Quiet, dispassionate, and cold,
        And other than his form of creed,
        With chisell'd features clear and sleek.
                                (from *Juvenilia*)

taken by the critics—to say that writing for an occasion is bad.
        give examples of writing for occasion—Beethoven
(*Bach*, everything almost) Mozart etc. etc. etc.
    The failure lies with the men not with the occasion

[12a]   [torn typescript, blue ribbon]
        not much has been
        the status of their art. The r
        real singer, as distinct from the mere   as
        Critics of music have in this country a difficult task, inasmuch
        as their work has to be hurriedly displayed or, in the opinion
        of the editor,——or as music is of course utterly unimportant,
        its fate regarding its position and time of appearance is left
        to the tender ignorance of the sub-editor.
        [marginal note in pencil] *its value cer*
        BUT the gentlemen who write for the daily press do, and
        have done their best to elevate the 'tone' of the press music
        generally: it is necessary to say the daily press because in the
        interests of cleanliness and honesty it m one must exclude the
        needy inebriates of the weekly reviews.
        BUT critics should have a free-er hand in the selection of
        things to be written about and should not be expected to
        mix up with a seriou matt [cf. p. 165]

[13]
        [δ Critical]
            Nothing should be more gratifying to a [δ creator] maker
        of music than to read a wise & just criticism on his work.
        Happily we have those with us who can [δ & will] help
        [See p. 177.]

The University,
Birmingham.

Messrs Russell, Cork & Co.

P.T.O.

Ms. 1   Composers
          Executants
                &
          Critics

Ms. 2   Composers
[C.A.E.   Executants
& M.G.]   Critics

Ms. 1   [δ I have been so much misquoted—sometimes without meaning apart from the context, have been help up as t] This has naturally . . .
. . . accused of [δ omitting] *ignoring* audiences [δ from the] *as a* . . .

Ms. 2   . . . the *indiscriminating* crowd
. . . the *well-being of the* whole art . . .

Ms. 1   critical; [δ that audience is not worth performing to] But [δ in the general mind] the word critic *usually* calls *to mind* [δ all the] only WRITER [δ only] of criticism—

Ms. 2   . . . calls to mind only a writer of criticism—
Let it not be assumed . . . is, or shd be, the critic [*caret* in Ms. 1, interleaved and written by E. in pencil, marked *]
[δ it is my business] it has been my happiness

Ms. 1   we, who are criticised, know the [δ value] differing value of [δ criticism] written criticism

Ms. 2   [δ know] *feel*
The hurried criticism . . . slowly-wrought opinion. [*caret* in Ms. 1, copied by M.G. on separate sheet, marked *]

           educational
Ms. 1   . . . musical events & [δ persons]

CRITICS

I divided the active musical world into three sections:— *Composers, Executants, Critics. This has naturally been misquoted* and I have been *accused of ignoring audiences* as a necessary part of a living art. I did no such thing. I expressly included auditors in the third section of which I discourse to-day.

I do not say that audiences (the *indiscriminating* crowd of a concert room) are necessary for *the well-being of the whole* art of music; but any good audience or better, auditor, must be in a measure *critical*; I therefore included intelligent audiences among the factors necessary to the working and well-being of a concrete art.

But the word critic usually calls to mind a WRITER of criticism—in these days of much journalism a newspaper writer. *Let it not be* assumed that I am about to endeavour to give advice to critics, it has *been my happiness and I trust* may continue to be, to receive advice from them. It is rather my wish to explain to the student the position the critic holds in his artistic life, the use and value which critical opinions may be to him. A student works through his courses of Harmony and Counterpoint—he submits his composition on his performance to the judgement of his teacher and of his friends and finds at last that his real teacher—the one *who gives* him the final polish—is, or *should be, the critic: we, who are criticised feel* the differing value of written criticism, and, that most read, that of the daily journal is from the very fact of its hasty production frequently of less value than the opinions more slowly evolved. *The hurried criticism* may be of value to the composer as showing the effect of a single performance of his work on a trained mind; but such an opinion may be reversed or modified on a second hearing, and all our good critics—unless a work is hopelessly bad or immature—make a reservation in this way. But the real, lasting, *educational* good is gained from the mature *slowly-wrought opinion*. I know that some papers permit articles on *musical events* to appear sometime after the actual occurrence but the words I said in my inaugural address practically sum up the situation.

I said:— "Critics of music have, in this country, a difficult task,

Birm.   The editor, of course, wanted news, and he wanted
Post   that news quickly. Whether he wanted it correct or not was
         a matter for his own conscience—(Laughter)—as he had
         regretfully noticed during the past week (Renewed laughter).
Ms. 1   [δ The Musician a paper has recently begun][1]

Ms. 2   *serious*
Ms. 1   . . . their serious essays
Ms. 2   „ [δ serious] „
Ms. 1   It is just this combination [δ of] with journalism [δ &
criticism] which *occasionally* makes criticism [δ sometimes] fall
to a somewhat lower level than [δ one could] [δ *wish*] [δ the
writer] the ideal of the We need not go . . .
Ms. 2   . . . fall [δ to a] somewhat lower [δ level] than the ideal
Ms. 1   We need not go into the beginnings of this disastrous combination: it is the natural outcome of a hurried daily press &
the *want of musical knowledge enough* [δ ignorance] of Editors
generally [δ of anything musical]. [δ Notices of picture exhibitions, except the annual commercial show at Burlington
House, are not rushed in the same way.]
Ms. 2   . . . beginnings of this *apparently* [δ *somewhat*] *inevitable*
combination: . . . and the want of sufficient musical knowledge amongst Editors generally.

Ms. 1   But the journalistic side has been the mainstay of most of
the lesser critics: it is somewhat easier [in Ms. 2 as in type-
script]
     . . . definite object
Ms. 1   [δ such as the fitting of the hall—the number of the audience,
than of the actual music. One unwary critic, no longer with
us,] such as the size of the audience, or the amount of applause
bestowed rather than upon *such* an [δ indefinite] *intangible*
thing [δ like] *as* music.
Ms. 2   . . . [δ number] *size* . . . applause bestowed *dress & so forth,*
Birm.   "It is so much easier", remarked the speaker, amid laughter,
Post   "to write of a definite object. . . . Information was given,

[1] *The Musician,* an educational journal edited by Thomas Tapper and published by The
Vincent Music Co. Ltd., London, ran monthly from November, 1905, to September, 1906.
In the last issue was an interesting review of Newman's recently published *Elgar* by
Edmondstoune Duncan, in which Newman's judgments are contrasted with those of
Vernon Blackburn.

inasmuch as their work has to be hurriedly displayed, or in the opinion of newspaper editors, its value ceases". It is to be regretted that we have no musical review, a periodical devoting itself to the consideration of music and matters bearing upon music apart from concert-giving or concert-going. It would appear that the English people do not read much about music, except in snippets—serio-comic lectures or perhaps mangled telegraphic reports of isolated sentences from *serious* ones. Be this as it may, we have seen during the last thirty years, the inauguration and disappearance of several periodicals, devoting themselves to the art in the way I have mentioned:— Concordia, the Musical Review and several others.[1] There has been no real support for these ventures, and our serious writers distribute their essays over the reviews and magazines. This dissemination would be a source of satisfaction to us if we knew that musical articles were welcomed by all Editors in the way that articles on painting and the drama are received, but except in RARE cases, (there ARE one or two Editors who know something of music)—the articles refer only to some sensation of the moment or to some special event. The whole panorama of music is not kept before us except in the columns of the Daily press. *It is this combination* with journalism which occasionally makes criticism fall somewhat lower than the ideal.

We need not go into the beginnings of this apparently inevitable combination; it is the natural outcome of a hurried daily press and the want of sufficient musical knowledge amongst Editors generally.

But the journalistic side has been the mainstay of such critics who, inadequately equipped, have to report on matters musical; it is so much easier to write of a definite object, such as the number of the audience or the amount of applause bestowed, dress and so forth, rather than to describe such an intangible thing as music.

[1] *Concordia*, dealing with the arts in general and edited by Joseph Bennett, was published weekly by Novello in 1875-6, but lasted only one year. The *Musical Review*, also a Novello venture and intended for educational use, came and went in 1883. *The Musical Gazette* lasted from 1899-1902, *The Musical Home Journal* from 1905-8, and in October, 1905, there appeared *The Musical Era* (the official Gazette of the Musical Reform Association Ltd., and sponsored by the so-called National College of Music, London, founded in 1898). These journals had little intrinsic merit, but, with strongly marked radical overtones, they represented a genuine desire for musical opportunity on the part of the then under-privileged.

for instance, as to the numbers of the audience, which was often quite unintentionally misleading. For instance, they read of 2,000 people present in Worcester Cathedral as 'a small audience', while 1,900 people gathered together in Birmingham or Leeds Town Hall was described as 'an enormous audience' (Laughter)".

Ms. 1   I could, in the way of lectures, conveniently . . .
Ms. 2   „   „   [δ in the way of lectures]   „
Ms. 1   in this sort of thing
Ms. 2   „   „   [δ sort of thing]

Ms. 1   . . . one of these [δ early] severe critics . . .

Ms. 2   *To read . . . of the critic* [*caret* in Ms. 1, given in Elgar's
                             hand on facing page in Ms. 2, fair
                             copied by C.A.E.]

Ms. 1   Critics *can*
Ms. 1   after only [δ reading the w] reading it. I supposed . . .
Ms. 2   after [δ only reading it] a mere perusal of it. I suppose . . .
Ms. 1   to whom [δ we have been long] *in the seventies & subsequently
             we were* indebted for illuminative analyses & criticisms.
Ms. 2   . . . to whom we were, in the . . .
Ms. 1   It is in the form . . . in our library [*caret.*]
Ms. 2   . . . and criticisms.
                     Analyses of Schubert, *masses* [in pencil]
                     & Raff
                          My own education [in pencil]
                          M.M. Review
                          Shedlock   C. A. Barry ★ [1]
             [on facing page [E.] in pencil] ★ It is . . . our library
             pure and simple★ [on facing page [E] in pencil] *music . . . facile
             description.*

                a Brahms' Symphony was given for the first time—

---

[1] Charles Ainslie Barry (1830–1915), was pupil of T. A. Walmisley, at Cambridge. He subsequently studied in Cologne, Leipzig, and Dresden, was editor of *The Monthly Musical Record* from 1875–9, and for long contributed programme notes to the Richter Concerts. He was a supporter of Liszt, and modern music generally, and a composer.

Usually an article on musical criticism contains many acid references to mistaken judgements. *I could conveniently* fill up an hour by reading you mistaken and bitter judgement on Berlioz and Wagner—written in the fifties. I see little *value in this*; it may be amusing to see how a later generation has reversed those decisions, but it is nothing more.

It would be seriously instructive if we were able to read, in his own words, the conversion of *one of those severe critics* of Wagner and Berlioz.

To read the gradual awakening of the soul, the opening of the mind to new impressions; or the closing of the heart against old prejudices as the warm feeling of the man and artist (as Hanslick from whom I quote presently says)—the warm feeling of the man and artist conquers the austere severity of the *critic*.

Critics CAN be converted, we know; I seem to remember a noble and sincere notice of Parsifal in the Athenaeum,[1] long ago, written after hearing the work—withdrawing much that had been said against the composition after a mere perusal of it. I suppose this was from the pen of Professor Prout *to whom we were*, in the seventies and subsequently, indebted for the illuminative analyses and criticisms.

It is in the form of analyses that the critic can do so much. I referred to some oversights in the analyses of Brahms' symphony. I find on looking through Mr. D. F. Tovey's exhaustive essay[2] that the motto theme is given due prominence. I am glad to say that a complete set of these analyses will be in our *library*.

There is a real difficulty in writing about music; *music pure and simple —music* connected with words opera and so forth and music written to a programme naturally lend themselves to a more facile *description*. I will not pretend to give my own views on this point but prefer to quote from an acknowledged master critic, Edward Hanslick of Vienna, premising that the translation is from the Musical World, December 22nd, 1883. The occasion was a concert at which a *Brahms Symphony was* given for the first time. I choose this also because the Symphony was *un*published and therefore not available for study. I

[1] See pp. 149–50.
[2] See p. 101.

Ms. 1   Brahms' 3rd Symphony was produced   follow on
[Here are interposed two sheets in Lady Elgar's hand
number 6 and 7, commencing] . . . conversion of one of
these severe critics of Wagner & Berlioz. Critics can be converted . . . *its various beauties* [E.]
[Various marginal annotations by E., of which the only one
not shown in some form elsewhere refers to the Brahms
Symphony] *Choose this also because the symphony is unpublished
therefore not available for study*
[The passage] *I would only say . . . Hanslick says:—* [is in
Elgar's hand on page facing no. 7. Sheet numbered 8 follows
with a quotation from Hanslick deleted. This is followed by
reduced version of quotation given in main text. Page 11
follows page 8, and the portion of the lecture succeeding the
quotation.]

Ms. 2   [Marginal note] *'tiefer' lower explain*
"Spoken language . . . render the latter" [marked by double
line in margin; see p. 158]

would only add that in this case, a critic's task was lightened by the knowledge that the work was by a famous master. The work of an unknown, or less known, man naturally requires careful attention to many details which may be taken for granted in the work of an established composer.

Hanslick says,

a perfect feast—but rather for the delighted man, and musician in us, than for the critic, who had afterwards to say what Brahms' new Symphony was like and describe its various beauties.

Now it is nothing either uncommon or incapable of explanation, for the critic's eloquence to sink the lower, the higher the composer has soared.

Spoken language is not so much a poorer language as no language at all with regard to music, for it cannot render the latter.

This was, perhaps, felt less in former and more easily satisfied times. But if, at the present day, we read the best criticisms, which appeared immediately after the first performance of Beethoven's Symphonies, and place ourselves mentally in the place of the first readers, we are compelled to confess that we have seen the announcement of some grand and beautiful music, but have gained no definite idea of its individual physiognomy.

It was not till Beethoven's Symphonies had spread far and wide and subsequent critics were able to connect what they said with something the reader knew, to assume that the reader had himself [δ also] heard and felt that we were really taught anything by the admirable Beethoven criticisms of modern times.

Brahms' Third Symphony in F major, performed on the 2nd December for the very first time, and still unpublished, has as yet no such bridge between the mass of the public and criticism, and so the latter has to rely principally upon COMPARISON with earlier and known works by the same master.

Here follows a most able and picturesque account of the work, which I do not read but I make a list of the references.

Ms. 1/2   (not Tchaikowski's not written)
Ms. 2   *the word* [Pathetic] *probably in connection with Beethoven*
                                          Sonata [in pencil]
Ms. 1/   C Minor Sym. Brahms
Ms. 2   IN 25 LINES   Faust [Ms. 2 only] (*Goethe's*)
                                         Ninth Symphony Beethoven
                                         2nd Sym Brahms
                                         Beethoven   thunder
                                         Mozart ⎫
                                                     ⎬ voices of
                                         Haydn ⎭
              [Ms. 1] only thirteen   Schumann & Mendelssohn
              references to extraneous things
Ms. 1   [δ After] The *masterly* & vivid descriptive [δ reference to]
              ends & Hanslick [written into Ms. 2 as Hauslick by C.A.E.]
              proceeds

              [At this point followed by sheet numbered 13 in Lady Elgar's
              hand with passage] feel aggrieved . . . 'talent for' [See below.]
Ms. 2   "As, however, . . . entire work" [*caret in Ms. 1, on sheet*
                                         formerly marked 13, renumbered as 12]

              This is a somewhat . . . his own work as unsatisfactory from an
              incompleteness which is unavoidable [δ *incompleteness*] . . . *com-*
              posers, PERFORMERS & *readers . . . sometimes feel*   [in Elgar's
                                                                    hand]

Ms. 2   Hauslick [*sic*] proceeds: *after suggesting music type*
              "another   method . . . 'talent for' [on sheet numbered 13]

              I pause here [δ to remark upon the last sentence]: Hauslick

Eroica—the word probably in connection with the Beethoven
   Sonata.
Pathetic. Beethoven not *Tschaikowski*, as that was not written.
Appassionata.
Pastoral.
C. Minor Symphony. Brahms.
Beethoven, thunder, 13 references.
Voices of Mozart, Haydn, Schumann and Mendelssohn.

The masterly and vivid description ends and Hanslick proceeds:—
"All this is properly speaking idle talk—the Symphony must be heard
and not read.

   "It is certain that a few short examples in musical notation of the
principal themes in the new Symphony would tell the reader more
about it than all our description."

   This is an amplification of the opening sentences of this article:—
"Spoken language is no language at all etc."

   "As, however, Brahms runs over with surprises, and as what he
develops from the motives is often a great deal more important than
the motives themselves, a musical paper—(and only such a paper can
indulge in the luxury of examples in musical notation)—would have
gradually to print half the score, and then refer us, after all, to the
entire *work*."

   This is a somewhat disappointing view to take. If an expert critic
looks upon his own work as unsatisfactory from an incompleteness
which *is unavoidable* it is not surprising that *composers, performers and
reader sometimes feel* aggrieved at the inadequacy of some of the musical
criticisms.

                                    (*after suggesting* music type)
"*Another method,* the poetically pictorial which renders the impression
received into a series of finished pictures, subjects for ballads, and
chapters of romance, is repugnant to my conviction of the purely
musical significance of an instrumental work; besides I do not possess
the 'talent for sound pictures' of which the otherwise musical Heine
could boast, and which, a poet by the grace of God, he proved practically in many a genial description of music he possessed.["]

   I pause here; Hanslick will not, in describing a purely instrumental

[*sic*] will not . . . pictures. * *In the face of* . . . 'elevates &
refreshes us' [in pencil on facing page]

Ms. 1   [page formerly 16, renumbered as 15]   [δ orchestral music
                    After all] *In conclusion* Hanslick [δ critic &]
                    practised critic . . . AND musician; [δ concludes]
                    frankly, but it must *also* be admitted, rather
                    lamely, *but* lamely only . . .
[On facing page] * *It is true* . . . '*refreshes us*' [cf. Ms. 2 as
shown above]

Ms. 2   Hauslick [*sic*] [δ practised] keen critic, & [δ cultured]
practised writer AND [δ practised] *cultured* musician; . . .

Ms. 1   "Thus . . . instrumental music" [written in by C.A.E.]

Ms. 2   *Then follow* Some references
Ms. 1   on this [δ criticism] *article* at some length because it [δ appears
          to me to] throws much [deletion] light
Ms. 2   article at [δ some] length
Ms. 1   musical criticism, & [δ to] explains *why* [δ if explanation
          here *is* necessary, the reason that so m] so much extraneous
          matter . . .
Ms. 1   . . . anxious to [δ hear read] learn

          current of apology [δ etic comment for the poverty of the
          writer [?]] for the impossibility . . . in [δ mere] *bare* words any
          notion [δ of] the *beyond mere* scope . . .
Ms. 2   * "*Language* . . . *music*" [on facing page]

Ms. 1   [δ I have no wish to] *Now if this difficulty is*
          . . . journalistic criticism?
                    [δ I do not refer to We get too often a [?] variety &
          this excepts & excuse? But it is upon a foundation of journal-
          istic criticism that that]
Ms. 2   *or to the writer*

Ms. 1   . . . one instance of *what may be considered an absolute* [δ mis]
          a—judgement [δ which]; this, written

[Marginal note] M.M.R. Nov. 1879

work, read into it, or out of it, a series of pictures. In the face of this disclaimer we must note that Hanslick allows himself to call the opening theme of the last movement 'a sultry figure' foreboding a storm—a storm which breaks forth into a magnificent tempest which clears the air—'elevates and refreshes us'.

It is possible that, in allowing themselves great freedom in this respect, critics have done much more than is sometimes suspected to encourage and develop the modern descriptive tone-poems. *In conclusion*, Hanslick keen critic, practised writer AND cultured musician, frankly, but it must also be admitted, rather lamely but lamely only in comparing the necessary limitations of musical criticisms with any other, says, "*Thus*, nothing is left for me save simply to express my delight at the new Symphony, in which we have gained one of the most beautiful and ripest creations of modern instrumental *music*".

Then follow some references to the orchestration, COMPARATIVE only; and some general remarks—also comparative—conclude the notice.

I have dwelt *on this article at length* because it throws *much light* on the difficulties of musical criticism, and explains why *so much extraneous* matter is inserted in some critiques.

Here we have seen an important occasion—the production of a symphony by the greatest living composer of his day—we have the musical world *anxious to learn* everything possible regarding the new composition, and through the whole of the article, admirable though it is, runs a strong *current of apology* for the impossibility to convey in bare words any notion beyond the mere scope and tendency of the work.

"Language is less than no language at all when used in reference to *music*".

Now if this difficulty is always present, if it is felt when ample time is allowed a writer to prepare his article, how much more must it tell upon hurried *journalistic criticism*?

I suppose nothing can be more irritating to an artist or *to the writer* than a misjudgement, and as such things have occurred and will in all probability occur again, I give *one instance of what* might be considered an absolute mis-judgement: this written in all seriousness, seems surprising. I regret to say I am old enough to remember its appearance in 1879.

Ms. 2   [On facing page in pencil] *The occasion was the first per-*
formance in England of the Suite from Sylvia by Léo Délibes. Now
if there is anything modern French—it is Délibes

Ms. 1   the Suite [δ arranged] from
but this [deletion] w^d scarcely be perceptible

Ms. 2   „   „   [δ would scarcely be] *is not*

Ms. 1   . . . in the Suite,—[δ *it*] *the* [δ *use of the leitmotiv*] [δ *is of course,*]
the use of the leitmotiv obvious [δ *obvious*] in the whole work.
The score includes 2 cornets with *in addition* to the usual
2 trumpets . . .

Ms. 1   The [δ passage] *critique*
        A *take in*
                Returning to the . . . to do so.
                It is not so very long ago   [on inserted sheet]
        . . . idea of a composition. **A** 22 *take in*
Returning to the journalistic / dual nature of newspaper
cutting side / It is not easy to keep the two par / I have always
kept the two departments, in my own mind HOWEVER quite
distinct. I wish / that critics w^d do so also / it could always
be so
        [followed by]
                                It is not so *very* long ago . . . [see below]

Ms. 2   *Returning . . . does for instance* [in pencil on facing page]
        [δ contrast Wagner & Délibes
        In journalistic work we [in pencil]]
        There are some details which detract from the dignity
        of musical criticism. For instance to say there was an
        'average attendance'
Such [in pencil] [δ Such] information [δ *is often quite mis-*
leading] regarding the enumeration (real or implied) of the
audience *is often quite unintentionally misleading* [in pencil]
trouble to hear it [δ *is*] *must be considered to be*
★ *Leaving . . . uncultured audiences* [in pencil on facing page ★]
as evinced by attendances
([δ holding] *seating* say 3,200) [See *Birm. Post*, p. 166.]

"The form in which '. . . . .' " (I omit the name for the moment) "casts his thoughts and modes of expression has already been made familiar to the public by Herr Richard Wagner: but there is sufficient evidence of originality to justify the hope that time will show him the need of self-reliance." Further:— "It is very cleverly written, capitally scored, and full of attractive melody".[1]

The piece referred to was the Suite, taken from the Ballet 'Sylvia' by Leo Delibes.

Delibes used the LEITMOTIV to a certain extent but this is not perceptible in *the Suite,—the use of the leitmotiv* is of course obvious in the whole work. The score includes two trumpets and a harp but there is nothing

unusual in such additions. *The critique* is wholly inexplicable to me and I quote it only to show how it is possible for a serious judgement, entirely well-meant to give a quite erroneous *idea of a composition.*

Returning to the dual nature of newspaper criticism, it is not easy to keep the two departments quite distinct. In journalistic work we are sometimes given details which may be necessary but in no way add to the dignity of musical criticism—audiences, receipts and *dress for instance. Such information* regarding the enumeration (real or implied) of the audience is often quite unintentionally misleading. Every person devoted to good music and taking the trouble *to hear it, must be considered* to be of the same importance—it matters not if they pay a guinea for a seat in Birmingham or Liverpool or one shilling in Gloucester or Hereford. *Leaving for a* moment the question of cultured or uncultured *audiences.* But, accustomed to judge of the size of audiences in halls which they frequent most, critics sometimes make some curious remarks regarding the success or popularity of a work *as evinced by attendances.* We read of a performance in Worcester Cathedral *seating say 3,200*[2] "a small audience gathered to hear etc. etc." showing that ["]* * * has not penetrated to the country etc. etc." Of a performance in Birmingham Town Hall (holding 2,300)—"An

---

[1] *The Monthly Musical Record*, November 1, 1879, p. 174, in a contribution entitled "Crystal Palace Concerts".

[2] See p. 75.

... the works of ... [δ have] *has on an enlightened etc. etc.*
present) *Statistics* (Number *present* 1900
So ...

... performances [δ in the provinces ...]
of the [δ London] papers ...

Ms. 1   [Main text resumed]
It is not so *very* long ago that [δ they]
writers were called reporters

Ms. 2   ... writer of *even* musical criticisms [deletion] were called
reporters:

Ms. 1   [δ Now when the recipient of a criticism is pleased he calls
the man/ The dignity of their position [δ should] requires all
critics to devolve the journalistic [δ side] work as much as
possible upon journalists. Mixed to / with musical criticism
such things as 'average attendances' [δ are out of place] jar
somewhat & *detract from the interest & dignity of criticism.*
Besides the information given is often quite misleading
regarding [δ numbers] enumeration ...
[passage previously missing in Ms. 1] ... 1900
enormous
[Emendations in this passage] [δ Leeds] *Liverpool*;
[δ Gloucester or Norwich] Gloucester or [δ Worcester]
Hereford.
[Continuation]
[δ I will not pursue the
To turn to the critical side [δ we next] we may congratulate
ourselves [δ on the personal [?] of]
It will be said ... presentation of a work.
The dignity of the musical critic is now assured [δ & it is to]
we will now consider [δ ation of] what we owe to the [δ great]
men [δ who have occupied & still happily occupy the place
and not only occupy but fill & fill nobly the place of our
leaders] who should help us ... function of the critic [δ It is
surely within their power / the power]

Ms. 2   ... * *running* ... *complex art* on facing page

Ms. 1   ... that we [δ sometimes let] *occasionally* expect
we are inclined

enormous audience assembled showing the hold the works of ★ ★ ★ *has on an enlightened etc.* etc. Number present 1900. So we see that, for the purposes of enthusiasm, 2,000 is a small audience and 1900 enormous. It will be said that this is a trivial point: so it is, but this sort of thing is to be deprecated on account of the effect it has on the prospects of a new work. *Subsequent performances* depend in a large measure upon the *reports of the papers* and anything tending to depreciate the general effect has an influence in deciding committees and conductors who cannot be present, as to their presentation of a work.

It is not so very long ago that writers of even musical criticisms were called reporters: the Times used to print notices of provincial Festivals and so on,—"From our own reporter"—Now we say "From our own correspondent".

This dignity of the position of the musical critic is assured and we will proceed to consider what we owe to the men, the true critics amongst them, who help us, guide us and lead us to higher things— such I believe to be the true function of critics. We are happy in seeing this function nobly fulfilled in some of the writers of our day. Culture, style, and a picturesque fancy *running* side by side with an experience born of practical acquaintance with the many sides and sidelights of

our *complex art.* The sphere of the critic has been so many times defined and so variously *that we occasionally* expect too much. We *are inclined,*

[inserted page numbered 26]

it is only natural we should expect
. . . met with [written by C.A.E. Continued by E.] These
gentlemen or [deletion] ladies confine themselves usually to
the comparison of pianists—an exhilarating & amusing
pursuit but which after all does not do much for art.

Now [δ it is] I have said [δ that we expect from our critics]
that in the equipment of a critic we wish for experience. In
their written   [end of page 26]
exposition of *containing* [followed by page beginning]
inclined unconsciously [See p. 188 **E**]
[page numbered 27] the virtues of each school

Ms. 2   „   „   „   „ [δ school]
Ms. 1   . . . we do not find
Ms. 2   . . . we do not [δ often] find
Ms. 1   . . . and we ask
Ms. 2   . . . and we *dare* ask
Ms. 1   musical *prodigies* it is only natural we should [δ have] *expect*
critical prodigies also—at any rate there are to be met with a
few such—whose only recommendation for their self-chosen
task w^d· appear to be [δ an en] a certain amount of ungram-
matical leisure.

[Page [page also numbered 27] continuing from] In their
written [above]
[δ critics I will now slightly [δ st] go over what we receive]
written word we ask for reasons. We do not want to be
merely told that this or that thing is wrong: we would like
to know why it is wrong or why the critic thinks it wrong.
Many of our best men tell us this. I have never known
criticism to hurt or to annoy if a reason is given. In the days of
unsigned articles this *want* was more felt than now when
many articles are signed: we know, or should know, the likes
& dislikes of the signatory & the school of thought in which
he was brought up & we know therefore in many instances
the cause of his praise or condemnation.

Nothing delights me, as a musician [page numbered 28]
and as a student of English than the prose of Mr. Joseph
Bennett: I have the greater pleasure in saying this as we do
not agree on many points— & some of his most drastic
sentences have been in [δ directed against] *my* direction; but

unconsciously, to fuse together a number of ideal critics and expect to find in one critique a crystallised *exposition containing* the virtues of each.

Naturally we *do not often find* this; we cannot insist on the qualifications of our teachers and we dare ask for only one thing—experience: happily most of our critics have this to give us.

It is true in these days *of prodigies,—musical prodigies*—it is only *natural we should expect critical* prodigies also—at any rate, a few such are to be met with.

the full & clear—the *sane* & reasonable fullness [δ & clearne] make his criticisms always valuable & I will add, as far as I am concerned, welcome: we have here a strong man, of clear & decided views, views which are not trimmed to suit occasions writing in clear nervous English *at its best* a type of what English criticism [δ shd. be at its best] shd. be: honest fearless & reasonable.

Ms. 1   [on facing page *]

            * There are many younger writers of whom I could write in the same [δ strain [Ms. 2 similar strain]] *& with very similar admiration* but I instance Mr. Bennett as the patriarch & [δ model] DOYEN [[Ms. 2] head] of the profession

It would be pleasant to give extracts from various writers on the same work . . .

Ms. 2   [Above passage on pp. 26–29, but on reverse of p. 26—]

* We have won our way through [δ some] the use of unnecessary technical terms & *a somewhat uneconomical use of* foreign expressions which have an equally valuable counterpart in English.

The use of

[interpolated sheet by E. in pencil between pp. 26 and 27] The use of English words, sweet old words used in their primal sense [δ has grown to be] is now [δ correct] *returning* & I have watched with pleasure that some of our younger critics are saying a 'PIECE' of music as did our forefathers. A portion of an immeasurable whole is a piece.

Erasmus writes, a German, 'I have learnt to love Rhenish wine. & I will so deal here that every year I will have a little piece of Rhenish wine'.[1]

Not confusing, as does the child, the word with the actual piece of paper on which the music is printed.

[cf. the whole of the above with *Birm. Post*]

Birm.   "They did not want to be merely told that this or that was
Post   wrong; they would like to know why it was wrong, and why the critic thought it was wrong. Many of the best men of the present day told them this: and he had never known criticism to hurt or annoy if a reason was given. In the days

---

[1] Erasmus ". . . delighted in . . . everything English, in fact, save the beer and the draughty rooms" T. M. Lindsay, *Cambridge History of English Literature*, 1909, III, p. 2.

English criticism should be—honest, fearless and reasonable.—There are *many younger writers* of whom I could write in the similar strain and with very similar admiration but I instance Mr. *Bennett as the* patriarch and head of the profession.

of unsigned articles this want was more felt than now, when many articles were signed. They now knew, or should know, the likes and dislikes of the signatory, and the school of thought in which he was brought up, and, therefore, in many instances they knew the cause of his praise or condemnation. They had won their way from the use of unnecessary technical terms and the somewhat uneconomical use of foreign expressions which had their equally valuable equivalent in English (Hear, hear). Criticisms of the critics were now to be extended to the people, and the use of English—sweet old words used in their primary sense—was now returning. Nothing delighted him more as a musician and as a student of English than the prose of Mr. Joseph Bennett (Applause). He had the greater pleasure in saying this because they did not agree on several points, and some of Mr. Bennett's most drastic sentences had been in his direction (Laughter). There were some younger writers, too, of whom he could speak in somewhat similar terms. Sir Edward was of the opinion that a most interesting and useful volume could be formed of the writings of the critics of the past twenty years, a volume formed not with the idea of setting up one critic against another, but with the idea of gaining wisdom from the multitude of counsellors. There was no such work extant, and, with a sufficient index, it would be of the greatest possible use.

Ms. 2   It [δ would be pleasant] *is invariably interesting* to [δ give extracts from] *read the opinions of* various writers on the same works: I venture to suggest *that such a collection* [δ this] might form a volume [δ far more *and a most* valuable contribution to musical literature if] of extracts . . . gathered together * [in pencil on facing page] It wd. form . . . literature ; not *formed* with any view . . .

Ms. 1   . . . in Manchester I should [δ say he was the best critic we have ever had] *place him very high*
Ms. 1   gave him [δ a] *great* distinction
of men—[δ acted upon his] assisted his . . .

It is invariably *interesting* to read the opinions of various writers on *the same work*: I venture to suggest that such a collection might form a volume. If extracts from various criticisms on the same work, or on the same performance of a work, could be gathered together, it would form a valuable contribution to musical literature; not formed with any idea of playing off one critic against another, but to arrive at the result, which from a multitude of such counsellors should be wisdom.

I do not agree with all the views, held by the late Arthur Johnstone, and I have never read a word of his criticism on my own works; but referring only to his own writings on the classics and large works produced in *Manchester, I should place* his very high. His training at Cologne Conservatorium *gave him great* distinction and his knowledge of things outside music—things and forces which go to make human beings *of men*—assisted his judgement in literature, art and music in a

* A collection . . . expressed by the writer [* on facing page]

	naturally [δ so great a] so fascinating

naturally [δ so great a] so fascinating
the truth it [δ much] somewhat needed

Ms. 2   the truth [δ was] it [δ somewhat] needed *in some quarters.*

Birm.   (Laughter)
Post

Ms. 1   . . . of practical matter, [δ a solidity] or to put it chemically [δ there was in solution in the] volatile & pellucid fluid [δ matter/ a solid] *held in solution matter* which was precipitated . . .

Ms. 2   . . . introduction of [δ its] *the* reader's own common sense.
Birm.   (Laughter)
Post

Ms. 2   [δ The] *His* imitators give us the *watery* fluid without the *useful* precipitate.

Birm.   (Laughter)
Post

Ms. 1   [δ We have also the poetic prose of Vernon Blackburn]
              read Vernon Blackburn.
          . . . suffers [δ from] therefrom: poetical [δ cannot go into the varying other]

it must have been the [δ residue] atom

farther north".* [On facing page] * *It is true . . . less possible*

wonderful way. *A collection* of his criticisms is about to be published[1] and if any student here is going to devote himself to literature, I advise him to study the clear and incisive English, the absolute correct use of every word, without I may add, adopting all the opinions expressed *by the writer.*

The lively and unstable pen of Bernard Shaw fluttered over the page of the Star in 1890, and subsequently in the world to our great amusement: *naturally so fascinating* a writer produced a host of imitators and gave a new life to musical criticism which, to say the truth it *needed in* some quarters. But in Bernard Shaw's writing there was

always a substratum of *practical matter,* or to put it chemically to volatile and pellucid fluid, held in solution, matter which was precipitated into obvious solid fact by the introduction of the reader's *own common sense.* His imitators give us the watery fluid without the useful *precipitate.*

We have also the poetic writer: not poetic without knowledge of the practical side and I venture to read an article or portion of it, by a master of this style.

Quotation from Vernon Blackburn.[2]

The rhapsodical, poetical style has very much gone to seed in America and music *suffers therefrom*: *poetical descriptive* work is all very well but to be of value, it must *have the atom* of practical experience which is to be found in the extract I have read.

Other writers are known to you: I speak with admiration of a critic gone from among us, Mr. Ernest Newman—a champion of the new school and an author of repute; it is a regret to me that he has left Birmingham to take up an important post "somewhere *farther north*".[3]

[1] Arthur Johnstone, *Musical Criticisms*, Manchester University Press, 1905; see notice in *The Musical Standard*, December 23, 1905, pp. 401–2.
[2] See p. 164.
[3] cf. p. 154.

Ms. 2   *It is true . . . less possible* [* on facing page, in pencil, ending]
In connection with the library now forming thanks to Newman

Ms. 1   [δ But apart from these] I would mention

          . . . concerning [δ sol   solo singers] executants

in a small measure
some *quantity of bad* * *infinitesimal* . . . *criticism* [* on facing
page]

[δ That foul unforgettable article]
[δ some articles] that *event* was connected . . .

          [page labelled **D**, renumbered 35]
Ms. 1/   . . . English critics
Ms. 2   Orchestration
                    ―――
                    piano playing
                    ―――
                    pt singing
          [page labelled **E**]
Ms. 1   . . . not [δ meant] well meant

It is true we do not agree on several points, but I have never found difference of opinion make daily intercourse with real strong men *less possible.*

Mr. Baughan of the Daily News, another writer who gives reasons for his views, and Mr. Kalisch worthily represent the best side of musical criticism. *I would* mention all others in detail but I have said enough to show that in the matter of musical criticism we are, as I said last week *concerning executants,* able to hold our own with other countries.

I will not refer in detail to the shady side of musical criticism—but we know that it, *in a small measure* exists and we deplore it. It would be folly to ignore the fact that some quantity of *bad, infinitesimal* in comparison with the good, exists even now. The things to be regretted come [more] naturally from journalism than criticism.

That foul unforgettable episode—the article on the dead Sullivan—has happily found no counterpart In the lesser journals, *that event was* connected with journalism not with musical criticism and it is distinctly understood that the music[al] [critic] of the paper was in no way responsible.[1]

We have still articles purposely written for the annoyance, it would seem, of anybody in particular. One of our reviews prefers to use tryginonic ink in preference to the usual fluid, but on the whole the world is better and happier for the existence of *our English critics.*

In conclusion: I recommend the young artist not to run away with the idea that adverse criticism[is bad]—it MAY do him good. Above all, do not let him insist that it is not well meant.

[1] J. A. Fuller Maitland, "Sir Arthur Sullivan", in the *Cornhill Magazine*, March, 1901, pp. 300–9. Two excerpts indicate why Elgar expressed himself as he did, but it *was* the music critic, rather than the journalist, at fault:

"There is no need to assign a motive for the composer's increasing habit of writing down to his public; it does not concern us to decide whether the cause of his growing banality of style was the common one of financial ambition or the more laudable desire for even more popularity than he had" (p. 307).

"In 'The Lost Chord' he appealed to the most sentimental emotions of the masses, and in such tunes as 'Onward, Christian Soldiers' and 'The Absent-minded Beggar' he won the heart of the man in the street. These last two scarcely stand, indeed, on the same plane, for the hymn-tune, vulgar as it is for its own purpose, is not a bad march, while the setting of Kipling's words must surely rank as the least happily inspired of all the tunes that have ever attained wide popularity" (p. 308).

. . . opera of course excepted, and [end of page marked **E** followed by page marked 27, cf. p. 178]

inclined unconsciously,   to [δ put] *fuse* together [δ the] *a* number of ideal critics & expect *to find* in one critique [δ to find] *an* crystallised exposition of the [δ whole] virtues of each school. But we

[δ do] must insist on experience

[In margin] * We want our critics to teach us & to lead us: this can only be done I quote Leslie Stephen

'We must start from experience. We must begin by asking impartially what pleased men, & then again *why* it pleased them.

We must not decide dogmatically that it ought to have pleased or displeased on the simple ground that it is or is not congenial to ourselves". [cf. pp. 57, 155, 156]

[page labelled **F**]

. . . utterances of [δ our] critics:

Ms. 1	[δ my] words would allow
Ms. 2	,, [δ would allow] could say
Ms. 1	. . . executants, [δ words,] a tribute
	. . . here [δ & never will]
	. . . lecture I [δ tha] say
	gentlemen [δ who] to whom
	in great measure

Birm.	except in a few cases
Post	
Ms. 2	*the last of this series*
Ms. 1	[On reverse of final page, in pencil]
	[δ Some things arouse distrust as to the powers of the critics in the minds of the young—we know better, when the]

Things new do not always strike home and require consideration: perhaps judgements on music—music in performance—are sometimes too severe. As I said before preventing a second hearing. A musical work cannot be put on for a number of performances—opera of course excepted, and a little more leniency sometimes would be grateful.

Nothing would have been more easy than to collect and ridicule some of the *utterances of critics*: I have refrained from that cheap course, hoping to show how much we owe to and, I will add, hope from them.

Last week I paid the highest tribute *words could say* to our English *executants, a tribute,* I regret to learn which was unanimously rejected by the amiable persons who condense my lectures; my personal feelings have never *been obtruded here except* in my last paragraph.

Last week, then, I paid a tribute to English executants and at the close of this lecture I *say our thanks are due to the gentlemen* to whom is committed *in great measure* the keeping of artistic characters: to whom we look for guidance and help and from whom, except in *some notorious cases,* we obtain these things in full measure.

My lecture next week, *the last of this series,* will fitly cover the whole question raised in my inaugural address.

Professor Fiedler, remarked Lady Elgar, found the lecture a "great intellectual treat". *The Musical Standard* noted as improbable Elgar's abstention from reading notices of his own works:

"I do not agree with all the views held by the late Arthur Johnstone of 'The Manchester Guardian,' and I have never read a word of his criticism of myself; but referring only to his writings on the classics and large works produced in Manchester, I should place him very high amongst the highest." Thus Sir Edward Elgar in the course of his lecture on December 6 at Birmingham University. It seems very extraordinary to us that Sir Edward should have read only those of Johnstone's criticisms that did not deal with his (Elgar's) compositions. We have always found that composers are more anxious to read criticisms of their own works than criticisms of the works of others, especially when written by a man who should be placed "very high amongst the highest" in his craft.

At a later point the proposal for a new musical journal won approval:

We regret, too, that there is no musical review of the character outlined by Sir Edward. Certainly we ought to have the musical equivalent of—say—"The Fortnightly Review" or "The Contemporary Review." Musicians, however, are notoriously idle readers. A wealthy lover of music might, however, do worse than agree to stand the loss—if any—of such a review. There are signs of a growing interest in musical literature: the many books issued within the last few years devoted to the subject of music clearly show that this is the case, for we may assume that the London publishers know what they are about, and would not issue volume after volume if there were no financial gain thereby.[1]

[1] *The Musical Standard*, December 16, 1905, p. 383.

CHAPTER 9

RETROSPECT
(December 13, 1905)

ON December 9, according to Lady Elgar, Elgar received a "Nice telegram from J[oseph] Bennett re storm raised by E's lecture being wrongly or misleadingly reported". On the next day the preparation of the final lecture of the series began, Elgar being determined to answer his critics. He worked on the evening of December 10, was reported as "going on" on December 11, and "finishing" on December 12. Thus, for once, he finished with a day to spare. Living up to the tradition of reporting as noted by Elgar the *Manchester Guardian* of December 14 remarked: "There was again a good attendance."

Rough Notes

[Sheet 1]

[δ That suggestion has been the subject of some shallow [δ crit] remarks. which apparently shew the difficulty of talking about music [or is to be?]]

[δ That] The suggestion that young men sh^{d.} draw inspiration from their own country has been the subject of some shallow remarks
[δ They are] It has been said that all composers have drawn inspiration from foreign lands. True. But the nationality of the composer has not been obscured by his so doing. We know that 'Carmen' with its Spanish colouring is of the French school & that Moskowski's Spanish dances[1] are, with all their Spanish flavour by an Eastern European [See p. 203.]

[2]

2

See Discoverie of Errors p 717
"It is enough for me, that I have done this, and I have

---

[1] Moritz Moszkowski, *Spanische Tänze für das Pianoforte zu vier Händen*, Op. 12, 2 vol., Carl Simon, Berlin, 1876.

gained as much as I looke for, if I shall draw others into this Argument, whether etc. etc

"I will comfort my selfe with *Mimnérmus*[1] his Distich & so cease

(shd be Greek)

Oblectes animum, plebs est morosa legendo
Ille benè de te dicet, ut ille malè

———

Heart take thine ease,
Men hard to please
Thou haply mayst offend.
Though one speake ill
Of thee, some will
Say better:— There an end.   [See p. 225.][2]
[On reverse of last page of Ms. 2 of *A Retrospect*, in pencil:]

I would naturally prefer a good building to a bad one a perfect Queen Anne House is more satisfying to the eye than an imitation Gothic. A good symphonic-poem is much better than a bad symphony.

But if we give up absolute music where are we logically to end? Are we to be led back by symbolism to ideograms & *is* music to become a mere series of labels or chemical formulae of the emotions. The argument in favour [δ starts?] of pictorial music starts well & seems a broad open road— but I fear if followed up will be like a forest road—narrow into a foot way—for one & then dwindle into a squirrel track & run up a tree. [See p. 208.]

---

[1] For Mimnermus, see Thomas Gaisford, *Poetae Minores Graeci*, 3 vol., Oxford, 1814: I, pp. 419-20. Mimnermus, Colophonicus, Solonis aequalis: poeta mollis, suavis, et Gratiarum alumnus: . . . vixisse Olympiade XXXVII . . . See also Strabo, I, p. 80; XIV, p. 940; R. F. P. Brunck, *Gnomici Poetae Graeci*, 1784.

[2] Elgar here refers to the rarest book in his collection (of which there are very few copies to be found anywhere): *A Discoverie of Errours in the first Edition of the Catalogue of Nobility, published by Raphe [sic] Brooke, Yorke Herald, 1619 . . . by Augustine Vincent, Rouge-croix Pursuivant of Armes*, London, William Jaggard, 1622. The prose quotation in full runs: ". . . . *Boni venatoris est aliquid capere, non omnia*. Here is a good Huntsman that can catch some not all: Other men may finde out more. It is enough for me, that I have done this, and I have gained as much as I looke for, if I shall draw others into this Argument, whether they undertake a new Worke, or amend this, And therefore, neyther puft up with opinion that ought is well, neither dejected with Feare that it will not take well, I will comfort my selfe. . . ."

Hazelwood,
Coppice Road,
Moseley.

My dear Edward

You have done a fine thing for our English Financial Art. Your address was a noble effort and a notable achievement. Putting aside personal attitude — which I am not likely to

Thank you for all the kind encouraging you spoke. The future is hopeful indeed.

We are all proud of you & are likely tomorrow to applaud you. Forever

[3]

[δ & would] we naturally prefer a good building to a bad one. a perfect Queen Anne house is more satisfying than a mere imitation gothic. A good symphonic poem is better—much better than a poor symphony. But if we give up absolute music where are we logically to end? Are we to be led back by way of symbolism to ideograms & is music to become a mere series of labels, like chemical formulae of the emotions.

The argument in favour of pictorial music starts well & seems a broad open road, but if followed will—like a forest route—narrow into a path way for one & perhaps dwindle into a squirrel track & run up a tree

[4]

Is the idea that from these gatherings much real good [δ will] results & will result? I think not. They touch the people. [δ upon whom you know I depend.] When the Salvation Army[1] began [deletion] in a small way and even later when [δ in] its greater being, much was said against its *methods & its aims*. It has lived thro' this *stage* & it has reached the people in a way that religion—or it may be religionism—has not done [δ The competition *festival* in music will do what for music but] and it is now looked upon by most serious church-men as a valuable adjunct to their own mission. [See p. 217]

The competition festival [δ will] has in music [δ taken the same place] done similar work [See pp. 215, 219]

[5]

Is it fanciful to turn to the people when we see what their betters do? [δ when we survey] we are all tired of Macaulay's New Zealander: but [δ I tremble at] let us sadden ourselves with the thought that [deletion] the antipodean artist may have anticipated somewhat / may not be waiting to see [δ our] a figure of departed glory in the ruins of St. Paul's: he may have been sketching the English Opera House & alas!

---

[1] The Salvation Army was established under this name in 1878 by William Booth (1829–1912). George Bernard Shaw's *Major Barbara* was produced at the Court Theatre, London, on November 28, 1905.

Irving's theatre[1] in their new guise as music halls & he may
even have learnt something of our real musical [deletion]
taste & enthusiasms from a contemplation of the ruins of
St. James' Hall. [See p. 219.]

[1] Sir Henry Irving (b. 1838) died on October 13, 1905. The Lyceum became famous
during the period in which Irving was lessee and manager (1878–99). From 1899 to 1902
the theatre was controlled by a limited liability company, Irving still acting as manager.
In 1902 the company went into liquidation, and the Lyceum, now without Irving, lost
its glamour. For the next few years it was a music-hall.

TEXTUAL COMMENTARY

Ms. 1   the suggestion [δ was made to me that I]
[δ First] I doubted
After my own personal [δ fear] *doubt* was removed I still
hesitated for a reason which I will make clear to you

Ms. 2   And after I had been persuaded *that I might occupy the chair*
[C.A.E. *even if I could not fill it* I stil . . .
and M.G.]

Ms. 1   [δ I have heard with pain by almost every] We know have known . . .
[δ that the professional ranks of mus] among musicians the professional ranks are sadly overflowing

Ms. 2   sadly over [δ flowing] *crowded*

Ms. 1   . . . young artists [δ and alas! not only young artists]
of their art
Music has made

Ms. 2   „   *we know* [in pencil] has made

Ms. 1   . . . in England [δ we know]

Ms. 2   . . . or less years *we know* [in pencil]

Ms. 1   . . . of this [δ joyful]

that [δ our] *the* multiplicity of *our*
. . . mediocrities: [δ I will not contest that point but it is not
ser absolutely necessary for]
* *although . . . the situation.*   on facing page *

Ms. 2   *or never comes at all* [in pencil]

Ms. 1   [δ Certa] It is certain

Ms. 2   *It is* [δ C] *certain* [δ it is] that

Ms. 1   if we do *take infinite pains to* produce mediocrities *in music*

Ms. 2   take infinite pains and *yet produce* . . .

Ms. 1   . . . we must put up with them

Ms. 2   [δ take] *bear* the responsibility:

RETROSPECT

A year ago *when the suggestion*, a very flattering one, was made to me, that I should be the first occupant of the Richard Peyton Chair of Music in the University, I hesitated for several reasons.

I doubted very seriously my own abilities and I pondered equally seriously upon the possibilities of working for any good in this new sphere. *And after I had been persuaded* that I might occupy the Chair even if I could not fill it, I still hesitated for a reason which I will make clear to you.

We have known for a long time reminders have reached me, post after post, for the last five years at least, *that among musicians*, the *professional ranks are sadly overcrowded*: that there is a difficulty for *young artists* in every department *of their art*, to find what I will call simply remunerative employment. And this difficulty does not apply to young artists only.

Music, *we know, has made* vast strides *in England* during this last thirty *or less years*— that side of the question need not detain us now; but by the side of *this very gratifying* increase of music in the way of performances and the rest, we appear to be face to face with the fact that artists of all kinds are educated for public life in excess of any demand likely to be made for their artistic services. It has been said, not by me, that *the multiplicity of our music-schools* up and down the country tend to produce *mediocrities*: *that statement* I will not contest now, and it is for the moment, beside the point, because it is not only the mediocrities who suffer from excess of numbers *although* it might be possible to prove that the absence of mediocrities would simplify the *situation*. Many good and capable artists are sorrowfully waiting for a time of recognition which comes so *slowly or never comes at all. It is certain that if we do take infinite pains, and yet produce mediocrities* in music, we must *bear the responsibility*; *we have no Upper House in music, we cannot make them peers.*

Ms. 1   [δ we cannot make them peers, *neither can we* / cannot make them fellows / wearily make the best of: we are]

Ms. 2   *we have no Upper House in Music* we cannot make them peers [δ We cannot make them fellows]

Ms. 1   encourage [δ not in the wa]

Ms. 2   [δ not in the way of musical education]

Ms. 1   . . . presents [δ small] *lessening*

Birm. Post   . . . aspirants (Applause)
                    . . . Professor of Music (Renewed applause)

Ms. 1   *for reasons I have given*
Birm. Post   for others; (Laughter)
Ms. 1   apparently [δ every] any one
          I have no doubt . . . shews [*sic*] the . . . [deleted and rewritten]

Ms. 1   . . . feels to a University
Ms. 2   concerning music as a profession
Ms. 1   . . . gowns and hoods [δ & degrees]: usually suggesting a list of *immediate* recipients of honorary degrees [δ which list contained very naturally / containing / *included* the writer.] Which lists gracefully & easily . . .
Birm.Post. . . of the writer (Laughter)
Ms. 1   evidently *from* disappointed students
                    plan
Ms. 2   [δ plan] *scheme*
Ms. 1   . . . which they thought wd. be
Ms. 2   [δ thought] *were kind enough to think* wd. be
Ms. 1   *my own being unknown.*
Birm. Post   . . . unknown. (Laughter)

Ms. 1   I am here to [δ make] *ask* you *to* think

I asked myself then, should I be justified in encouraging the erection of another centre, as it were, from which music should be definitely encouraged; *encouraged, not* in the way of actual teaching—the Midland Institute School of Music was seeing—and is seeing to that—but a centre from which might radiate some influence for good, and—this was the thought—perhaps attract young people to attempt success in an Art, which, as we have seen, *presents lessening* possibilities for a successful life.

But after much thought, it seemed possible to me that I might in some way help those engaged in their studies and pledged to an artistic life, and perhaps clear the way a little here and there, and perhaps set some sort of an ideal—and it may be, in due time, be fortunate enough to help on to success some of its struggling *aspirants*. And so I, the idle singer of an empty day, became a Professor of Music.

I was in Germany at the time and I was pursued from town to town by suggestions, advice and threats: the Chair which I hesitated to accept *for reasons I have given*—had no *terror for others*; *apparently any one* except myself was anxious to be Professor of Music.

I have no doubt each gentleman and lady—for in the spirit of the age, ladies offered to relieve me of the difficulty of decision and accept the post themselves—would have endeavoured to improve things vastly, but I have not taken their advice.

Why do I mention this? *Because it shows* the feelings which the ordinary Briton *feels concerning music as a profession*. Most of the letters ran on millinery—*gowns and hoods; suggesting a list of immediate recipients on* [of] *honorary degrees, which lists gracefully and easily included the name of the writer*: this matter of degrees seems to be the acme of musical desire among many people. Some suggested bitter things about existing institutions; these *evidently came from* disappointed students, as I pointed out in my inaugural address. A third order ventured to sketch *out a scheme* for teaching which they *were kind enough to think would be an improvement on my* own, my own being *then unknown*.

These were evidently gifted with divining powers as I do not teach. I am not here to teach, I am here to suggest. I am here *to ask you to*

With this view *has been* [δ I / have endeavoured] set before you
[δ in my inaugural address] "A future for English Music".
A [δ future not the] future, not THE future.
[δ As I then said] I had no wish to *attempt to* dictate,
I have *now* no *such* desire [δ now]
. . . incidentally [δ of] *on*
will find it [δ more useful &] helpful
of [δ actual] present day . . .
actualities [δ than to hear a tragic account for the fiftieth time
of some musician who had no effect on his career or on any
one elses /next page/
    I divided the active musical world into Composers,
Executants & Critics, & I have considered them with a view
always to the assistance of the student. Naturally much has
been read into
    It struck me that] There [δ was] is no [δ more] *apparent*
reason *why* a musician should not discourse *usefully* [δ profit-
ably] on his own time.

Ms. 1   because [δ some] we

Ms. 2   are not all living in the present *it*.

Ms. 1   . . . each of these. *Through this musical world we have travelled.*
These remarks
    [δ In the first I held up a]
      were addresses to & were intended [δ solely] merely for
[δ the use / *help* of students] young musicians: you have
accompanied me on the journey: we have noted the living
[δ thi] & it may be blossoming things & *hoped for rich fruit in
due time*; *but* we have not set down [δ &] to admire[δ d] milestones.

Ms. 2   * *These remarks . . . accompanied . . .* [* on facing page]

Ms. 1   *It is* have been said that the young musicians have, [δ in this
room] been too much praised [δ I think not. That is]

Ms. 2   It [δ is] *has been . . .* too much praised *in this room*.

Ms. 1   Merely the[δ ir] doings *of the young school* have been mentioned & [δ I claimed for the younger men the honour of
being produced]

think—(you need not think too furiously)—and to show, as occasion may arise, some paths not too much overtrodden, and yet not necessarily new—in which our young musicians may walk and find encouragement and help.

This view has been set before you, 'A future for English Music'—A future, not THE future. *I had not wished to attempt* to dictate, I have no wish now. I had no desire to prophesy (in the sense of prediction, the world is sadly misunderstood) and I *have now no such desire.*

The object of that address was to show what might be—and touched *incidentally on the past and on* the present. A young man, in the midst of his education, or just completing it, *might find it helpful* to know something of *present day actualities.*

There is no apparent reason why a musician should not discourse usefully on his time. In other arts, the modern side is freely handled and it seems to be only in music that the practical everyday life is ignored—ignored I suppose, *because we are not all living in it.*

I divide, as you know, the active musical world into Composers, Executants, and Critics, and I have devoted a lecture to *each of these. These remarks were intended* primarily for young *musicians. Through this musical* world we have travelled, and you who have accompanied me on the journey have noted the living—and it may be blossoming things—and hoped for rich fruit in due time: but we have not sat down to admire milestones.

It has been said that the young musicians have been too much praised in this room. If my remarks had been accurately reported or accurately understood, that idea could not have arisen. Merely the *doings of the young school* have been mentioned *and their claim.*

their claim to the production of serious work

Ms. 2   . . . their claim to [δ the production of serious work] ⋆ *recognition as the producers of serious work* [⋆ on facing page]

Ms. 1   a school of [δ English music which shall wort] composition which [δ shall hold its own] shall have . . .

Ms. 2   I take [δ a] *an old* definition

Ms. 1   . . . to English art". [δ for . . .?

                                 this absence of English material tradition . . .]

This is

Ms. 2   [δ is] was

Ms. 1   . . . suffices to explain [δ one] the position [δ and I] of music.

Ms. 2   [δ explain] *define*

Ms. 1   young men to [δ take] *draw*

           their own [δ land] *country*

Ms. 2   country *climate* OVER

⋆ [δ *That*] *This suggestion* [δ *that young men sh*ᵈ· *draw inspiration from their own country*] *has been the subject . . . of a Frenchman &* [δ *that*] *we feel . . . Eastern European.*

                     Italy . . . Strauss [in pencil]

Ms. 1   We have always had composers of whom we are justly proud: we have many now but a school has not existed [δ in the way th]

Ms. 2   We have *now and* always *have* had [δ composers of whom] *music of which* we are justly proud: [δ we have many now]

Ms. 1   A [δ passage] sentence occurs to me, which I read [δ when in touch with the law] before . . . "see p. 384"

We wish to see in this *country a school of composition which shall have* "*some* hold on the affections of the people and be held in respect abroad".

What is a school? I *take an old definition* from Chesneau:[1]— "Generally it (the word school) is used to designate a special collection of traditions and processes, a particular method, a peculiar style in design, and an equally peculiar taste (in colouring)—all contributing to the representation of a national ideal existing in the minds of artists of the same country (at the same time). In this sense we speak of the Flemish School, the Dutch School, the Italian School and the French School—but NOT of the English School. We cannot apply the word to English art".

This was of course applied to painting but with the alteration of a word, it suffices *to define the position of music.*

I have asked *young men to draw their* inspiration from their own country, from their own literature and in spite of what many would say—from their *own climate. This suggestion* has been the subject of some shallow remarks. It has been pointed out that all composers have drawn inspiration from foreign lands. True, but the nationality—the school—of the composer has not been obscured by his so doing.

We know that 'Carmen' with its Spanish colouring is unmistakably the work of a Frenchman and we feel that Moskowski's Spanish Dances, with all their characteristic flavour, are by an Eastern European.

Italy. Tchaikowsky, Raff, Berlioz and Strauss . . .

But such inspiration has been the cause of the individuality of the foreign schools and may be of our own.

We have now and always have had much music of which we are justly proud: but a school has not always existed: we have had what I will call "an egotism of several"—which is a different thing.

Confusion has been caused by some of our younger spirits complaining violently of laws of harmony and crying out against pedantic tyranny. To an open mind this would seem an unnecessary outcry seeing that the complainants do not feel themselves bound to follow the rules. Truth to say, these complaining are not new—they have always occurred and not only in music. *A sentence which I read before* I

[1] Ernest Chesneau (1833–90), Inspector of Fine Arts in France, and author of *La Peinture anglaise* (1882), *Artistes anglais contemporains* (1882), and *Joshua Reynolds* (1887).

Ms. 2   [Comments in parentheses in pencil]

Ms. 1   . . . the best [δ educate]
          . . . artistic few [δ Let the young writer / The situat]
          Personally I would ask young composers to use . . .
Ms. 2   [δ Personally I would ask] *But* young composers [δ to] *should*
Ms. 1   . . . they can [δ get] *obtain*
Ms. 2   ⋆ *passages so written . . . easier manner* [⋆ on facing page]

Ms. 1   [δ At] *Today* [δ a] *At* any rate [δ today / in these days] those
          spirits most ardent [δ spirits]
          [δ they need] innovators need . . .
          or [δ to follow a] *that the pundits*

          . . . upon [δ that] music
          foundation of our
Ms. 2   ⋆ *As four-part harmony* [δ *is*] REMAINS STILL *the* [δ *ideal*
          harmony foundation] FOUNDATION OF CHORAL WRITING . . .
          absolute music the real [δ *essence of music*] *staple of our art*
Ms. 1   No arguments I have yet read [δ can] have alter*ed* this view.
Ms. 1   . . . beginnings of music: [δ that w^d· be useful as consider-
          ing how primitive man invented a circle or a sphere, a subject

deserted the flowery paths of legal life for the deserts of art, occurs to me, from Jeremy Bentham:

> "Tyranny and anarchy are never far asunder. Dearly indeed must the laws pay for the mischief which they are (thus) made the instruments. The weakness they are thus struck with does not confine itself to the peccant spot; it spreads over their whole frame. The tainted parts throw suspicion upon those that are yet sound. Who can say which of them the disease has gained, which of them it has spared? You open the statute book (the harmony primer) and look into a clause (consecutive fifths are [forbidden]): does it belong to the sound part, or to the rotten? How can you say? By what are you to know? A man is not safe in trusting to his own eyes. You may have the whole statute book by heart, and all the while not know what ground you stand upon under the law. It pretends to fix your destiny, you must learn it, not from the law, but FROM THE TEMPER OF THE TIMES".

That is it after all: the temper of the times: not the unreasoning and unquestioning temper, but the *temper of the best*, the educated, the reasonable and the artistic few.

Let us say WHAT SOUNDS WELL IS WELL: and trouble no farther. *But young composers should use* correct harmony and legitimate means when *they can obtain their* effect by so doing: *passages so written* offer little difficulty to the performer and the effect is obtained in an *easier manner*: but if the effect is good and true, other means may be justified by the ends gained.

To-day at any rate, those spirits most ardent for innovation need not think that Academic teachers do more than pity them: *the innovators* need not flatter themselves that they are upsetting everything,—that they are to be acclaimed as martyrs *or that the pundits* are holding back "Debarred by the infidelity of the age from that most exquisite of repasts, the blood of heretics", as Jeremy Bentham has it.

Turning to the question of absolute music: I still *look upon music* which exists without any poetic or literary basis as the true foundation of our art. *As four-part harmony* remains still the foundation of Choral writing, as the Cantilena of the Violin is the real essence of the genius of the instrument, so is absolute music the real staple of our art. *No arguments I have yet read have altered this view.*

I will not go back too far and speculate on the *first beginnings of music*; but leaving legendary and poetical traditions and coming to the

we proposed to ourselves at school. It was thought that he
waited for a full moon: my own opinion was that if *that
particular* primitive man was my own ancestor he evinced a
little more invention & probably depressed his great toe &
spun round in the sand.] But leaving [δ idle] poetical views
of music & coming to [δ later] the last 3 or 4 centuries . . .
Views [δ taken] to the contrary

Ms. 2   are [δ usually] *we shall often
find*

Ms. 1   . . . ear for music. [δ At all events they do not appear to
possess it.]
but [δ it is understood to mean] we all know . . .
the greatest genius of our day, & for many a long day past,
Richard Strauss, [δ devotes] recognises
for his [δ astound] splendid orchestral achievements
dead. [δ It is unfortunate they want]
    Perhaps it is dead: but when the genius comes looked for
genius

Ms. 2   [δ Perhaps it is dead], *the form is somewhat* ⋆ *perhaps the form*
. . . *admirers*, [⋆ on facing page in pencil], although some
modern Symphonies . . .

Ms. 1 *absolutely*
give us *a* [δ the finest]
Think of the architecture,

Ms. 2   *I know the danger of analogy* but Think of the Architecture . . .

Ms. 1   Gothic: [δ we know how it grew]

Ms. 1   [δ Just as] *In this way*
lends itself to [δ easy] cheap imitation

Ms. 2   [δ imitation] *travesty*

Ms. 1   not certain [δ if] that

suspicion that the Epic Poem fell into.

last three or four centuries, we seem to know that music was first vocal, and secondly used for rhythmical exercises, marching and dancing. Out of these beginnings were evolved the suite and similar collections of pieces, until we come to the Sonata and the Symphony. I hold that the Symphony without a programme is the highest develop-

ment of art. *Views to the contrary are, we shall often find,* held by those to whom the joy of music came late in life or who would deny to musicians that peculiar gift, which is their own, a musical ear, or an *ear for music. I use,* as you notice, a very old-fashioned expression *but we all know what* it conveys: a love of music for its own sake.

It seems to me that because the greatest genius of *our days, Richard Strauss, recognises* the Symphonic Poem as a fit vehicle for his *splendid achievements,* some writers are inclined to be positive that the symphony is dead. Perhaps the form is somewhat battered by the ill-usage of some of its admirers, although some modern Symphonies still testify to its vitality; but when *the looked-for genius comes,* it may be *absolutely* revived. I am sure Richard Strauss could give *us a symphony to rank* among, or above the finest if he chose.

I know the danger of analogy: but *think of Architecture,* conveniently but not quite correctly called *Gothic:* I quote:— "What is called Gothic architecture is in reality nothing more than the logical outcome of the progressive Romanesque—the transition is a natural one, just as in English architecture, is the transition from the round-arched Norman to the pointed style of the thirteenth century".

In this way the Symphony was evolved out of preceding art works: and just as Gothic architecture so-called lends itself to *cheap travesty,* so does the Symphony. After the glorious centuries during which the art of ecclesiastical architecture blazed forth and covered Europe with those buildings which are still our wonder and delight, the inevitable time of pause came. I say pause, because we are not *certain that it is death.*

Just as in our day what has been called 'Suburban Gothic' from its mere imitation and baldness gives us only a dismal amusement, so the Symphony became the prey of the would-be sayer of wise things, and fell into *the same sort of suspicion.* Gothic Architecture may only be

Ms. 1   deciding *if it is dead*;

Ms. 1   quote Edw A. Baughan Chord No. 2[1]
Ms. 2   quote Baughan ★ *You have heard much on the other side:* [in
                                                                pencil]
                              We will hear a voice on the [δ *other*] *side . . . of*
                                  the Symphony   [in pencil]
                              [printed version of quotation affixed, below
                              which in pencil]
                                  Shall we go back to musical microglophany?
                                  | *Ideograms* | *Ideographics* [all from ★ on
                                  facing page]
Birm.   A good symphonic poem was much better than a poor sym-
Post   phony, but if they gave up absolute music, where there they
          logically to end? Were they to be led back by way of sym-
          bolism to ideal ground, and was music to become a mere
          series of labels like the chemical formulae of the emotions?

Ms. 1   *in this place*
Ms. 1   . . . composition [δ in this place]

          great artists, some [δ people like myself] *some*

[1] E. A. Baughan, "A Plea for the Symphony", in *The Chord* (no. 2), a quarterly
journal issued from The Sign of the Unicorn, Cecil Court, London, 1899–1900. After
four numbers it ceased publication. Elgar quotes from the peroration of Baughan's essay
(*The Chord*, pp. 36–47).

resting and we must wait and see the new Liverpool Cathedral[1] before *deciding that it is dead*; at any rate a cursory glance at the plans shews that we are on the eve of something great and grand. May not the Symphony, when the genius comes, in a more modern way hold the place it has never really lost?

You have heard much on the other side: we will hear a voice on the side of the symphony:—

When a great genius comes let him speak with a great voice, and we will hearken to him; but to be bored by the platitudes of mediocrity is more than we can patiently bear. And it is because mediocrity has singled out the Symphony as its own, and has copied the symphony style of the great masters, a style largely caused by the technique of their day, that there is a disposition among the young men of real talent to shirk writing symphonies. My plea for the Symphony is that it should once more be made the vehicle of emotional expression, as it was with Beethoven, or has since been with Tschaikowsky, for the present symphonic-poem with its vague form and unworthy reliance on the meaning of its programme has been an utter failure. Let the young composer make what modifications he will, and turn a deaf ear to the protests of the learned doctors in music, but let him recognise that the essentials of the symphony-form are not barren formalism, but are based on the unalterable logic of human expression.

E. A. Baughan

In noticing my remark made incidentally in the Lecture on Brahms' Symphony, some one has said "my views are astounding seeing what things I have written myself".[2] I have never referred *in this place to* my own efforts in the way of *composition*, save once to give a practical illustration of the cost of publication and I would not do so now save that my opinion has been asked. I HAVE written Overtures with titles more or less poetic or suggestive: am I then so narrow as to admire my own music because I have written it myself? Certainly not.

In the decoration of the temples, in addition to the glorious marbles of the great *artists*, *some* were allowed to present their little leaden images, as I have done. Let me say definitely that when I see one of

---

[1] Giles Gilbert Scott's design for the new Cathedral at Liverpool was recommended by the assessors, G. F. Bodley and R. Norman Shaw, in 1902. The Foundation Stone was laid by King Edward VII on July 19, 1904.

[2] See p. 105.

... or as a mason [δ may do] when he [δ *still*] see[δ s]—well—
the Campanile

Manc.   University of Birmingham (Laughter)
Guard.

Ms. 1   [δ This work was found] *It was found* impossible [deletion] *to
take the work on tour* [δ The symphony by Brahms was
suggested by a member of the orchestra not by me]

with *a* [δ vast] *immense*
weights

Ms. 2   *Such as at the People's Palace*

But in many cases there is

Ms. 1   But too [δ many] *often a* people's concerts [δ are] *is* stupid
music which we *ourselves* should . . .
Ms. 2   people's concert[δ s], in the country
mostly, . . .
[δ stupid] squalid music . . . [δ should] *would* avoid . . .

Ms. 1/2 . . . on the road [δ &] we
Ms. 1   *A certain writer* At a friends *house* [δ I am] is requested to do
[δ my] *his* pen work in the Italian garden: [δ I love] the
Italian garden *is lovable* & in the *early* morning [δ I] *he* walks
there & *no doubt* thinks of [δ Petrarch] *Dante* . . .
[δ I] *he* . . . stays . . . feels . . . inspiration & [δ I climb] I go
out of that garden, & into the park. I climb . . . I can find &
work there
[Final version in Ms. 2]

my own works by the side of, say, the Fifth Symphony, I feel like a tinker may do when surveying the Forth Bridge, or as a mason when he sees the—well—*Campanile of the new Birmingham University.*[1]

All the same, I look upon Richard Strauss as the greatest living composer and I chose 'Don Quixote' for the tour which I conducted. It was found however impossible to take the work on tour on account of the size of the orchestra required.

I turn now to the question of cheap concerts. It must not be thought that I have any particular place or district in view. I think I know where music really exists and people need not burden the Post Office *with an immense* weight of circulars giving particulars of local concerts. I said sometime ago that I would like to see that vast working population of this country able to have and enjoy the same music we possess and enjoy ourselves. Many concerts are given called People's Concerts,—some of these are as good as anything we could desire—*e.g. those at the People's Palace* where great works are given and the Sunday concerts at Liverpool.

But there is too much labelling of the people. We give them a sight of the same pictures, and we give them the same literature: the public picture galleries, loan collections wisely arranged, are the same for the people as ourselves: the free libraries contain, even if they are not read, the same literature we read or sometimes pretend to read ourselves. *But too often a people's concert, in the country mostly, is a collection of frivolous and squalid* music which we ourselves would avoid like a plague.

We dislike being labelled. You know of works and factories where gardens are laid out with trees and seats for the workmen to sit and eat and smoke during the dinner hour. Well, they do not sit and smoke there, much—they go outside and *stand on the road*—we sympathise with them. *A certain writer at a friend's* house is requested to do his penwork in the Italian garden.[2] The Italian garden is very lovable and in the early *morning he walks* there and no doubt thinks of Dante, after lunch *of Petrarch* and after dinner of Boccaccio. But he never *stays there.* He feels labelled for inspiration and goes out of that garden and into the Park, climbs the *ruggedest tree he can find and works there.*

---

[1] The then new buildings of the University of Birmingham at Edgbaston were designed by Sir Aston Webb and erected between 1900 and 1909. The "clock tower [was] built as a memorial to Joseph Chamberlain and modelled on the Campanile at Siena". *History of the County of Warwick*, ed. W. B. Stephens (*Victoria History of the Counties of England*), O.U.P., 1964, p. 45.

[2] Probably that of Frank Schuster, at Bray (see *Letters of Edward Elgar*, p. 350).

Again good music

Ms. 2   [δ Again] When good music

Ms. 1   much pleasant thought gave him etc. etc. [passage to "in giving him one" omitted]

Ms. 2   much [δ pleasant] thought

Ms. 1   ... working men [δ (*are not asses*)] do not want treating sentimentally

Ms. 2   ... [δ working men are not asses] *working men are intelligent; they* do not ...

Ms. 1   real thing without enquiring with too much sentiment

Ms. 2   [δ „   „   „   „   „   „   ]

Ms. 1   I repeat that what we do ...

Ms. 2   [δ I repeat] what we do

Ms. 1   ... suggest that [δ anything] everywhere concerts shall *will*

Ms. 2   *should*

Ms. 1   diverting [δ our small means] any of our small national means [δ & make]

hopeless case. [*P. 27a*] (take in 27b) For the purpose ...
                                        exhibition of pictures
                                                        [P. 27b]

audience as I [δ have] wish to see

When good music is offered to the people, there is too much of the attitude of Sterne about the givers. When Sterne saw the hungry ass— he, *after much thought* gave him a macaroon. His heart, he says, smites him that there presided in the act more pleasantry in the conceit of seeing how an ass would eat a macaroon than of benevolence in giving him one. *Now—the English working-men are intelligent: they do not want treating sentimentally,* we must give them the real *thing, we* must give them of the best because we want them to have it, not from mere curiosity to see HOW they will accept it.

What we do in literature and art, we might do in music. I know the difficulty of expense and that in many districts this difficulty is insuperable, and above all, I do not *suggest that everywhere concerts should* spring up like mushrooms, but I do ask that these things should be thought over and when occasion arises that something on the lines suggested may be done.

In these days of much tribulation and of much hunger and distress,[1] it is difficult to think of diverting any of our national means devoted to art, to the channel of music. In these moments too, when a general election is in the air, we know that for the time being public men must not think of art: we know that any candidate who ventured to mention the words "art and music" to his constituents would never have a chance of accepting the Chiltern Hundreds: he might give up his contest at once: if indeed his Committee did not desert him as a *hopeless case.*

For the purpose of giving such concerts,—we want halls—large halls such as are built without hope of their being successful commercial speculations in some newer regions. I venture to say that if such a hall were only filled twice in a year with such an audience *as I wish to see,* the building of such a room would be justified and the loss need not be accounted waste, any more than a corresponding loss which is cheerfully borne upon an exhibition of pictures.

[1] On December 17 a Service for the Unemployed, at which Canon Newbolt preached on the text "The Kingdom of Heaven is at hand" and "impressed on the congregation the need for patience", took place in St. Paul's Cathedral, London. This was at a time when the Conservative Party was on the point of collapse, and when the Independent Labour Party, led by Keir Hardy—bitter and vocal, was active. The situation in Russia increased anxiety in Britain: on the one hand censorship of the press was in force, on the other anti-Semitism was strong. Conditions were such that Wilhelm Backhaus cancelled a concert tour. Further away there was alarming news of a bank collapse in Chicago, and of riots in Shanghai.

Ms. 2 ... frequently made *known*
Ms. 1 than mine: not much seems to come but I join
Ms. 2   [δ ,,   ,,   ,,   ,,   ,,]

Ms. 1 If larger audiences are *not* being made, listeners are being
       educated by the great competitive festivals ...
Ms. 2 [δ If] Larger audiences are [δ not] being made & listeners
       [δ are being] ... by the [δ great] Competition Festivals ...

         [δ I do not think ... music and good music too [May
           Grafton's hand] & *not a word mentioned* [E]]

Ms. 1 musical critics [δ pretend to give] make pretensions to give

10,000 people were gathered together during four days

... considered [δ but then much as we might like to see music
on a]

Ms. 1 *multitude of* remains & ruins [δ of the many temples, it was
       impossible to forget] *glorious in their surroundings* [in margin ★]
       ★ *their nobility and their history and association* the scenes of
       rivalry in athletics [δ & song] poetry & song *were vividly*
       brought to mind.
       Let [δ me] *us*

The need for National Opera is frequently *made known* by voices and pens more eloquent and powerful *than mine*: but *I join* in in the hope that some day not far distant, the British Public may find itself desiring opera: when it does, we may venture to promise that the performers, and adequate performers will be found. *Larger audiences are being made and listeners educated by the Competition Festivals* now, I am glad to say, being established throughout the Kingdom. When properly conducted,—and the English competitions are properly conducted on artistic lines, these gatherings are productive of good.

I do not think the press has taken a sufficiently serious view of the importance of these gatherings. I ventured to point this out some two years ago[1] and many things were said upon it. My point was this, the London papers—not the *musical critics*—*make pretensions to give* us the news of the country. Columns are headed with the names of districts, news is tabulated and so forth. I read concerning one watering-place the following remarkable news:—

"Another lovely day: the corpse of a foreign sailor was washed up on the foreshore this afternoon and will be buried on Sunday".

Whether this remarkable piece of information was worth telegraphing I know not; but it seemed strange that the fact that in another place nearly *10,000 people were gathered during* four days for the making of music and good music too and not a word mentioned.[2]

I hope that soon England will be covered by these Societies—there are many existing now and some need more support than is accorded to them, while others are happier in the possession of local influential people with goodwill towards music.

It is a mistake to think that these competitors meet, in England at least (of the Principality I say nothing now), for the value of the prizes. They meet primarily—and this fact at least should ensure them a favourable eye from the critics—they meet primarily for CRITICISM. The actual value of the prizes is so small that it need not be *considered*. And then the competition element—why should it be looked upon askance? On looking on Grecian land, two months since,[3] and surveying the *multitude of remains* and ruins glorious in their surroundings, their *nobility, their* life history and their associations, the *scenes of rivalry* in athletics, poetry and song, were *vividly brought to mind*. Let us recall to ourselves:— "Very anciently a contention for a prize in poetry and

---

[1] See p. 154.   [2] See p. 154.
[3] Elgar had been on a Mediterranean cruise in September of this year, see *Letters of Edward Elgar*, p. 146 f.

[Marginal note] *Symonds p. 164 etc*
. . . remembered [δ Pindar] Symonds'

              and this *a* dreary journey by train *railway*
Ms. 1   . . . the chivalry & the song. [δ From]
                    [δ Let us then hope that]
                        From these competition festivals much is hoped:
              statistics . . .
Ms. 2   * *Is the idea . . . similar work* [* on facing page to 38]
              . . . good results [δ & will still further result?]

Ts. [1] J. A. Symons [*sic*]. The Greek Poets. Chapter XI Pindar. (Vol. 3rd Edition) [E.]

music was a favourite entertainment of the Grecian people . . .
A Festival of this kind held in the little Island of Delos, at which Homer
assisted brought in numerous concourse from different parts by sea;
and Hesiod informs us of a splendid meeting for the celebration of
various games (at Chalcis) in Euboea where he himself obtained the
prize for poetry and song. These gatherings have been the subject of
much poetry and have always commended respect and admiration".
"Let us pause to imagine the scene which the neighbourhood of
Olympia must have presented . . . The full blaze of summer over-
head,—plain and hillside yield no shade but what the spare branches
of the olive and a few spreading pines afford. . . . Epic poets and
rhapsodists are furnished with tales of heroes freshly coined from their
own brains . . . With the lute and with the various voices of flutes,
they travelled by the bed of Alpheus, tawny in midsummer with dusty
oleander-blossoms, the pilgrims pass to the contest".

I have seen this land and *remembered Symonds'* prose. But I remembered also with joy that we have our own music—like this among the
people. True, it cannot be picturesque in the way that ancient Greece
was picturesque and *a dreary journey by railway* cannot compare to
Pindar's journey, but the feeling is the same—the rivalry—the chivalry
and *the song.*[1]

Is the idea fanciful that from these gatherings much real good results? I
think not.

When the Salvation Army began in a small way, and even later,
when its greater life astonished us, much was said against its methods
and its aims. It has lived through this stage and it has reached the people
in a way that religion—or it may be religionism has not done, and it
is now looked upon by most serious churchmen as a valuable adjunct
to their mission.

---

[1] J. A. Symonds, *Studies of the Greek Poets*, 2 vol., 3rd ed., 1893: "Then too there is the
picture of the poet, gorgeously attired, with his singing robes about him, erect upon the
prow of a gilded galley, floating through the dazzling summer-waves toward the island
of his love, Rhodes, or Sicily, or Aegina. The lyre and the flute send their clear sounds
across the sea. We pass temple and citadel on shore and promontory. The bands of oars
sweep the flashing brine. Meanwhile the mighty poet stretches forth his golden cup of
song to greet the princes and illustrious athletes who await him on the marble quays.
Reading Pindar is a progress of this pompous kind. Pindar, as one of his critics remarks
was born and reared in splendour: splendour became his vital atmosphere . . ." I,
pp. 330–1.

The competition festival [δ has] *is*, in music, [δ done] *doing*
[δ From these . . . much is hoped] [Ms. 1, see above]

Ms. 1   . . . the [δ amount] number of voices
           . . . to keep the [δ mus] standard of music chosen high

Ms. 2   „   „   „   „   „   „[δ chosen] „

Ms. 1   to preserve the [δ best & *truly* elevating] *ennobling*

Ms. 2   *Is it fanciful . . . sketch them* [on inserted sheets 39a, 39b]

as [δ music halls &] *the home of*

[δ Let us hope he did not sketch them]
           „ „ „ „ „ „ „ „ „ „   „   [in pencil]

Ms. 1   . . . these Lectures will, [δ I trust] understand

Ms. 1   To the student much has been said about modern things:
           next year we may look at the old . . .

Ms. 2   [δ To the student . . . modern things] * *I have tried . . .*
           modern things [* on facing page in pencil]

Ms. 1   In bygone days much [δ is / *has been* taught in the way of]
           much has been insisted upon

Ms. 2   *But* [δ I] *in* bygone days [δ much] *a great deal* has been insisted
           upon . . .
           the strictest

Ms. 1   student must know

Ms. 2   „   „ [δ know] *have a knowledge of*

Ms. 1   language he [δ writes] *uses*

Ms. 2   orchestration. *letter*
                                   "*appear to have masterie*"
                                                        [in pencil]

Ms. 1   composition: *to do*
           . . . if not impossible [δ *to do*]

The competition festival is in music doing similar work. Statistics are in some cases available as to *the number of voices* trained: we know in some places large choruses can now be got together where ten years ago no chorus was. It only needs *to keep the standard of* the music high, and the prize list low, *to preserve the ennobling qualities of these institutions.*

Is it fanciful to turn to the people when we see what their superiors are capable of? We are all tired of hearing of Macaulay's New Zealander: but let us sadden ourselves with the thought that that antipodean artist may have anticipated somewhat; he may not be waiting to see a figure of departed glory in the ruins of St. Paul's: he may have been sketching the English Opera House and alas! Irving's theatre in their new guise,[1] as the home of variety entertainment; and he may even have learnt something of our real musical taste and enthusiasm from a contemplation of the ruins of St. James's Hall.[2] *Let us hope he did not sketch them.*

And now, you who have followed the whole of *these Lectures will understand* the trend of them: it is impossible to make things clear in a few detached paragraphs. I have tried to shew you things as they are: the place of the young musician in his own country and what he may hope for in it, *so necessarily much has been said to the student on modern things,* next year we may look on the old. *But in bygone days* a great deal has been insisted upon in the way of *the strictest* harmony and counterpoint which can be of no practical use now: but the *student must have a knowledge* of these things even as the literary man must know the bases of *the language he uses.*

Many people have asked me to devote some portion of my Lectures to composition—that is, the explanation of the actual labour *of composition: to do* this is difficult, if *not impossible.* Tschaikowsky says in a letter:—

[1] See p. 52.
[2] See p. 195.

Ms. 2   [Quotation extracted from book and affixed to facing page,
          beneath:]
                    TCHAIKOWSKY
                    Letter
                    We find the same view in Emerson: viz—
          [Emerson quotation without ascription given in Ms. 1]

"It is delightful to talk to you about my own methods of composition. So far I have never had any opportunity of confiding to anyone these hidden utterances of my inner life, partly because very few would be interested, and partly because, of these few, scarcely one would know how to respond to me properly. . . . Do not believe those who try to persuade you that composition is only a cold exercise of intellect. The only music capable of moving and touching us is that which flows from the depths of a composer's soul when he is stirred by inspiration. There is no doubt that even the greatest musical geniuses have sometimes worked without inspiration. This guest does not always respond to the first invitation. We must ALWAYS work, and a self-respecting artist must not fold his hands on the pretext that he is not in the mood. If we wait for the mood, without endeavouring to meet it half-way, we easily become indolent and apathetic. We must be patient, and believe that inspiration will come to those who can master their DISINCLINATION. A few days ago I told you I was working every day without any real inspiration. Had I given way to my disinclination, undoubtedly I should have drifted into a long period of idleness. But my patience and faith did not fail me and to-day I felt that inexplicable glow of inspiration of which I told you: thanks to which I know beforehand that whatever I write to-day will have power to make an impression, and to touch the hearts of those who hear it. I hope you will not think I am indulging in self-laudation, if I tell you that I very seldom suffer from this disinclination to work. I believe the reason for this is that I am naturally patient. I have learnt to master myself, and I am glad I have not followed in the steps of some of my Russian colleagues, who have no self-confidence and are so impatient that at the least difficulty they are ready to throw up the sponge. This is why, in spite of great gifts, they accomplish so little, and that in an amateur way.

You ask me how I manage my instrumentation, I never compose in the ABSTRACT, that is to say, the musical thought never appears otherwise than in a suitable external form. In this way I invent the musical idea and the instrumentation simultaneously. Thus I thought out the scherzo of our symphony—at the moment of its composition—exactly as you heard it. It is inconceivable except as PIZZICATO. Were it played with the bow, it would lose all its charm and be a mere body without a soul".

We find the same view in Emerson:—

Ms. 1   own method". A true man never acquires after College
      rules.—(not in College—but afterwards)

Ms. 2   [δ A true man . . . but afterwards)]

Ms. 1   it *seems to* sums up

This [δ mus] real [δ bit of] poetical . . .
To the many *executants* who have
      [δ I hope to arra]   asked to be shown a royal
road—a road which knows no boundaries [δ enclosures]
fences or the like—

Ms. 2   . . . a road . . . the like *or toll-gates* [in pencil]

Ms. 1   [δ Now] we [δ have been told] know the position . . .
      The erection of numerous orchestras in all the . . .

Ms. 2   The *establishment in the 18th century* [in pencil] of numerous
      orchestras

Ms. 1   We [δhave] *had* no such help

Ms. 2   We [δ *have*] had *at that period* . . . musical life [δ in the 18th
      century]

Ms. 1   But we may hope that if all young England work together . . .

Ms. 2   „ „ „ „ „ „ all *true artists, composers, executants &*
      critics [ink over E.'s pencil insertion]

"Each mind has its own *method*". "What you have aggregated in a natural manner, surprises and delights when it is produced. Intend your mind, without respite, without . . . in one direction: your best heed may for a long time avail nothing. Yet thoughts are flitting before you. We all but apprehend, we dimly forebode the truth. We say, I will walk abroad and it will take form and clearness to me. We go forth but we cannot find it. It seems as if we needed only the stillness and composed attitude of the library to seize the thought. But we come in, and are as far from it as at first. Then, in a moment, and unannounced, the truth appears".

This passage seems to be written for the encouragement of composers as well as poets. I know not if this poem is printed, I hope it is: *it seems to sum* up the matter of inspiration:

> He hears the music of his heart,
>   But knows not whence the breath is blown;
> It comes from regions far apart,
>   With power beyond his own.
>
> A presence at his side alights,
>   A whisper at his ear is heard;
> Amazed he takes the pen, and writes
>   The inevitable word.

This real poetical description is from the pen of Alfred Hayes.[1]

To many executants who have asked to be shewn a royal road—a road which knows no boundaries, fences or toll-*gates—I* can only say I know of no such road in art. Hard work is apparently the only way to achieve success in art business or politics.

We know the position England held musically in Purcell's time and earlier: that position was soon lost—it can be regained.

The establishment in the 18th century of numerous orchestras in all the little Capitals of Germany had the greatest effect in fostering and in many cases, creating a love for orchestral music. *We had at that* period no such help to a musical life. *But we may hope that if all true artists, composers, executants and critics* work together, setting aside small differ-

---

[1] Published as "Poesy", in *The Vale of Arden and other Poems*, John Lane, 1895, p. 74.

Ms. 1   ·we may [δ yet] once again
          produce [δ a s] what we do not possess at present a school
Ms. 2   ,,   [δ ,,   ,,   ,,   ,,   ,,   ,,   ,,] ,,   ,,
Birm.   . . . in respect abroad   (Applause)
Post
Manc.   (Loud applause)
Guard.
Ms. 2   In an old book [etc. to end, added by E.]

[On reverse of last page in pencil]
        I would naturally
                        prefer a good building [etc see
                                            p. 192]

ences of opinion, *we may once again* be a musical land and *produce a 'school'* (not an egotism of several) of serious English music which shall have a hold on the affections of the people, and SHALL be held in respect *abroad*.

In an old book of Heraldry, which, with its mixture of symbolism, philosophy, poetry and romance, sometimes lightens a too-full hour, Rouge-Croix ends his work thus:—

"If I have given you something on which to think I have gained as much as I looked for: if I shall draw others into this thought, whether they undertake new Worke, or amend old. And therefore, neyther puffed up with Opinion that aught is well, neyther dejected with Feare that it is not well, I comfort myself with Mimnermus[1] his distich, and so cease:—

> Heart take thine ease
> Men hard to please
> Thou haply mayest offend:
> Though one speake ill
> Of thee, some will
> Say better: There an end.

[1] Mimnermus, Greek Elegiac poet, about 634–600 B.C. [E.]

On the day following the lecture Elgar wrote from Hereford to Peyton:

My dear Mr. Peyton:
    I am sorry I did not see you to speak to yesterday but you know I get very hot & must run away to change.
    I am writing now to say that I had an interview with Mr. Williams,[1] the father of the boy composer concerning whom you wrote. I am arranging to see the boy as soon as possible: for the present I will keep the letters & other information sent to you.
                        With very best regards
                            Yours v. sincerely
                                Edward Elgar

For once the report of the lecture that appeared on December 14 contained one palpable inaccuracy, which provoked *The Musical Times* to anecdote: "No wonder that Sir Edward Elgar complains that his lectures are misreported. In a *Birmingham* newspaper (!) he is actually credited with a reference to 'Brahams's Symphony', a work doubtless inspired by the death of Nelson, though Sir Edward seems to have been silent on that point. This reminds us of the tradition that when the Requiem of Brahms was first performed in this country some (surely not so many as 'some') of the musical critics referred to the work as 'a forgotten composition by Braham'!"[2]

The misprint no doubt annoyed Elgar. A leading article in the same issue of *The Birmingham Post*, however, must have proved infuriating. This represented a distinctly cold climate:

In commenting on Sir Edward Elgar's inaugural lecture as Richard Peyton Professor of Music in the University of Birmingham, we spoke of the keynote of modernity then struck. It would give the musical world, we said, something to think about. The course of lectures that followed, and was concluded yesterday afternoon, has amply justified our forecast. These lectures have not only given material for thought, but have provoked discussion, and occasioned some heated correspondence. Now that the series has been completed, we may be permitted to notice some of the points that have, apparently, given offence. It has to be remembered that the University of Birmingham is a young institution, untrammelled by tradition and ancient usage. The Professor of Music is not tied down to the procedure of any predecessor. His aim, as explained at the outset, was to define music as a living art, and he gave as the three factors that went to the making of that living art—the composers, the executants, and the critics. The lecturer's modernity was shown by his selecting a very short period back as his starting point. His hope was in the young English school, now just beginning to make its influence felt, which should

---

[1] On January 23, 1906, Elgar wrote again to Peyton saying that he understood the "boy Williams" had been promised a scholarship at the Guildhall School of Music. His compositions, however, "are of no use at all, but they shew industry . . ."

[2] "Occasional Notes", Vol. XLVII, January 1906, p. 27.

remove the reproach that clung to our serious art and compositions—
that they had no hold on the affections of the people, and were held in
no respect abroad. That conviction Sir Edward Elgar has expressed more
than once. We can appreciate the opposition to such an idea. But we must
first consider the circumstances. Sir Edward spoke ex cathedra, from the
professorial chair; the lectures were free, and open not only to students
of the University, but to as many of the public as the lecture hall could
accommodate. Consequently much greater importance was attached to
the utterances than would have been the case had the lectures been given
with closed doors to students. As a result, this criticism of his contemporaries, in this public manner, has been resented. We think there is ground
for such resentment. English composers have been held in honour abroad,
and their works are not yet dead. We cannot begin with a "clean slate"
to-day, and wipe out the past altogether. The promise of the young
school now rising into notice need not obscure the work done by earlier
men. The past is the parent of the present; the age makes the man, not
man the age. The brighter prospects of the new composers are due in
part to the efforts of those who went before. Still, everything is not
altogether satisfactory even now; production exceeds demand, and composers of large and serious work cannot find publishers.

With the aims of the Birmingham Professor of Music and with the ideal
he would place before the student, we have the fullest sympathy. The
lecture on English executants was generously appreciative, particularly
in regard to orchestral performers. There was a misunderstanding concerning conductors, and we are glad to know that no slight was intended
to any of our English wielders of the bâton, though the reference to the
factory yard was unworthy of the speaker. When Sir Edward differenti-
ated the conductor pure and simple from the composer-conductor and
the organist-conductor he must surely have forgotten that the first
species is almost unknown. Lamoureux and Colonne are the only
names we can now recall as conductors of fame who were not composers. Dr. Richter was a composer, Mr. Henry J. Wood wrote many
pieces before he gave himself up exclusively to conducting; Nikisch,
Mottl, Weingartner, among Germans, and the leading conductors in this
country, are all, or nearly all, composers. What inducement can we offer
to an able man to give himself up entirely to conducting? And that
brings us to another consideration that we think the lecturer overlooked.
When comparing our chorus-singers with those of Germany, our
dramatic art with that of Germany and France, Sir Edward forgot that
ours is a free country—free to neglect as well as to accomplish. We may,
and do, neglect art, especially music, and leave it to those who treat it
commercially. Truly artistic enterprises mostly spell ruin. The chief
Continental nations are before us in education, and the art of music is
cared for and supported, as are the sister arts. But the peoples of those
countries are not free to do as they like, and such "free" lectures as those
of the Birmingham Professor would probably not be acceptable to the
heads of Continental Universities.

We need not say much about the critics, as seen from Sir Edward's point of view. In general his remarks were just, and his advice well meant. We do not know the degree of intimacy existing between editors and the lecturer, but we fancy there is more of imagination than reality in his picture of them. While on the subject of the press, we must express our regret that Sir Edward should have employed an expression in his letter to Dr. Cowen that is open to grave objection. To say that telegraphed reports were "wholly misleading, and perhaps made so purposely," is to charge the press with a deliberate attempt to mislead the public and injure the lecturer without any obvious motive—a charge that Sir Edward would have considerable difficulty in establishing. But we gladly turn to more attractive matter. The lecturer's attitude to "absolute music" was most ably explained yesterday, and it very clearly set forth what at first was easily misconstrued. His reasons for not mentioning his own compositions, and his modesty in connection with them, gave gratifying proof of the sincerity of his work in these lectures. His desire was to enable the student to see things as they are; to help forward the cause of true art. We are with him in the commendation of the musical competitions where "the standard is high and the prizes are low"; and we wish as greatly as he does to see the working man enjoying a fine concert. We have our Saturday evening concerts in the Town Hall, where oratorios and orchestral works can be heard for the merest trifle, but other towns are not so fortunately situated. Build suitable halls where possible, establish cheap prices, but do not allow those who can afford to pay more to take the places of those for whom the concerts are intended. Such things have been done. We end, as we began, by repeating that the Professor of Music in the University of Birmingham has given the musical world something to think about. Let the University and the city convert thought into action, and some of us may live to see even the establishment of opera in our midst. When the public wish for anything, they will obtain it. Let the wish take a musical direction, and the thing will be done.

If Elgar had wished to provoke discussion he had certainly succeeded. After *The Birmingham Post* came a less official voice, that of an anonymous student writing in *The Coxcomb* (the University of Birmingham unofficial organ) of February, 1906 (p. 12). His theme was *Pre-Raphaelitism in Birmingham*.

Sir Edward Elgar, in his last address at the University, made reference to the adequate provision allowed by the municipal authorities in the matter of free libraries, recreation parks, and art galleries, but insufficient provision for music with which to stir the feelings of the working classes.
This, no doubt, is one element of truth in Sir Edward's many diatribes against existing conditions, but the very existence of an art gallery is no argument in favour of their being much utilized.

It depended on who chose the pictures. In this case subservience to fashion almost resulted in artistic disaster, for members of the Art Gallery Committee wanted to invest in "works of contemporary painters . . . then considered the ideal collection, but Mr. [Whitworth] Wallis stood out in opposition to the desire for twentieth century talent, and by true persistency wrested from exclusion the Pre-Raphael School".

On December 14 Elgar went to a sale in the Cathedral Close in Hereford, and "bought some Dictionaries". Apart from renewing an interest in chemistry he devoted the remaining days of the month to *The Kingdom*, the Introduction to Part II being written on December 28. So ended a trying year. Lady Elgar summarised the Professorial aspect in the last entry in her Diary for that year:

> Much worry in some ways. E. oppressed with the Birmingham Prof-ship & worried & quite unable to write music. Very unwell over Inaugural Lecture, & again over Winter lectures, but did them splendidly & made a great mark, so can look back with clear content on his 1st year's work there.

CHAPTER 10

ORCHESTRATION
(November 1, 1906)

THE prospect of further lectures hung over Elgar during 1906 like a dark cloud. He was plagued with headaches and for ever threatening to "give up his work". On January 23 he summoned up energy to take the Chair at a lecture on Art in Hereford, and observed that "as in music religion was the founder of Italian Art, or rather art was based on religion": a vote of thanks seconded by "a dissenting minister", was proposed by Count Louis Bodenham Lubienski.[1] But on February 9 he showed "distinct traces of trials gone through" and was "less vivacious & more self assertive in opinion etc."[2] Nevertheless he pushed on with the completion of *The Kingdom*, which was interrupted by another visit to America during the summer. The first performance took place during the Birmingham Musical Festival, at the morning concert on October 3. The soloists were Agnes Nicholls, Muriel Foster, John Coates, and William Higley. The second part of the concert was provided by Bach's *Sing ye to the Lord* and Brahms's First Symphony.[3]

The nervous condition in which Elgar then was is indicated by the account of the performance "In conducting 'The Kingdom' yesterday morning, Sir Edward Elgar's emotions were so stirred by his own wonderful work that, according to the observation of the choristers, tears were streaming down his face several times during the oratorio."[4]

On October 30 he was "depressed". On the next day Lady Elgar reported that he was "busy with lecture—depressed". So far as the newspapers were concerned their columns on November 2 had to be given over to the municipal elections. Elgar's lecture therefore went unnoticed, as also did the Festival Choral Society's performance of *St. Paul*, which also took place on November 1.

---

[1] Diary.

[2] Ibid.

[3] In addition to *The Kingdom* Holbrooke's *The Bells*, Percy Pitt's *Sinfonietta in G minor* (evening concert, October 3) and Bantock's *Omar Khayyam* (October 4) had first performances at this Festival.

[4] *Birmingham Mail*, October 4, 1906.

Rough Notes

[Sheet 1]

Syllabus
Books on orchestration
limitations
simplicity   impossible to teach it
Motley quotation   text books *prevent*
Berlioz

————

Opportunities for hearing
orchestras
the true education[1]

———

playing in orchestras

———

The future of orchestral music.
Commercial considerations.

———

publishing performances

———

Gramophones

———

Copyrights

———

Beckford Vathek
politicians & music
[See p. 257.]

Municipal
orchestras   ———

The people. difficulty in hearing music:
a revolution—a peaceful one. the upper
classes not increasing musically
the lower classes are.

[1 sheet of rough notes in Elgar's hand, numbered 18 and
bound up into Ms. 2]

———

[1] Elgar tried to increase the opportunities for hearing orchestral music in Birmingham this year. On June 22 he wrote to Fiedler that: "There is a chance to get [the Queen's Hall Orchestra], with Wood for three concerts. I suggest that the idea should emanate from the School of Music—and the University join in . . ." A year later Elgar was still busy with this project. In spite of the support of Fiedler, Peyton, Bantock, and others, it did not fructify—largely through the opposition of a Halford lobby.

Mozarts

A fully equipped orchestra, capable of wrestling with any ordinary score, now consists

of

Wood Wind
{
picc
2 Flutes—or 3
2 Hautboys (or 3)
& [δ Cor] English Horn
                              Tenor Hautby
2 or 3 Clarts
Bass Clart
2 or 3 Bassoons
        & Double Bassoon
}

Brass
{
4 [δ C] Horns
3 Trumpets
3 Trombones
Tuba
}

Percussion or *ive*
U.S.A.
{
Drums of all kinds
    Cymbals Triangle
        Glockenspiel
}

Strings
    including 2 Harps

next page

[δ Some composers require more than]

[On reverse of p. 18]
[In pencil]   The Mozart Orchestra consisted of:—
                Normal Mozart Orchestra

2 Flutes, 2 Oboes, and in his later score, 2 clarinets,
2 Bassoons, 2 Horns, 2 Trumpets, Drums and string

[separate sheet following, unnumbered]
                Mozarts orchestra
This orchestra has now grown to the following by easy stages

[Pencil note on reverse of last page 35 of Ms. 2]

* Holmes & the Burgomeister playing without his coat in a quartet with 3 colleagues

The business of the town did not suffer: & it is possible that a [illegible deletion] *violin playing* Burgomaster wd. have come out of [δ the Koepeni] an interview with the Koepenick Captain as [δ one] a mayor who does not fiddle & a practical interest in music need not impair his value as a public servant[1]

---

[1] Edward Holmes (1797–1859), principally remembered for his *Life of Mozart* (1845), wrote many essays for *The Atlas, Fraser's Magazine, The Spectator,* and *The Musical Times.*

On October 16, 1906, a cobbler named Wilhelm Voigt (d. 1922) walked into the Town Hall of the Berlin Borough of Köpenick dressed in a Captain's uniform. He arrested the Mayor, seized the Treasury, and took over the administration of the Borough. This is the classic example of the alleged German respect for a uniform.

See Wilhelm Schäfer, *Der Hauptmann von Köpenick,* Leipzig, 1930; Carl Zuckmayer, *Der Hauptmann von Köpenick,* Leipzig, 1931.

TEXTUAL COMMENTARY

Ms. 1   O. [δ in its is defined]
instruments". [δ O. in its best sense is nothing of the kind.
That is precisely what orchestration, in its best sense, is *not*.]
. . . fundamentally wrong

Ms. 2   „   [δ wrong] *misleading*

[C.A.E.]

Ms. 1   . . . treat the enquirer

Ms. 2   „ [δ „ inquirer] *us*
. . . the Standard give *orchestration* "the act . . .

Ms. 1   COMPOSING

ARRANGING
. . . useful & necessary to make arrangements of such . . .

Ms. 2   „ [δ & necessary]
. . . and the like *are to be transferred from the piano*

Ms. 1   . . . not be considered [δ at present] now
Beginning with the fact . . .

Ms. 2   [δ Beginning with] *Accepting*
simply

Ms. 1   . . . we at once feel

Ms. 2   „ [δ at once] feel

Ms. 1   . . . wᵈ· lead us [δ to believe] think

Ms. 2   „ „ [δ us] *the enquirer*

Ms. 1   a mere [δ translation] *transference* of ideas

Ms. 2   a mere *labour*; a transference of ideas

Ms. 1   as it were, [δ in coul colour]
. . . dignified or possess [δ have a thousand] other qualities
—but this [δ last] is . . .

A musical idea then

ORCHESTRATION

Orchestration, *in the older edition* of the largest English musical dictionary, is defined thus:—

"The art of ADAPTING musical ideas to the varied capabilities of stringed, wind, keyed and other *instruments*".[1] This curious definition no doubt describes the method of a certain class of composers: but it is fundamentally *misleading*. Literary dictionaries *treat us better*, the Century and the *Standard give* "the art of composing OR arranging for Orchestra". This is correct: orchestration in its highest sense, is the art of *composing* for an orchestra: NOT the perfunctory matter of ARRANGING ideas for instruments. It is sometimes *useful to make arrangements, such* things as accompaniments to solos *and the like* are required to be transferred from the piano, but this avocation need *not be considered now.*

Accepting the fact that orchestration is not *simply* arranging for instruments but composing directly for those instruments, *we feel* that we are dealing with a real, living branch of creative art, not (as the erroneous definition would *lead an enquirer to think*), a mere labour: *a transference of ideas* from one medium to another,—or painting, as *it were*, a picture in colour from a mezzotint. A musical idea, whether phrase, theme, melody, or harmonic progression may have a certain value in itself apart from its presentation to the hearer.

It may be pleasing, *dignified or possess one* of a thousand other qualities; it may even be interesting because it is "scholarly"—but *this is so unusual* that we need not build upon it.

A musical idea may be interesting to read without hearing, or it may hold the attention when played on a keyed instrument: or by a combination of instruments, but its inventor must have had some definite

[1] *Grove's Dictionary*, 1880, Vol. 2, pp. 566–73, article on "Orchestration" by W. S. R[ockstro].

Ms. 1   . . . without [δ devising and] designing [δ in his own mind]
          simultaneously no-one [δ deliberately writes a solo for the 'cello
          &] in writing

          . . . the means are [δ the same] within limits the same

          they are both instruments [marginal note C.A.E.] *both*
Ms. 2   „   „   „   *wood-wind* instruments

Ms. 1   piano? [δ The absurdity is multiplied]
          they only *resemble each other* [δ resemblance / in so far as / point
          of contact is in the fact *that*] *in so far as* both . . .
          The piano [δ is a] however

          notion that [δ things are] *music is*
          . . . for orchestra afterwards★ [to] ★ [δ As] *This* we gathered
          . . . belief. [by-passing section marked **A**] I shall have . . . by
          themselves [See p. 239.]
          [at foot of page 6] above **A** [referring back to pp. 5b and 5c]
          I have said . . . often attempted
Ms. 2   This is *to be* gathered
Ms. 1   ★ and as you *probably* all play the piano and wonder what I
          mean I had better [δ sa] touch on this point now (back).
          [★ in margin]
          . . . only [δ one conce] *point* concerning . . .
          . . . of reproducing orchl. effects & pianists expect
Ms. 2   „   „   *not only* orchl. EFFECTS *but* *orchestral*
          HARMONY
          ★ and pianists expect . . . [★ on facing page]
Ms. 1   [δ one quality] *two qualities* of tone [δ at a time] *simultaneously*
          in the hands of a [δ very] moderate player

But he seems also unfortunately
the mere pedantic mechanic;
respectable men who would

have been equally successful as
schoolmasters ... they
... title ...

... keepers in a factory
... — Men who create
...

an orchestral work like a

problem of Euclid & therefore
at our birth might ...
without one thought of fate.
We have heard of the boy

who has to delighted

... the reasoning of Euclid
that he need to peruse

from
of
"hearing"

★ Think ... your ago or
... an explanation contradicts
but (certain.)

or, if they must keep time to
others they would figure
more inequality a timekeepers
in a factory yard

"Timekeepers in a factory yard"

Music examples for use in Mozart lecture

Miniature score annotated for lecture on G minor symphony

medium in his mind. It will be understood that I refer only to music of a high type, not to that of the market. Now I find it impossible to imagine a composer creating a musical idea *without defining inwardly, and simultaneously,* the exact means of its presentation. This seems easily understood when a SOLO for any instrument is in question: no *one in writing* a solo for 'cello deliberately thinks it out "on" the organ; or develops a piece for violin with the help of the piano. Such things are unthinkable and you assume that it is foolish of me to suggest such a thing. Wait—

It IS possible to transfer a melodic passage from one instrument to a kindred one—from the Viola to the 'Cello; *the means are* within limits the same. The pitch is altered: to take a theme from a clarinet and give it to a flute is not ridiculous: *they are both wood-wind* instruments and the phrasing of both is dominated and limited by the breath of the player.

But what are we to say of those who approach the Orchestra through the *piano*? *No* two things could be more dissimilar; they *only resemble each other in so far as* both are capable of complete harmony and not as in a single violin for instance, an extremely limited range of chords. *The piano however,* dominates music of the present and is responsible for many distorted ideas in music generally; everything is 'arranged' or arrangeable for the piano and this has given rise to the *notion that music is* in some way composed first and 'arranged' for orchestra *afterwards. This is to be gathered* from the old definition in Grove's Dictionary, and it is a very general belief. I have said the reign of the piano has given rise to some distorted views, *and as you all probably* play the piano and wonder what I mean, I had better touch on this now.

The *only point intimately concerning* our present subject is harmony. It is too easily assumed that the piano is capable of reproducing not only the orchestral EFFECTS but orchestral harmony also *and pianists expect* an orchestral piece to sound well on their favourite instrument. Now the rigid piano is capable of only two *qualities of tone simultaneously in the hands of a moderate player*—and most players are that. Better performers are able to produce further effects by allowing one part (one voice) to predominate in each hand, giving us four distinct weights of

variety of shades of tone, [δ & these shades]

[δ If this is remembered it is at once] We see [δ n] harmonies [δ was] *is*

To give a single instance
of a chord

Ms. 2	*by the heavy-toned ones*
Ms. 1	while the [δ mor]

the backbone, [δ as at] is . . .
suggested. [δ Of this point] [in margin] and every shade . . .
chord, *& this,*
simultaneously . . . possibility of modern harmony

Ms. 2	possibilit[δ y]*ies*
Ts.	sure [Ms. 1/Ms. 2] aware
Ms. 1	disastrous results to his [deletion] reputation by one of the critics . . .
Ms. 2	[δ to his reputation] [δ of the critics] . . .
	on its merits
Ms. 1	. . . hearing [δ it] *an arrangement*
Ms. 2	*of it*
Ms. 1	by [δ the] *an* orchestra
Ms. 2	*Simple harmonies . . . composed* [at foot of p. 5c]
	I am not assuming that other & [at head of p. 6, both added by E.]
Ms. 1	I am not assuming [follows "a very general belief." See p. 237]

true dignity. above **A**   I shall . . . themselves [marked **A** and within square brackets follows] for orchestra afterwards [on p. 6; See p. 236 above.]

Ms. 1	*the orchestra of the moment*

in its early days

Ms. 2	*it grew in its earliest years*
Ms. 1	. . . although [δ a further]

but [δ additions & occasionally] experimental additions, some to remain permanent

Ms. 2	[δ permanent]

tone. Beyond this the piano cannot go. The modern orchestra is capable of an unending variety of *shades of tone*, not only in succession, but in combination.

We see that a whole world of new *harmonies is at* the disposal of a composer for orchestra: harmonies which may sound execrable and impossible on the piano but which may give the greatest pleasure when scored for instruments. *To give a single instance*— The dissonant notes *of a chord* may be merely suggested by the soft-toned instruments, or they may be thundered *out by the heavy-toned ones, while the principal notes* of the chord, the backbone, *is merely suggested*. Every shade of dynamic force is possible for every note of every chord, and this simultaneously. We have only touched on the fringes of the possibilities of modern harmony.

I am quite sure of the harmonic invention of Chopin and others: I only say that the orchestra must not be studied through the piano. This was done with disastrous *results by one who* played (he said he played it) a work of Richard Strauss on the piano and criticised it from that stand-point. No one would dream of criticising a piano piece on *its merits as* a piano solo after *hearing an arrangement* of it played *by an orchestra*: this is naturally absurd: but it is not more absurd than the reverse process, which we know is often attempted. *Simple harmonies will* sound satisfactory by whatever means presented: but modern harmony must be heard and judged and played by the actual medium for which it was *composed*. *I am not assuming* that other and correct views are not known, modern writers especially have upheld orchestration in its *true dignity*. *I shall have something to say of the orchestration of* pianoforte players later: of Schumann, Rubinstein and Brahms, these three forming almost a class by *themselves*.

I ask you then to consider the ORCHESTRA as a thing distinct from anything else. The present day orchestra, the orchestra *of the present*, is a complex machine, not invented, but slowly evolved from very small beginnings. I do not treat of the orchestra as a finite thing: it grew in its *earliest years*, it has been enlarging, developing and strengthening itself during two centuries, and to-day, *although sufficiently* large to satisfy a moderate ambition, we cannot say that its component parts are fixed or in any way fixable. Certain instruments will always be and remain absolutely necessary, *but experimental additions, some to remain*, some to be discarded, will always be made. The machine that

Ms. 1   [δ I am n]

research; naturally with a want of candour, painful but not surprising, certain antiquarians omitted the word 'useless' [Marginal note] p. 7?

I am still here.
& I am going . . .
Ms. 2   And I am going to
particulars [δ of the history of such as these] may be found . . .
It may be said that the really great . . .
Ms. 2   [δ I will point out . . . said that the] *The* really great
endeavoured to ma[δ d]*k*e
Ms. 1   *by their compositions* [Marginal notes] age? [for time] p. 8
lesser [for less] p. 8
have been [δ made] *shaped*
Ms. 1   but [δ to] a stud[δ ent]*y* of it [δ at the present day] it can be of
[δ no] little practical use.
Ms. 2   but, to a student [δ of the present day] it can be of little
practical use.
Ms. 1   [δ Bach's] the orchestra
unchangeable. next p.
              [δ What alchemy is to modern chemistry,
—what astrology is to astronomy so is the older orchestration to that of the present day.]
The history of the orchestra [δ between] *from* Bach & Handel
to Mozart is dull; we shall find **A** [δ those instruments been
improved] [in margin] that the manufacture of instruments
improved & that the clarinet was invented . . . [δ admitted]
welcomed into *a so-called* the orchestra
[δ We have] It must be allowed
if not improved
Ms. 2   ⋆ We may remark . . . detail, [⋆ on facing page to p. 10]
Ms. 1   These apparent cessations [margin] ? [p. 10] have naturally
been caused by the appearance of a great master: we hear of

suits one generation is antiquated in the next, and this must always be so.

We must not claim that all additions to the orchestra have been successful: some have been discarded as hurriedly as they have been introduced, but we must not think for one moment that the orchestra of 1820 can in any way influence music in the twentieth century.

I said in a former lecture that too much time (in music) was spent upon "useless" antiquarian research. Some antiquarian quoted this, omitted the word "useless", preached a sermon on the mutilated text, and condemned me to unheard of punishment,—which punishments after all would be light compared with the possible agony of listening to a humorous antiquarian lecture (musical). I am still here.

I am not going to weary you with details of pre-Mozart orchestras, *particulars of which may* be found in many historical works. I will point out that at all times orchestration by the great men of their day, has been adequate to their ideas. *The really* great composers have endeavoured *to make,* to build, if you like, their orchestras *by their compositions,* while lesser men, men of the professorial, Capellmeister type, have accepted the orchestra of their day: their compositions have *been shaped,* built, if you like, by the limitations of the orchestra of the moment.

The orchestration of Bach, the father of modern music, is supremely interesting, *but, to a student it can be* of little practical use. While we admire his great qualities, his grandeur, reticence, pathos, ingenuity and clever orchestral *device, the orchestra* of that day is to us of anti-quarian interest only. But we can learn that Bach was not content to accept any limitations: new instruments were always tried and he did not look upon his orchestral machine or method as *fixed or unchangeable.*

The history of the orchestra from Bach and Handel to Mozart is dull: we shall find that the manufacture of instruments improved, and that the Clarinet was invented and after some tentative trials, was finally welcomed into the (so-called) classical orchestra. It must be allowed that the Orchestra has always developed, if not improved, but there have been times when a pause has apparently been made. *We may remark* that Mozart's Orchestra was generally sufficient for his purpose, while Beethoven is frequently overweighted by the master's ideas. This is a point for consideration in detail. *These apparent arrestments* have naturally been caused by the appearance of a great Master: we

the Mozart orchestra . . . Wagner orchestra [δ & this has
given] & this vast machine . . . we pause

Ms. 2   These apparent [δ arrestations] *arrestments*

Ms. 1   [δ I propose to commence my review of the orchestra] p. 11
The orchestra is divided . . . and is now allotted [missing at
this point in Ms. 1, see p. 243]

Ms. 2   rhythm [δ and] *of*
and of [δ giving] *adding* to

Ms. 1   It is scarcely worthwhile to [ρ consider] *dwell upon* proposed
additions to the orchestra

Ms. 2   [δ It is . . . to the orchestra]

Ms. 1   Those instruments which [δ are ?] have
* *occasionally . . . lack of it* [* in margin]
. . . special [δ mission] work
[δ That *beautiful* sweet-toned instrument t] The saxophone
. . . is penetrating

Ms. 2   * *Saxhorns . . . in the orchestra*   [* in margin]

Ms. 1   I [δ wrote for] *introduced*

. . . rehearsing [δ expense & so forth]

[δ home] *permanent home*

. . . in [δ score] orchestral scores

& not [δ so much in the direction of] *its*

hear of the Mozart orchestra: this was spoken of as a complete and final thing: but there grew out of it the Beethoven orchestra—to this day spoken of as a complete and final thing: then came the Wagner orchestra and this vast machine was considered the "last word" by his contemporaries, but now we have the Richard Strauss, and, for the moment, we pause.

The Orchestra is divided now as it was 200 years ago into four principal groups; strings, wood-wind, brass and percussion. Each of the divisions has received additions. The strings stand much as they were: the wood-wind now numbers among its permanent members, the English Horn, or tenor hautboy, the bass clarinet and the double bassoon. The abiding addition to the Brass section is the Tuba: this replaces the Ophicleide, one of the experimental additions to which I referred.

I need not mention the "Battery" in the percussion department demanded by modern composers: it includes everything capable of emphasising rhythm, of lending explosive force and of adding to picturesque colour. The harp has taken a permanent place in the orchestra and is now allotted a more dignified position than was its lot earlier in the last century. Those instruments which have found a permanent place have a power of 'blending' with each other in a marvellous way. Extra instruments, introduced for special effects, have been used irrespective of this quality: occasionally chosen for some special effect on account of their lack of it, but when their special work has been accomplished they have departed. The saxophone will no doubt some day be established among us; its tone is beautiful and expressive and, if you wish, subdued. Saxhorns, a valved or keyed modification of the horn family, chromatic instruments, do not 'mix' and they can never take a permanent place in the orchestra. I introduced four saxophones in a work (Caractacus) in 1898 but there was a difficulty in getting players, rehearsing and the extra expense prevented my experiment coming to a hearing. Richard Strauss has within the last year or two, written for these instruments. Apart from their permanent home in military bands, the saxophone had an occasional appearance as a solo instrument in orchestral scores—Delibes, and, earlier, Bizet.

Concerning possible advantageous additions to our present orchestra, I shall have something to suggest later. For many years apart from mere novelty, composers have aimed at increasing the SONORITY of the orchestra and not its purity of tone and sweetness: I hope the addition of saxophones may be the first step of many in this direction.

... moderate share of [δ ancient] musical history was [δ known] *common*: I now assume that [δ the] a certain ...

A   What alchemy ... [See p. 240 above] [δ was] *is* [δ was] *is* to astronomy

so is [δ a ...] *the older*

... present time [δ **B**]

... & as [δ the] art

... profiting by the EXPERIMENTS & ERRORS as well as the noble achievements of former artists, we [δ can/must] *can* ...

Ms. 2   [δ noble] successful

Ms. 1   I propose [δ to go no further] to [δ be] commence no earlier than Mozart. We will not be blind—[δ Mozart orchestn] or deaf—the latter calamity is likely to fall on us first—to the claims of the modern school

[Marginal note in pencil] *More? p. 14*

Ms. 2   ... certain distance. [δ I propose ... earlier than Mozart.]

[Marginal note in pencil] *Stet*

Let us look ... Wagner says: [inserted on sheet numbered 15] [Following quotation in typescript on p. 16] (*Ashton Ellis partly*) (+ *back*)

Ms. 1   *after Wagner extract*

This is [δ of course] *too* highly coloured ...

... freedom [δ & an expression]

... the orchestra a [δ poetic] *more plastic*

... has landed the [deletion] orchestra *somewhat below its real position*—the [δ f musical] *mighty* engine [δ of absolute music];

In my former lecture I assumed *that a moderate share of* musical history was common: *I now assume that a certain* knowledge of the orchestra is in your possession. *What alchemy is to modern* chemistry—what *astrology is to astronomy,* so is *the older* orchestration to that of the present time. But as *the new grows* out of the old *and the art progresses,* profiting by the experiments and errors as by the successful achievements of *former artists, we can profitably look back* a certain distance. *We will not be blind, or deaf,—the latter* calamity is more likely *to fall on us first—to the claims of the modern school.*

I propose to commence no earlier than Mozart. Let us look at the scores of Mozart's most important symphonies: for several reasons this is a convenient starting point for a consideration of the modern orchestra. In his Artwork of the Future (1849) Wagner says:

> "He (Mozart) breathed into his instruments the passionate breath of a HUMAN VOICE, that voice towards which his genius bent with overmastering love. He led the staunchless stream of teeming harmony into the very heart of Melody; as though in restless care to give it, only mouthed by Instruments, in recompense the depth of feeling and of fervour that forms the exhaustless source of human utterance within the inmost chambers of the heart. Whilst, in his Symphonies, Mozart to some extent but made short work of everything that lay apart from this his individual impulse and, with all his remarkable dexterity in counterpoint, departed little from those traditional canons which he himself helped forward to stability: he lifted up the singing power of instrumental music to such a height that it was now enabled, not only to embrace the mirth and inward still content which it had learned from Haydn, but the whole depth of endless heart's-desire."
>
> 'The Art-work of the Future', by Richard Wagner, translated by William Ashton Ellis (1892), Vol. I, page 121.

This is too highly coloured and rhapsodical but the underlying truth is solidly there: Mozart extended the "expression" of the orchestra. From that day onward there has been an ever-*increasing freedom,* there has been no cessation from the endeavour to make the orchestra a *more plastic vehicle,* and, thankful as we are to pioneers we cannot help feeling that the unreasonableness of some non-musicians in pursuing a perfectly vain and empty argument, *has placed the orchestra somewhat below its real position*—the mighty engine, the vehicle of the highest

[δ 14]   [δ We may therefore look with equanimity
                has landed the orchestra, I say, bound over to the torturers]
            is degraded into a machine for painting pictures for hopelessly
            unmusical people.

Ms. 2   [δ is] *could be* degraded . . . painting pictures for hopelessly
            [δ commercial] *unmusical* people.

Ms. 2   ★ *Therefore . . . edition*   [facing p. 16] (★ *back*)
            [followed by] *Today we are concerned with general principles
            only. to p. 17*
            . . . we will [δ begin] *commence*

                The Mozart orchestra [in pencil at foot of p. 17 formerly 16,
            misplaced in bound volume and shown above on p. 232]
            A fully equipped orchestra . . . Strings including 2 Harps
                                [on p. marked 18, see p. 232 above]

Ts.   Strings including 2 Harps [omitted]

Ms. 1   For special purposes . . . to be ill". [on pp. δ 19/20 **B** bound
                                                                    after p. 20]
Ms. 2   on p. 19
Ms. 2   . . . sufficient [δ for the present]
Ms. 1   The tendency of the [δ present day] *moment*

                . . . to [δ many] works
                . . . nationality [δ I am continually reminded of the phrase
            quoted by Motley]

form of art ever known to the world, would be degraded into a machine for painting pictures for hopelessly unmusical people.

Therefore, when we begin *our analytical work we will commence with Mozart*: next week I propose to consider the three larger symphonies of Mozart: E flat, G minor and the so-called Jupiter: I shall use the miniature of the C minor symphony and it will be more easy for you to follow my remarks if you provide yourselves with copies of that edition.

The Mozart orchestra consisted of 2 flutes, 2 oboes, and in his later scores, 2 clarinets, 2 bassoons, 2 horns, 2 trumpets, drums and strings.

This orchestra has now grown to the following by easy stages: - a fully equipped orchestra, capable of wrestling with any ordinary score, now consists of:—

> Piccolo
> 2 Flutes or 3
> 2 Hautboys or 3 & English Horn
> 2 or 3 Clarinets
> Bass Clarinet
> 2 or 3 Bassoons and Double Bassoon
> 4 Horns
> 3 Trumpets
> 3 Trombones
> Tuba
> Drums of all kinds, Cymbals,
> Triangle, Glockenspiel
> Strings including 2 Harps.

For special purposes, some composers require more than this: but for general purposes this force is sufficient.

The *tendency of the moment* is to use this great machine too continuously at something approaching the full power, full in numbers if not in strength. In *listening to works* by young composers of any *nationality, it is impossible not to feel* that the orchestra is kept at white heat for too long a time, complication is piled on complication, it would seem to

Ms. 1   **B** If the composer . . . to be ill"

. . . room in [δ our] *some* hearts

The [δ average] young composer

Ms. 2   *The list given last* [in pencil] [δ This] then . . .
Ms. 1   . . . how [δ is it to be written for] *are we to* write for it?
in many books [δ but] as the rudiments
Ms. 2   [δ as]

Ms. 1   . . . real orchestrators [δ being produced] *resulting*
Ms. 2   *from   the*
efforts [in pencil]

Ms. 1   . . . other arts [δ may be]
Ms. 1/Ms. 2   . . . available for English readers
Ms. 1   it is [δ not] *no longer* PRACTICAL in many ways * [To lower
part of page.]
[δ & deals, chiefly as all books of the class must with analysis.
It deals chiefly with analysis.]
    A A most useful [δ book] *work* is the small handbook of
Prout, [δ but that also goes & there are several others] & this
can be recommended for beginners.
    * The great development in the [δ playing of] execution of
our string players, for instance, renders many of the [δ directi]
recommendations for the division of difficult passages
amongst the strings unnecessary.
All works . . . Berlioz' book. **A**
    [δ An old fashioned view of the art is
        I read the following as shewing how much we have to]
        I [δ knew] *felt* that *my condemnation of*
Ms. 1   to [δ read you] *give*
Ms. 1/   [Pages [22 and 23 respectively] with quotation from
Ms. 2   Macfarren *carent*]

be for the sake of complication only. *If the composer* finds he has written at all simply, he seems to be possessed with a nervous feeling that something is wrong—that he has fallen from some ideal and faltered in a noble task. He need not fear: there is *still room in some hearts*, if not in some heads, for the pure and beautiful in music.

The young composer may still write music inspired by the higher feelings with acceptance: the opposite class remind me of the sentence quoted by Motley from the sarcastic Padovaro, "When he finds himself SOBER he believes himself to be ill."

The list given last then is to-day the ideal orchestra. How are we to write for it?

The question is answered in *many books: the rudiments* of painting can be taught, but we cannot make painters,—as grammar, prosody etc. can be ground into many millions of youthful people without producing a poet, so can the general idea of orchestration be induced into many thousands of students without *a real orchestrator resulting from the efforts.*

But the study of orchestration will always help to a better appreciation of instrumental music: so the teaching or attempted teaching, of orchestration, is justified in the same way as is the study of the *other arts.* Berlioz's book has been *available for many years and* still remains the most inspiring work on the subject. It is no longer practical in many ways. The great improvement in the execution of our string players, for instance, render[s] many of the recommendations for the division of difficult passages unnecessary—a small point.

All works on orchestration must deal chiefly with analysis and much music has been written since Berlioz penned his inspiring volume. A most useful work is the small handbook of Prout, and this can be recommended for beginners.[1]

I felt that my condemnation of the definition of orchestration with which I commenced, would surprise you. I am anxious not to misrepresent and to avoid "reading into" anything which is not there. But at this point I find it convenient *to give an extract* from Macfarren, a noteworthy writer on many branches of our Art.

(Quotation of book not to be found.)[2]

---

[1] Berlioz's *Modern Instrumentation and Orchestration*, translated by Mary Novello, was published by Alfred Novello in 1854. Prout's *Instrumentation* was issued in 1878, *The Orchestra* (Augener), 2 vol., in 1898–9; the former was published as *Stromentazione*, by V. Ricci, of Milan, in 1901.

[2] Possibly from lectures on Bach and Handel contained in *Addresses and Lectures*, 1888.

Ms. 1   *after extract* [in pencil at head of p. 23]
    . . . I should say it is the [δ sustaining/varied] "simultaneous . . .
    . . . at once. [δ When I said that the orchestra must not]

    [δ When I said] *I now explain the sentence*

    . . . but that the fact . . .
Ms. 2   . . . but *I insist* that the fact

Ms. 1   . . . of that kind. [δ I now say in a general
         A mistake often made by pianists who
         write for orchestra—Rubinstein was
         frequently did so was the ineffectively]
    Give examples in works [foot of p. 25: P. 26 begins—] We
    frequently hear [See p. 253 below.]
Ms. 2   *Write a crotchet in the bass. ped sustains. this must be a semibreve in the orch* [in pencil at foot of p. 26.]
Ms. 1   [δ To a practical player] Good orchestration . . .
    . . . to present *the musical idea in an* [δ adequately] entirely adequate way
        [δ the musical idea] [δ I assure you that this is a part of the original in]
    . . . means used [δ by Mozart]

Ms. 2   . . . so few [δ in number]
    or thin [in pencil]

Yes, the treatment has been modified. Larger works have demanded larger orchestras, or larger orchestras have demanded larger works; I leave it to historians to decide, if it be worth discovering, which force was the moving power.

Strings—larger numbers possible division.
Some pizzicato, some arco, some sordini.
    Wood-wind, endless combinations.
    Brass—   ,,   ,,
Harps, Mandolines, Guitars (Schumann) etc.

If it be required to define the 'genius' of the orchestra in one sentence, I should say it is *the "simultaneous,* varied sustaining power"—the organ can sustain, but only with three or four varieties of the colour *at once. The* sustaining power of all orchestral instruments (except of course pizzicato instruments, harps or the percussion) is the chief thing to be considered.

I now explain this sentence. "WE MUST NOT APPROACH THE ORCHESTRA THROUGH THE PIANO", I do not mean that a composer must not play over his ideas before committing them to paper *but I insist that the fact* that the piano is capable of full harmony must not lead a composer to transfer his piano ideas— ideas conceived on the piano—bodily to the orchestra. But this has been done and is still frequently done. In the consideration of specific works, I may be able to point out distinct passages *of this kind. Speaking* generally: Rubinstein's orchestration is an example— Schumann's also—they forget that in playing the piano they used the 'sustaining' pedal, or as people will call it, the loud pedal.

Give examples in works.

Write a crotchet in the bass, pedal sustains, this must be a semibreve in the orchestra.

Good orchestration is the fitness of the means to the end: that is to say, the accurate choice of the *vehicle to present the musical idea* in an entirely adequate way.

With the *simple means used at* the end of the 18th century and the beginning of the 19th, it was easy to decide if the use of the instruments was good or bad. They *were so few that* the smallest error in choice of tone—in the filling out of chords was disagreeable *or thin.* In our enlarged orchestra the case is different: it is possible for a novice to

Ms. 1   . . . are to an expert nothing but
Ms. 2   . . . are to an expert [δ every] *nothing*

Ms. 1   . . . does not sound [δ bad] *at all bad*

          . . . absence [δ wd. be missed]
          dissatisfaction. ★ ★ *take another sheet* **B** [See p. 248.]
          ★ ★ ★ **B** Passages are often written . . . exploit them
          [on page wrongly numbered 27 and placed after] the orches-
          tration is not good [See p. 255; followed by pages numbered
          28, 29, 30.]
              Good orchestration . . . clarinet for instance [See pp. 251–3.]

Ms. 1   Orchestral instruments . . . [continues on p. 30 after
                                              interpolation of **B**]

Ms. 2   *they are*
Ms. 1   always [δ readily] *ready*

          We frequently [δ read] hear

          . . . impossible. [δ Certainly] *often*
          [δ writer] composer
          some of
          This is simple
Ms. 2   This is *a* simple *case* [pencil insertions]
          more or less prominently

pile one mass of tone on another absolutely wasting his means, without the effect being painful or absurd. But from a practical point of view this is not GOOD orchestration. "Whatever sounds well, is well"—true, but there must be a consideration for the players. Many works, much praised by critics, who know nothing of the technical part of the orchestra, *are to an expert, nothing* but childish experiments. It is possible to see what Strauss is driving at when he superimposes one mass on another: but his imitators frequently blaze the whole orchestra in an immature way, trusting that something will 'turn up' as it were; out of the whole mass there must be some result: and truth to say, there often is a result—of noise and bewilderment—and—it *does not sound at all bad.*

But this is scarcely orchestration. Much is of course written which is not intended to be *distinctly* heard: *filling in* which is not noticed, but its *absence would cause* a sense of *dissatisfaction.*

Passages are often written for strings by Wagner which are not suited to the genius of those instruments, but these are only to add to the general effect and are not intended to sound brilliant. When Wagner wishes a passage to stand out effectively, he writes something playable.

Weber—perfect orchestration played without expression.
Delibes—wastes nothing.
Berlioz—accused of inverting effects and then composing music to exploit them.

Orchestral instruments must be kept in the player's hands, *they are* intimate things.

Solos must be prepared.

Again the piano—*always ready*—but soloists do not plunge into a concerto, they play with the tutti.

A few preparatory unimportant notes for the clarinet for instance.

We frequently hear that such and such a work is badly orchestrated. How is it possible to decide one way or another? How do we know what the composer intends? The answer in most cases is easy: in some doubtful, and in a few impossible. Often in a "tutti" passage we know that *the composer* wishes to give us a fine resonant succession of chords: if *some of* these chords are not full and resonant, we can only say that the arrangement is bad. *This is a simple case.* When a passage is written for a solo orchestral instrument we may assume that this solo is intended to be heard *more or less prominently*; if the accompaniment is

18—AFFEM

but . . . doubtful case. [in pencil]
* *A difficult case . . . solo work* [* on page facing p. 32]
        . . . as I [δ have referred] referred to
Ms. 1   [Continued on p. 31]

I have today confined myself to general considerations only leaving the analysis of scores to future lectures. I therefore conclude with a few observations on the future of orchestral music in this country.

Ms. 2   I have today confined myself to general considerations [δ only] leaving . . . future lectures. I therefore [δ conclude with a] *I think fittingly give* few observations . . . in this country. [pencil insertion]

Ms. 1   . . . amongst our rulers
Ms. 2   . . . amongst our [δ lawgivers] *public men (there are notable exceptions in Birmingham)*

Ms. 1   and [δ above] *without*

that no [δ polit] statesman

too heavily scored and obscures the main idea we may say again that the orchestration is not good: *but the importance of the accompanying figure may be paramount with the composers: this is a doubtful case. A difficult case* may be such a passage as I referred to where tone is piled upon tone without effect. Sometimes such passages are written merely to keep a 'treacherous' instrument in the player's hands preparatory to some *solo work.*

I have to-day confined myself to general considerations only. I will therefore, I think fittingly, give a few observations on *the future of orchestral music in this country,* leaving the analysis of scores to future lectures.

Orchestration can be best learnt or assimilated by listening to orchestras: the opportunities in this country are comparatively few, and it is a matter of surprise and congratulation that we have so many composers who are good orchestrators among us.

In Germany it is different. I need not go into the many circumstances which have led to this, they are well known.

Commercial considerations are always at the root of any art movement and in the present lack of musical taste and education *among our public men (there are notable exceptions* as in Birmingham) we must only wait and hope for a better day. We can scarcely hope for municipal orchestras at present.

The position is anomalous: we have seen during late years a great deal of theoretical philanthropy in the domain of music. Teaching institutions have been founded under royal patronage *and without it also.*

We have been educating and turning out a vast number of musicians generally better equipped than was the case or was possible, a few generations ago.

We have seen the difficulty of obtaining a copyright bill to protect the rights of those composers whom we have been at great pains to produce. That bill is now happily an accomplished fact.[1]

But while we musicians are thankful to the movers in this much-needed act of common honesty, we cannot but feel aggrieved that music is still in such a curious position in the eyes of business men in this country, that *no statesman* of the first rank dare lift up his voice in the House of Commons in favour of the protection of our rights. A question affecting literature or painting would have been treated differently, not that it was always so. Let me remind you that in 1783,

[1] See p. 76.

Ms. 2   . . . House of Commons.   *next page*   [in pencil]

[δ *Authors are now welcomed amongst
our legislators & we may take heart from this fact & trust that
music may be also treated with respect*]   [in pencil]

[Ms. 2 ends at this point, for note on reverse of
final page see p. 233]

Ms. 1   . . . no serious statesman would [δ ever again] *continue to* be
considered serious [δ amg] *by*   [in pencil, as all subsequent
insertions and emendations]

[δ *Thinking so*] *But the vast majority of our public men are
unmusical &*
. . . municipal orchestras [δ *in the*] *in the near future* [δ *as being
within reach* / *the range of* / *near steady realisation*]
an annual [δ small] loss
Great concerts . . . and opera
so few copies sold * [* on facing page] * *At this point I had much to
say here twelve months ago & I see that Sir Alex^r· Mackenzie
referred to the subject yesterday*

[δ How can] *Why should* . . .

seem to progress [δ *in the way*] in proportion *to the growth of
the population.*
largely
Are we . . . like ourselves [in margin]

We must [δ give] *meet* them [δ *something better*] *in a nobler
way* than *by* [δ songs] publish[δ ed]*ing* [δ *at*] *songs* & [δ 2^d]
pianoforte music at twopence a sheet

[William] Beckford, the author of 'Vathek', printed a volume entitled 'Dreams, [W]aking Thoughts and incidents', really one of the earliest and most poetic travel-books.[1] Before publication, his friends represented to him that the fancy and imagination of the work would prejudice the author's success in the *House of Commons*. Their advice prevailed and all copies were destroyed except six.

This sort of thing has been lived down and a man need not fear his position in the House on account of authorship. But with music it is still different: *no serious statesman would continue* to be considered serious by the business men of this country if he made an important speech in favour of our art. *But the vast* majority of our public men are unmusical and *it seems difficult* to see the advent of municipal orchestras in the *near future*. A city like Düsseldorf looks upon its orchestra as an asset and does not mind an *annual loss*; the music is a feature of the town life and draws many residents.

Great concerts, popular concerts, choral concerts and opera.
Publication of orchestral works unremunerative necessarily so, *so few copies sold*. Few orchestras in existence. Piano arrangements dwindling sale. Gramophones reproducing instruments. Long records reproduce the singer. Orchestral records, no particular orchestras.

This may seem outside the point but it is really vital. *Why should we* 'lure' young men on to writing that which will pauperise them?

A revolution is with us, a peaceful one, rather, a gradual change.

The "upper classes" music *does not seem to progress in proportion to the growth of the population*. We have been educating the poorer classes *largely*. They must have music: otherwise our education fails. How is this to be done? *Are we going to leave them to their own pianos, their gramophones, their comic songs and Music Halls? or shall we ever attempt to give them what we like ourselves? We must meet them in a nobler way than by publishing* songs and pianoforte music at twopence a sheet. In 1871—I said literature must be provided for the newly educated people

---

[1] *Dreams, Waking Thoughts and Incidents; In a Series of Letters from Various Parts of Europe*, London, 1783 (no author given). The first Letter begins: "Shall I tell you my dreams?—To give an account of my time, is doing, I assure you, but little better. Never did there exist a more ideal being. A frequent mist hovers before my eyes, and, through its medium, I see objects so faint and hazy, that both their colour and forms are apt to delude me. . . ." For Elgar's obsession with dreams see p. 89. Beckford has much to say in this book about the state of music in Italy.

. . . but it is not. [next page]

       [δ I propose to take Mozarts G minor sym-
       phony]

But we hope for better days.
I propose to take Mozarts sym } [in margin]
miniature score

    The writer of successful *high-class* orchestral music can look
forward to the usual comforts of the work-house &, I fear,
nothing more. I speak advisedly

—a fortune could be made.[1] No fortune is possible in providing good orchestral music—we want larger halls and municipal orchestras, the loss must be cheerfully borne at first. Why should not Birmingham lead—or follow Bournemouth?[2] This may be considered outside the subject but *it is not*. A modern University must be practical, or at least suggest practicality. I am not here to say that orchestration is a desirable thing—you know that: or to tell you simply how to perpetrate it—some of you know that also.

The result of your work must be considered, and I fear that the enlightened beneficent country which founds institutions and scholarships to train you will do little for you when you have produced those great works which it demands.

But we hope for better days.

[1] The date 1871 is quite clear in Elgar's MS. He was then a schoolboy!
[2] A municipal orchestra was instituted in 1893.

CHAPTER II

MOZART'S G MINOR SYMPHONY
(November 8, 1906)

In his Inaugural Address Elgar had projected the detailed study of particular works. In the event he discussed only those two which had exercised the greatest influence on him in his formative years. Mozart's Symphony in G minor (K. 550) had been his inspiration as a boy and his own first venture into symphony had been with an essay (incomplete) closely modelled after Mozart. This exercise had been undertaken in 1878.[1]

This lecture was delivered more or less extempore, and under trying conditions. It was given in a "small room, more people than cd. well find place—no light for piano".[2] The lecture was, however, covered by the press—which brought further cause for misunderstanding. In view of everything that had happened since his inauguration as Professor Elgar felt that he could take no more. On November 19 he "found he really cd. not give the lectures . . .", and on the next day he was "happier feeling clear of Birmingham".[3]

From the account of the lecture given in the *Birmingham Post* on November 9 it is clear that the introduction was that intended for (and possibly delivered in connection with) the previous one:

ORCHESTRATION

Sir Edward Elgar delivered the second of his series of lectures on orchestration at the University last evening. He pointed out that orchestration was defined, in orchestral works to which we could refer in these days, as arranging ideas for instruments. He did not think this was the correct view. Orchestration was composing for instruments, it was a great creative part, and not an extra to the composition at all. He further pointed out that the orchestra had never remained still; it was not finite. It began growing in the earliest days, and had been developing and enlarging—he did not say improving—until it arrived at certain pauses. These pauses were exemplified by the orchestration of Mozart, Beethoven, Wagner, and Strauss, which was the pause of the present. Each pause had been brought into being by some exceptionally great man. Dealing with the subject of harmony, the lecturer said it was too easily supposed that the piano could produce all harmony. It was well known

---

[1] See reproduction of part of score in section following p. 236.
[2] Diary.
[3] Ibid.

that it could produce orchestral effects, but it could not produce orchestral harmony.

Sir Edward then proceeded to deal in detail with Mozart's G Minor Symphony, which he described as an epic in sound. The whole thing was kept within certain well-defined limits; to his mind it was an example of consistency. Proceeding, he expressed himself in favour of a revision of the works of the old masters so that the omissions due to the deficiencies of the orchestras of their day might be supplied from our ampler resources. It was not from reticence, he observed, that Mozart or Beethoven did not employ certain natural effects, but simply because they were unattainable with the orchestral instruments of their time. He believed that, much as had been achieved, we were only on the verge of possibilities of modern harmony.

Rough Notes

[Numbering of sheets by Elgar.]

[Passages within () show the notes as copied on sheets stamped by Elgar as 2 and 3. Figures preceding notes correspond to those marked by Elgar in his score. In each case the bar number is added.]

2 [in pencil]   Bassoons left for the moment: Entry of the Hautboys
6 [bar 22]   *same pitch* as violins so almost unperceived. Bassoons added leading up to the pendant in B♭ (leading by cumulative effort, to the pendant (outburst—new themes) in B♭)

7 [bar 28]   only a little added force possible

8 [bar 28]   Horn—plays the 2 (two) important notes & is carried on two bars farther *see p. 16*[1]—corresponding passage (.) where, after the two bars the Horns are (perforce) omitted

(3) 9 [bar 28]   Quavers in Basses(;) continue sense of restless movement. Bassoons col Bassi almost careless (?)

10 [bar 29]   Violins in unisoni: (*not*) in octaves (as) 1mo. wd have been too high & out of keeping with the rest (out of keeping with the Violin passages throughout the work) [for continuation see below, p. 263]

_____
[1] cf. miniature score.

[unnumbered
sheet]

[Notes in ink, pencil insertions shown ——]
points of difference in G minor.
a general subdued effect.

——

in E♭ Sym [δ Violins] strings mostly violins, have
brilliant long runs

——

'cellos *occasionally* separate part, but only over a pedal—
Double Basses too weak *& uncertain* to be capable of
dealing with a moving bass effectively—changes of
harmony unsatisfactory without a firm bass.

——

in E♭ sym a great deal of repeated notes

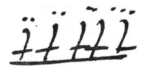

——

C major sym.
Brilliance attempted by endless

Trpts & Drums

I   I [bar I]   Violas divided, subdued accpt observe the care with
which the harmony is disposed so as to avoid doubling
the notes of the theme in the violins
Violins in 8$^{ves.}$

2 [bar 10]   Bass sustained—giving a new atmosphere & leading up
to the half close 5$^{th.}$ bar p. 2.

3 [bar 16]   Ingenious '*manipulation*' of the Horns. Open notes

4 [bar 16]   *Formal.* four bars cd. be omitted unmeaning bursts of
noise Grove[1]

5 [bar 20]   Bassoons. lovely

2   See p. 261 above

3   „ „ „   „   up to and including 10

11 [bar 28]   Really the climax before 2nd subject

12 [bar 42]   A great deal to be learned from a comparison between
p. 4 and p. 18 Strings simply transposed except the
Basses. great increase of weight of tone: Basses often
written too low

[Marginal note]
note 2$^{nd.}$ *violin* CHANGED *in one bar*

4   *Brahms.* often lumbering. looks well on paper but does
not sound well

5   *Andante*
One of the many movements beginning with repeated
notes—

---

[1] It would not appear that "Grove" is meant to relate to the previous statement, which
is not to be found in *Grove's Dictionary* (1st ed.) in the essays on "Mozart", "Orchestration", or "Symphony", nor yet in Grove's own analytical note on the symphony for the
St. James's Hall Richter Concert of June 14, 1880. There, in fact, "G." states: "The score
as it stands is a perfect gem. May no vandal ever add a note or an instrument to it."

Beethoven first Symphony

[δ seems] notice the rise to the *fourth*. in so many movets
[*sic*] of this kind.
as, for instance, 2ⁿᵈ subject part of the andante of the
E♭ (Mozᵗ) symty.
suggested by Bach
[in pencil] play them
(See illustration facing p. 236]

[separate sheet bound at end of Ms. 1]
    Mozart orchestra
  Mozarts three greatest Symphonies

I *in G minor*;—1 Flute, 2 Hautboys, 2 Bassoons, 2 Horns
                (Strings)
              no Clarinets
                    no Trumpets or Drums
          Mozart himself
          (Clarinets added later)   *violas divided.*
  no *other divisi* in Strings: Celli & Bassi always in unison
      orchestra *the same in all movements.*

II in E♭ ;—1 Flute, *2 Clarinets*, 2 Bassoons,
        2 Horns, 2 Trumpets & Drums.
        (Strings)
        no Hautboys
  orchestra reduced in Slow movement
        Violas divided
      Celli & CB divided—but only over a pedal.

III in C. Jupiter (so called), 1 Flute, 2 Hautboys
                2 Bassoons, 2 Horns,
                2 Trumpets & Drums

(no *clarinets*)
orch: reduced in Andante: upper strings are *muted*.

[Miniature score (London, E. Donajowski, supplied through Schott & Co., 187 & 188 Regent Street, London, W.) used by Elgar for lecture, with his annotations. Clarinets not shown in this score.]

[1 *Allegro molto*]
[At head of score]

Symphony in G minor.

(Composed 1788.)

.... p. 54 [last movement, bar 114, see p. 269]

[Bar no.]

1	[Figure 1 as on p. 263]	div. subdued accpᵗ·
10	2	[Vcl. & CB.] sustained
16	4	[Ww.]
	3	[Horns]
20	5	[Bassoons]
22	6	[„] left for the moment
28	7	[Ww.] a *little* added force
	8	[Bassoons] col Bassi
		[Horns]
	9	[Bassi] Sense of quaver movement kept up
29	10	[Vl. 1 & 2] *Vl. unis* 8 va wd have been too high
31–33		Sense of harmony & avoided fifths
34–35		[Vl. 1 & 2 ringed]

[Note at foot of page:] Horn carried on, see p. 16 [bar 195]

34–35   clever distribution of parts. Violins practically between chord

Bar

38	11	really the climax before 2nd sub.—but 2ⁿᵈ Horn has no note weaker here than preceding bar

39   [Bassi] $\dfrac{6}{4}$

[Horns]   compare p. 18
[bar 231 f.]

41   [Bassi] $\dfrac{6}{4}$

42	12	
44		Str. 2 & 3 pt. harmony effective
46–50		(4 pt. Harmony in mus [?] p. 19 [bar 231 f.]) answering strgs & wind
46–47		[consecutive fifths between vla. & vl. 2 marked]
64		violas col Bassi
70	[Fl., Basson, Vl.]	3 8ᵛᵉˢ
72–75		counterpoint in the same octave
76–77	[Vl. 1]	*not* 8ᵛᵉˢ—otherwise 6ᵗʰˢ. (I & II) in next bar wd. sound weak as it is they sound stronger
79	[Vl. 1 & 2]	6ᵗʰˢ. sense of fullness p. 21–22 [bar 276 f.]
81–83		inversion
86–87	[Vl. 1 & 2]	p. 22 [bar 284]
93–100		ordinary formal ending. with vigorous & triumphant sort of rhythm asserting itself
102–105	[Ww. ringed]	Analyse this passage modern tendency to complete the 'families of wind
107	[Bassoons]	sustained chords again mark change of harmony
114	[Fl., Ob.]	Harmony recurring
115–116	[Horn 2 ringed]	Horn follows theme to upper note see next p.
117		Working out
123–124	[Horn 2 ringed]	Horns cannot give upper note here

Bar			
134		[Fl. ringed]	movement kept up
		[Bassoons ringed]	odd writing for Bassoons
140			2$^{nd\cdot}$ ob & 1st Bassoon in unis in choice . . . [?] tone
153			2 Horn *luck*!
		[Ww. ringed]	this movement in w$^{d\cdot}$ wind truly orchestran.
178		[Bassoon]	new part added for poetic effect
199		[Vl. 1 & 2]	down not up to F—too high
201		[,,]	in 8^{ves} pitch allows them effective
203			Horns stop abruptly
213			Cross rhythms. Vio. 1 sufficient to answer va. Fag & Basses—5 accents—crotchet rhythm in Fl Ob
221			serious—keeps the sad dignity forward serious sound violins low in unis nearing the end
227			again clever distribution of chords
231	12	[Str.]	no 7^{ths} in IIs compare p 4 bar 38
235		[Str.]	jumps up not down as before
239			compare p. 4 [bar 46] 4 pt harmony
252			5th higher than 1st time but [. . . ?] Vl II & Vle in 8^{ves}
257			alive W. wind
276		[Vl. 1 & 2 ringed]	same points as before p. 6–7 bar 76 f.
284		,,	see 6–7 bars 86–87
295		[Horn 1]	better omitted
298			*sum up—consistency of convention* & [A . . . ?]
299		[Horn 2]	poetry [marked with] < [and] >
309			analyse last chord
[2 *Andante*]			
		[At head of score]	One of the many movements beginning with repeated notes
9		[Vl. 1]	possible germ of Dvorak's high violin parts

Bar

18	[4th quaver Ob. 1 ringed, marked] d	
19		analyse—no movement in Ob Bsn Hrns or Bass
29–32		these four bars (& in 2nd. plc. rewritten.

33 Schumann pointed out in the old score—C♮ in flute ex. of orch harmony

35	[Vl. 1]	compare p. 38 [bar 106]
41	[Str. ringed]	notice how the jump of an octave is managed
42	[vla.]	d? compare p. 39 [bar 113]
44	[Horns]	in E♭ Horns useful
58	[2nd quaver]	Fl & Fag omitted too high
60	[„ Fl., Bassoon]	∨
74		as before
103		Fl & Fag omitted
106	[Vl. 1]	Compare p. 29 bar 35
107	[„]	Vn. passage wd. have been too low or too high if merely transposed ends now on 1st string wd. have ended on 2nd. *dull* or if 8ve. higher, too *shrill*
112		Fl omitted
113	[Vla.]	? B compare p. 30 [bar 42] 8ve. jumps again. (The old scores had B♮s here J.A.)[1]
115	[Fl.]	G♮ written into rest bar

[3 *Menuetto—Allegro*]
[*Trio*]

4	[Vla. & Bassi]	entry of parts

[4 *Finale—Allegro assai*]

1	[Bassoon]	careless
15		enlarge on Brilliant writing generally. a sort of 'virtuos'

[1] Note in another hand: John Austin? See *Elgar O. M.*, pp. 127, 239.

Bar		acquentance [?] leads to cheapness Weber very brilliant about as far as one could safely go
21		In violin passages M. never repeats the wrong note quote Schumann
80–84		full rich sound quite modern. notice low B♭ in Horn
89	[Horn 2]	

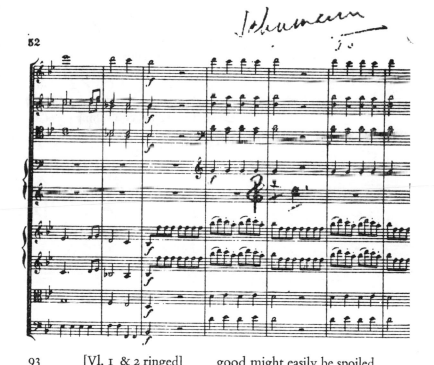

93	[Vl. 1 & 2 ringed]	good might easily be spoiled
104–110	[Wind ringed]	movement of wind pts. good
110–111		unison passages analyse brilliant unis.
114	[triplet figure]	only one. Jupiter full of it.
115		solid
147	[Fl.]	"Elijah"
158	[Bassoon & Vl. 2]	Consecutive 8ves.

161		Fl & Ob doubled
164–167	[Wind ringed]	cumulative effect altho' *not* doubled
176		Fag with vl.
178		Fl Ob with Bassi
240	[Vl. 1]	varied
249	[Horn 2]	an effect in a small room lost in a large hall
257) 259)	[Ww. Vl.] }	imitation
272	[Vla.]	This sound (violas) always carries my mind back to the opening of 1st movement
280	[Ob. 2 Vl. 2 ringed]	E$\natural$ dissonant note emphasised
284	[,,]	E$\natural$
287		movement of 2nd. Ob & 2nd. Horn —also Flute, 1st. Ob & Bassns / orchestral effect nothing *dead* no dead weight

Mozart's G minor Symphony

... from a modern score
to this small, Mannstein orchestra, — a pitiful array of
instruments, we may wonder how
it is possible that a perf orchestra could be evolved from
such crazy material.
However, "Sculptor does what
... ...
... a figure by its bulk"
as Gilbert makes Pygmalion
say.

I have read, in Otto
Jahn, sufficient proof of
this symphony that is not
necessary to trace it in
its place amongst the
... ...blest achievements
of art. ...

TEXTUAL COMMENTARY

Ms. 1   [δ Looking] *Turning* from a modern score [δ on] to
from such sorry materials

Ms. 2   „   „ a sorry *mass* of material[δ s]

[C.A.E.]

Ms. 1   [δ Works of art, however, are not 'judged by their bulk']
However, a sculptor
[δ highest] & noblest
[δ Then by reason] We have to marvel that with a [deletion]
such selection of instruments, sufficient variety

Ms. 2   . . . [δ sufficient] variety and contrast can be found
sufficient

Ms. 1   [In margin]

E♮	543
G mi	550
C	551

. . . thirty minutes.

[δ The compos]

MOZART'S G MINOR SYMPHONY

Turning from a modern score to this small, attenuated orchestra:— a pitiful array of instruments, we may wonder how it is possible that a great art-work could be evolved *from such sorry material.*

However, "a sculptor does not test the beauty of a figure by its bulk", as Gilbert makes Pygmalion *say*.[1]

I have read in Otto Jahn[2] sufficient praise of this Symphony, and it is not necessary to insist on its place amongst the *noblest* achievements of Art.

We have to marvel that with such a selection of instruments, variety and contrast can be found *sufficient to* hold the attention for *thirty minutes.*

---

[1] *Daphne* (wife of the patron Chrysos):
Why bless my soul, young man, are you aware
We gave but fifteen hundred not long since
For an Apollo twice as big as that?
Pygmalion:
But pardon me, a sculptor does not test
The beauty of a figure by its bulk.

Pygmalion and Galatea, Act II, Haymarket Theatre, 1871, Comedy Theatre, 1900, see *Original Plays*, 1876.

[2] Otto Jahn (1813–69), Professor of Classical Philology and Archaeology in the University of Bonn, and writer on music. His four-volume work, *W. A. Mozart*, was published in Leipzig (1856–9). Elgar read the English translation (*Life of Mozart*) by Pauline D. Townsend, with a Preface by George Grove, issued in three volumes by Novello in 1882.

See III, pp. 35–6: "The G minor symphony affords a complete contrast to all this E flat symphony. Sorrow and complaining take the place of joy and gladness. The pianoforte quartet . . . and the Quintet . . . in G minor are allied in tone, but their sorrow passes in the end to gladness or calm, whereas here it rises in a continuous climax to a wild merriment, as if seeking to stifle care. . . . This is the most passionate of all Mozart's symphonies; but even in this he has not forgotten that 'music, when expressing horror, must still be music' . . . And in the same sense in which Goethe ventured to call the Laocoon graceful, none can deny the grace of this symphony, in spite of much harshness and keenness of expression."

    . . . except [δ perhaps] the *Celli*
    . . . they [δ are ? to] play . . . Double bass or alone. [δ The]
Ms. 2 *Violin somewhat brilliantly written for.* [in pencil]
    [δ Mus. ex. as on p. 265]

Ms. 1 Smallness of orchestra . . . [Marginal note] *enlarge*
    too weakening [misread by C.A.E. and given as "necessary"
    in Ms. 2 but corrected by E.]

    The bassoons are
Ms. 2 The Bassoons [δ are] *appear to be*
Ms. 1 . . . & we shall find several places where we could wish some
    thing different.
Ms. 2 . . . & we shall find several places [δ which] *where* we could
    wish *the Bassoon parts* had been written differently.

Ms. 1 any note [δ on the] that will . . .
    . . . musical harmonic climax
Ms. 2 . . . musical [δ harmonic] climax
Ms. 1 When Beethoven
Ms. 2 [δ We see] *When* Beethoven
Ms. 1 noticeable. [Remainder written in train?]
Ms. 2   ,, [Ends at this point.]

Ms. 1 . . . omitted. [δ Hard on this so
        Mozart a mas]

      [Followed by one page of rough notes. See
           p. 264.]

Notice first that all the instruments are treated 'generously' *except perhaps the 'Celli.* Throughout the work *they play only* the bass either with the *Double Bass or alone. Violin* somewhat *brilliantly written for.*

Smallness of orchestra made 'division' too weakening.

Moderate compass for strings: upper range very limited. Mozart, a solo violinist, must have avoided high flights which he would well know how to write easily and effectively to prevent any feeling of thinness.

The Bassoons appear to be carelessly written for sometimes.

It seemed *so* easy to put *col Bassi* without regard to the actual passages, and we shall find several places where we could wish the Bassoon parts had been written differently.

Horns—Open notes only are used, and great ingenuity is shown in 'dodging', to use a schoolboy's [term]—to get a useful note: the series of harmonics same as on the violin string.

The horns are crooked in B flat alto and in G, two keys never used now.

This limitation sometimes has disastrous results: it being impossible to find *any note that will* 'fit' the chord, the Horns have to be silent: so it happens that the *musical climax* is often not the climax of tone.

When Beethoven used trumpets *and* Horns in the same way, the cessation of the brass is naturally more *noticeable.* Look at page 9, last two bars, 2nd horn goes with the important figure in the Bass ascending to C (sounding G). Now turn to page 10, 2nd line, bars 2 & 3. Observe that the 2nd horn plays only C—the A (sounding E) was not possible on the old horn, so it is perforce *omitted.* Can anyone say that Mozart would have omitted the upper note of the phrase if he had an instrument which could play it? No.

The whole question of 'improving' the orchestration of the old masters might turn on this very simple point.

One might well think that a lecture on Mozart's fortieth symphony could hardly raise a ripple of controversy. But in this respect at this time Elgar was distinctly accident-prone, and his capacity for tact was all but drained away. In casting aspersions on the accuracy of newspaper reporting he was courting disaster. What Elgar was reported as saying has been shown, as also the main lines of what he intended to say. What he was interpreted as saying caused a storm on November 10, which blew itself out in the *Birmingham Daily Mail*:

SIR EDWARD ELGAR AND THE OLD MASTERS
"AN ASTOUNDING STATEMENT" DISCLAIMED
WHAT SIR EDWARD DID SAY

Sir Edward Elgar has once more fallen foul of the newspaper reporters. In a lecture on orchestration . . . he was reported to have ["The report of my lecture in to-day's 'Post' is in one passage entirely misleading. It runs thus:" He] expressed himself in favour of a revision of the works of the old masters, so that omissions due to the deficiencies of the orchestras of their day might be supplied from our ampler sources.

Sir Edward, as on a previous occasion, claims to have been misreported. Writing to today's "Post", he says:—

"This astounding statement was not made by me. I simply said that the question, which occasionally arises, of modifying certain passages in some of the older scores might be discussed in connection with the horn parts of the G minor symphony, and instanced one note only which might be added with advantage. I am entirely opposed to any tampering with the scores of the great masters."

As Sir Edward has questioned the accuracy of the summarised version of his address, which appeared in our columns in common with those of our contemporary, we append a verbatim report of the disputed passage in his lecture, leaving our readers to judge whether it bears the interpretation placed upon it or not. Referring to Mozart's G minor Symphony, Sir Edward said:—

"With the horns open notes only are used, and a great deal of ingenuity is used in dodging, as school boys say, so as to get some notes that fit into a series of chords. The notes used on the old French horn are simply the harmonic notes. That dominated all the horn playing of that period—just the open notes were used. This limitation has occasionally disastrous results, it being impossible to find any note that will fit into the chord, therefore the horns have to be silent. So it happens occasionally that the musical climax does not coincide with the climax of tone. Where Beethoven uses trumpets and horns in the same way the cessation of all that section of the bass [*sic*, for 'brass'] causes some astonishment occasionally. That limitation is the point on which the whole discussion as to improving, or altering, or amending, or editing—whatever is the least disconcerting word—the scores of the old masters turns. Because we know perfectly well it was not reticence on the part of Mozart that made him leave the note out and spoil the phrase; it was simply because he had not the note there. We find that in some of Beethoven's scores it has been

TELEGRAPHIC ADDRESS,
"LANGHAM, LONDON."
CODES, "A.B.C." AND "UNICODE".
TELEPHONE Nos. {3571 GERRARD.
{11342 CENTRAL.

LANGHAM HOTEL,
LONDON.

May 15 1907

Dear Fiedler:

I am anxious
to further the Richter —
— Wood orch! scheme
I have written a
line to Sir Oliver
Lodge about it
& have asked him
to talk to you.
I don't know how
far

Westfield
Augustus Road Edgbaston
June 13 - 1907

My dear Sir Edward
                        Supposing that you may
now have returned home from London & I
write to express my regret at the trouble
you are experiencing with your Eyesight
which I trust will be only temporary —
I was troubled in the same way myself
many years ago & know how inconve-
nient & disconcerting it is —

              As to the concert I am not in the
least surprised at the letters in the
newspapers & am sorry for Mr Halford
but we want to obtain the best we
can get & I much hope that the new
series will stimulate & encourage the
study of music & result in a great
advance both as to the performance &
appreciation of art in the city & neighbourhood - with my kind regards to Lady
Elgar & yourself believe me
                    Yours very sincerely Richd Peyton

suggested that a phrase given in skeleton form for the trumpets should be given in detail now we have the instruments to do it. I am sure Beethoven would have been the first to do it."

Sir Edward went on to relate, with evident satisfaction, how when Sir August Mann [sic] gave, according to previous announcement, an "arranged" version a few years ago, all the critics condemned it, but that arrangement played unannounced afterwards by a foreign conductor at Queen's Hall was pronounced by the critics one of the finest things they had ever heard.[1]

[1] In a controversy started by "C.A.B[arry]." (see p. 166) in the *Monthly Musical Record* of April 1, 1874, Manns—who "always set his face sternly against any 'tinkering' with the classics"—when chidden for not using Wagner's alterations to the "Choral Symphony" declared "that Beethoven's works require no such alterations as are suggested by Herr Wagner, considered as they are by all, excepting a small minority, as the most perfect monuments of musical art in existence". Manns, however, had no inhibitions concerning Handel, whose scores "were left in a deplorably incomplete state as regards the modern orchestra". H. Saxe Wyndham, *August Manns and the Saturday Concerts*, London, 1909, p. 102 f.

CHAPTER 12

RESIGNATION

THE Elgars spent the early part of 1907 in Italy. In the summer Edward went to America, returning in time to take the Chair at a meeting of the University Musical Society.

Westfield,
Augustus Road,
Edgbaston,
Birmingham.
June 21, 1907
If the longest we will still hope
not the hottest day

Dear Sir Edward

I hear from Dr. Fiedler that you will be in Birmingham at the University for a little ceremony *at 5 o'clock* on 5 July—also that you will be here [δ also] on the morning of *the 6th* for the important ceremony in the Town Hall & I write to ask if we may have the pleasure of receiving you here & whether we may also hope to see Lady Elgar as probably on so important an occasion she will be willing to be present.

If we may look for the pleasure of seeing you please let me know whether I shall meet you at or before the meeting at the University at 5 p.m. on the 5th July also whether Lady Elgar will like to attend that meeting or whether my carriage shall meet her at the station & bring her direct to this house where you & I should find her at or before dinner time

Yours very sincerely
Richd Peyton

The reason for the Meeting on July 5 was the presentation of a piano to the Society. Elgar was in buoyant mood. His wife approved his speech, and both enjoyed the dinner party at the Peytons which followed. Among the guests was Neville Chamberlain.

The next day the *Birmingham Daily Mail* picked up the Professor's *obiter dicta* and commented:

> There's many a true word spoken in jest, and what Sir Edward Elgar said yesterday at a gathering of the Birmingham University Musical Society may prove more accurate than he, in jocular mood, anticipates. A piano has been presented to the Society, a fact which caused Sir Edward to observe that some day the instrument might be

looked on as a curiosity, for mechanical players were multiplying in such
vast numbers that the human piano-player would probably disappear.
Ever since the piano came into vogue there have been mechanical players,
but of the human variety, and there is one point upon which we may
congratulate ourselves, viz., that music from an instrument of which
you merely [have] to turn the handle, so to speak, is almost invariably
better than that produced by a pianist who simply strums on the keys.
No wonder Sir Edward Elgar advised students to take music seriously.
There is no art in which mediocrity becomes so palpable, and the piano
is an instrument which refuses to be cajoled by a bad player. It would
sooner respond to the barrel-organ arrangement.

In another column of the same issue was an account of the Degree Ceremony
(with some comment on the levity with which the then students of Birmingham
regarded this grave affair), and "there was much cheering as the distinguished
composer, Sir Edward Elgar, Peyton Professor of Music, stepped forward to
receive the degree of Master of Arts".

The Peyton Professor was now thinking how he might gracefully slip out of
office. While he had been abroad Lady Elgar had seen Fiedler (who was now
on the point of departure from Birmingham) and it had been accepted that
Elgar should merely supervise the arrangements for a series of lectures by other
speakers.

27 Calthorpe Road,
Edgbaston
Birmingham
23.ix.07

My dear Elgar,
   I am 'dreaming' till Monday next when my successor will be elected.
   Your list of lectures must be approved by the Faculty before we can
advertise or send out circulars. I will put the matter on the agenda for
the meeting on Monday and if you will let me have the list in time for the
meeting I will get it passed.
   You can have the large lecture theatre on Fridays at 5^{30}, but it would
be well to fix the exact dates as soon as possible.
   The Vice Principal Prof Heath has been elected Chairman of the
University Musical Society in my place. I believe they are going to have
their first concert on Wednesday October 30th "In memory of Grieg".
   It is a great wrench for us to leave Birmingham & it makes me quite
sad to think that I shall not be at the University to welcome you when
next you go there. I shall always remember with pleasure and pride our
association as colleagues and our fellowship in work at the Birmingham
University.
   With best wishes for Cardiff[1]

Yours ever
H. G. Fiedler.

[1] For a performance of *The Kingdom*, on September 26.

The scheme for the lectures was now passed on to the Principal, Elgar also advising him of his intention to winter in Italy.

The University,
Edmund Street,
Birmingham,
7 Oct. 1907

My dear Elgar,

Thank you for your letter. I had heard of the scheme through Professor Fiedler, who knows my mind in the matter, and I am quite contented with whatever arrangement you have made with him, provided always that any scheme submitted has to be approved by the Faculty.

I trust very sincerely that the winter abroad will renew your health and do you good in every way.

Believe me, with very kind regards,
Faithfully yours,
Oliver Lodge

The following announcement was then issued:

THE RICHARD PEYTON PROFESSOR OF MUSIC (Sir Edward Elgar, M.A., Mus.D., LL.D.), has arranged the following series of Lectures to be given by

MR. THOMAS WHITNEY SURETTE,

(Lecturer on Music for the American University Extension Society,
Teachers' College of Columbia University,
and the Extension Delegacy of Oxford University)

DR. H. WALFORD DAVIES, Mus.D., LL.D.,

(Organist of the Temple Church, London)

and MR. ERNEST NEWMAN.

Friday, Oct. 18th "The Music Dramas of Wagner" (I.) Mr. Surette.
   „   Oct. 25th "Church Music"   –   –   – Dr. Walford Davies.
   „   Nov. 1st "New Forms in Music"   –   – Mr. Ernest Newman
   „   Nov. 8th "The Music Dramas of Wagner" (II.) Mr. Surette.
   „   Nov. 15th "Russian Music"   –   –   – Mr. Surette.
   „   Nov. 22nd "Modern Harmonic Basis"   –   – Dr. Walford Davies.
   „   Nov. 29th "The Fifth Symphony of Beethoven" Mr. Surette.

The Lectures will be given in the Large Lecture Theatre of the University, at 5.30 p.m.

Admission will be free by ticket to be obtained from the Secretary.

On October 9 Elgar was a guest at the Dinner of the Association of Leeds Professional Musicians, and in the course of his speech reminded his audience: "As they probably knew he did not think much of critics—(laughter)—he had not read any criticisms since 1900—but he liked to talk over his thoughts with his fellow composers and musicians." The reference to 1900 is enlightening. For it was after the first performance of *Gerontius* (as correspondence with Jaeger shows) that Elgar's bitterness with what he took to be the perfunctoriness of criticism was extreme.

Elgar took the Chair at the first two Peyton lectures of the 1907–8 series and "explained that the only reason he was not delivering them that year was that, unfortunately, his eyes were of no use to him. He trusted this ailment was only a passing one."[1]

So too did Ernest Newman, whose lecture, given in fact, on November 8 took place three days after Elgar had left for Italy. Newman spoke on musical forms, and concluded as follows:

> One other possible form Mr. Newman mentioned was that of Sir Edward Elgar. His idea was for a new combination of orchestra, acting, and pictures. The idea was not exactly new. Liszt had thought of using it in his Dante Symphony, the pictures being thrown upon a screen. It would be of interest to see what Sir Edward Elgar would do with the idea.[2] He was not in a position to say more about Sir Edward's new work,[3] but would express a hope, in which he was sure they would all share, that he might be restored to health to finish it.[4]

Completely absorbed in composition Elgar reviewed his Professorship in the summer of 1908. On July 31 he was "depressed at Birmingham prospects."[5] A month later he wrote his resignation,[6] and felt a "weight lifted".[7]

Peyton also felt a weight lifted, but in a different way. He wrote to G. H. Morley, Secretary of the University, on August 28, saying: ". . . I am pleased to think that there will be now a prospect of some satisfactory results attending the existence of a musical professorship in the University . . . The actual result & virtual waste of time has, I need not say, been a great disappointment to me . . ." When news of Elgar's resignation got around two aspirants to the Professorship wrote to Peyton offering themselves. They were John Francis Barnett (1837-1916), a composer less unknown in Birmingham than elsewhere, and William Wallace (see pp. 81, 113).

In the event, however, the obvious choice was made, and on November 4 Granville Bantock was appointed to the Chair.

[1] *Birmingham Mail*, October 19, 1907.
[2] Lord Abingdon had attempted something similar in his *Mary Queen of Scots* (1790), see Percy M. Young, *History of British Music*, p. 388.
[3] Reference probably to the first Symphony.
[4] *Birmingham Mail*, November 9.
[5] Diary.
[6] Ibid., August 29.   [7] Ibid., August 31.

According to the witness of Havergal Brian Bantock had, in a sense, been there all the time:

> Elgar had recently accepted the Chair of music at Birmingham University and there was an expectancy in the air as to what was to happen next. Elgar talked of making Birmingham an English Leipzig with a magnificent Conservatoire of Music, staffed by professors of modern outlook and to establish a permanent symphony orchestra of 100 players. Bantock was the moving spirit behind Elgar's talks— Bantock was the prompter.[1]

[1] *Foreword*, Bantock Memorial Concert, Midland Institute, November 12, 1946.

INDEX

INDEX

Albert, Prince Consort, 2
Amsterdam, 94
Argyll, Duke of, 176
Aristotle, 156
Arne, Thomas Augustine, 43
Atkins, Ivor, 18
Austin, John, 268

Bach, Johann Sebastian, 37, 39, 67, 69, 74, 77, 160, 230, 240, 241, 264
Bantock, Granville, 11, 14, 45, 48, 68, 71, 76, 92, 93, 230 n. 3, 231 n. 1, 283, 284; Bantock Memorial Concert, 155, 284
Barnett, John Francis, 283
Barry, Charles Ainslie, 98 n. 1, 166, 279 n. 1
Baughan, E. A., 49 n. 1, 187, 208, 209
Bayreuth, 149
Beale, Alderman, 76
Beaumont, Francis, and Fletcher, John, 80, 81
Beckford, William, 89 n. 1, 231, 257
Beethoven Ludwig van, 33, 35, 37, 63, 69, 95, 105, 107, 108, 139 n. 1, 146, 150, 151, 160, 169, 170, 171, 209, 243, 260, 261, 263, 274, 275, 276, 279, 282
Bell, William Henry, 64
Bennett, Joseph, 165 n. 1, 178, 180, 181, 182, 191
Bennett, William Sterndale, 4, 6, 43
Bentham, Jeremy, 205
Berlin, 94
Berlioz, Hector, 145, 167, 168, 203, 231, 248, 249, 253
Birmingham: Amateur Harmonic Association, 9; Art Gallery, 9, 100, 228; Central Library, 62; Clef Club, 13; Festival Choral Society,

19 n. 1, 55, 230; Mechanics' Institution, 2; Midland Institute, 2, 9, 13, 14, 16, 18, 22, 45, 62, 68, 76 n. 2, 80, 104, 112, 199; Music Festival, 6, 9, 10, 19 n. 1, 121 n. 1; Oratory, The, 11; Snow Hill Station, 112; Town Hall, 2, 3, 9, 11, 13, 67, 71, 166, 175, 228, 280
Bishop, Alderman, 7
Bizet, Georges, 243
Black, Andrew, 136, 137
Blackburn, Vernon 108, 164 n. 1, 184, 185
Boccaccio, 211
Borwick, Leonard, 128, 129
Bossi, Enrico, 133
Bournemouth, 259
Bradford, 111
Brahms, Johannes, 37, 42 n. 1, 43, 51, 63, 64, 92, 95, 96-110, 111, 130, 149, 150-4, 158, 167-73 passim, 209, 210, 226, 230, 239, 263
Brian, Havergal, 155, 282
Bristol, 4, 129
Brodsky, Adolf, 16, 111
Bruch, Max, 9
Brussels, 66
Buckley, R. J., 144
Bülow, Hans von, 145

Cambridge, 64
Carracci, Agostino, Annibale, Lodovico, 26, 38, 39, 59 n. 1
Cardiff, 279
Carlisle, 155
Carlyle, Thomas, 142, 143
Chamberlain, Joseph, 8, 10, 211 n. 1
Chamberlain, Neville, 280
Chappell & Co., 76
Chesneau, Ernest, 203